THROUGH NATURE TO ETERNITY

Through Nature to Eternity

Chaucer's *Legend of Good Women*

Donald W. Rowe

UNIVERSITY OF NEBRASKA PRESS

LINCOLN AND LONDON

Copyright © 1988 by the University of Nebraska Press
Manufactured in the United States of America

The paper in this book meets the minimum requirements of
American National Standard of Information Sciences—
Permanence of Paper for Printed Library Materials,
ANSI Z39.48–1984.

Library of Congress Cataloging-in-Publication Data
Rowe, Donald W.
    Through nature to eternity.
    Bibliography: p.
    Includes index.
    1. Chaucer, Geoffrey, d. 1400. Legend of good
women. 2. Chaucer, Geoffrey, d. 1400. Legend of
good women—Sources. 3. Women in literature.
4. Mythology, Classical, in literature. I. Title.
PR1882.R68   1988   821'.1   87-5993
ISBN 0-8032-3882-7 (alk. paper)

To the two men with whom I first read Chaucer:

Dale S. Underwood

for the zest with which he constructed readings, and

B. J. Whiting

for his unfailing delight in the text's particulars

CONTENTS

Acknowledgments

C haucer's *Legend of Good Women* has long been a preoccupation of mine: I wrote a dissertation twenty years ago that dealt with the relationship of the Prologues to their sources in French courtly poetry and of certain of the legends to their classical origins; I first drafted a monograph nearly ten years ago in an effort to broaden the literary context in which it had traditionally been viewed; and finally, I reconceived and, intermittently, rewrote the whole yet again over the last two or three years. Though perhaps this revisionary process has only been throwing good money after bad, the *Legend* deserves, I have told myself, more scholarly attention than it has received. The fact that it holds little appeal (beyond the charm of the F Prologue) for modern sensibilities, in spite of its problematic character, suggests that the search for a literary and intellectual rationale that will account for it may bring us closer to the medieval Chaucer. Still, read as an effort to defamiliarize Chaucer and Chaucer criticism, the following pages will disappoint. One will meet there the familiar ironist of many voices, and they are written in the equally familiar language of modern, and on a rare occasion, postmodern criticism. My intention, however well achieved, has not been to enable us to experience the *Legend* as Chaucer's immediate audience did but rather to restore an awareness of aspects and dimensions of the poem that time has alienated and, seemingly, eradicated. I have assumed that our understanding of the past and its artifacts must be constructed in our terms.

The text's debts are many. The dedication acknowledges the longest-standing of these obligations. The most recent are to two of my colleagues, Sherry Reames and A. N. Doane, who have at one time or another either read or discussed with me virtually all its argument. (They are not to be blamed for having been unable to win me over to wiser points of view.) Between there lies all the scholarship immediately addressed to the *Legend* of which I am aware— much of it no doubt forgotten to my own peril—and whatever I have been able to assimilate from Chaucer criticism more generally and from the scholarship devoted to illuminating the medieval tradition of philosophical poetry to which the *Legend* ultimately belongs. I hope that those who recognize their ideas here will find their names in the notes, though no doubt much I imagine my own invention is in fact misplaced memory. For errors of fact, infelicities of style, or absurdities of fancy I alone am responsible.

Backgrounds

I

C haucerians have long been accustomed to finding a pleni-
tude of critical response to the god's plenty of the *Canterbury
Tales* and the diverse perspectives of *Troilus and Criseyde* catalogued
in each year's Modern Language Association bibliography. We are
equally accustomed to see the *Legend of Good Women* all but ignored,
even though it was written when we suppose Chaucer to have been
in full command of his genius, between the previously mentioned
works we find so amenable to elucidation.[1] The comparative thin-
ness of the *Legend's* criticism may well reflect an artistically thinner
work, but this disparity in critical response is too great to be explained simply by acknowledging that every Homer nods. Either
we have discovered a legion of unintended subtleties and layers of
imagined signification in the masterpieces, or we have missed intended complexities when reading the Legend. It is the latter possibility that prompts this study.

If interpretive diversity is evidence of the ingenuity of critics, it
also demonstrates the fundamental flexibility of literary texts, their
capacity to assume a variety of significant forms in the light of diverse assumptions, different contexts, and various textual relations.
Inevitably, as historical scholarship expands a text's network of relationships and discovers more and more of its manifold potentiality, interpretations that once seemed adequate appear partial: responses but to selected aspects of a text, the products of historical
and literary contexts that have been too narrowly defined and too
deterministically imposed. Readings seeking to be comprehensive
grow ever more complex and ever more elusive until, finally, we
are forced to choose between an integrated text achieved through

selectivity and the disintegration that results from language's irreducible plurality and indeterminacy. Still, nearly anyone studying
the *Legend* in the context of present-day Chaucer criticism would
no doubt judge most of its critical tradition needlessly reductive.
Three problems have dominated this tradition until recently. Which
Prologue is the revision? What autobiographical and historical circumstances are allegorically represented in the poem? What relationship exists between the legends and their sources on the one
hand, between the legends and the Prologue on the other? While
only the last of these questions evokes a lively interest in contemporary critics, the first two cannot be ignored: we must establish a
text, and localizing it properly—determining its connectedness to
its milieu—is a necessary guide to interpretation, a useful stay against
indeterminacy.

The two versions of the Prologue have, since F. N. Robinson's
first (1933) edition, been known as F (earlier B) and G (earlier A).
At one time much energy was expended to determine which was
the original, which the revision; Victor Langhans could observe in
1917 that virtually every major Chaucerian had expressed an opinion on the question.[2] This interest is hardly surprising, given the
need to establish a text; nor is the more recent absence of debate,
given the morass of conflicting opinion produced by the earlier efforts at resolution. The present silence apparently reflects a general
acquiescence in the view, one fostered by Robinson, that John Liv-
ingston Lowes more or less settled the issue by assuming that the
first version of a text is bound to be more like their shared sources
than a subsequent revision and then by demonstrating that F is closer
to the French sources common to both Prologues.[3] In fact, however, the question is far from resolved. Lowes's assumption may be
probable, but it is by no means necessary. The two texts most important for his argument, Eustache Deschamps's *Lay de franchise* and
Jean Froissart's *Paradys d'amours,* cannot even be assumed beyond
a reasonable doubt to have been sources.[4] Certainly, anyone who
has read much of the debate can appreciate Lowes's effort to find
grounds for determining priority other than the history supposedly being allegorized in the two or critical judgments as to which
is better, but Lowes's own practice—as opposed to his own characterization of what he was doing—demonstrates the impossibility

of determining which is the revision without recourse to subjective judgments.[5]

The absence of objective criteria for establishing priority does not free us to please ourselves in selecting a text, for there are seven surviving manuscript versions of F and only one of G; historically, F has been *the* Prologue. Though one can imagine any number of explanations to account for this disproportion, two seem to have a distinctly higher probability. One is that whichever was first and whichever the revision, Chaucer chose to "publish" F, making it for whatever reasons the preferred version. The other likely possibility, one discussed by Lowes, is that F was published along with the poem's nine legends and that the process of multiplication began before G was written, or at least before it was circulated.[6] If G does represent second thoughts and intended improvements (rather than an earlier version or an adaptation for a special occasion), the existence of a single surviving copy hardly suggests a vigorous effort on Chaucer's part to see that it replaced F. In short, since there is nothing in G itself or in the textual history of the two Prologues as we know it that establishes G as a repudiation of F, the predominance of the latter in the manuscripts makes it the necessary choice for a critical base text.

Though textual history rather than critical judgment should determine our text, my excursus undertakes a brief reexamination of the priority question. The purpose of that discussion is not to determine which version has, as the revision, Chaucer's imprimatur. The history of the debate demonstrates that interpreting the text to authorize a version is critically counterproductive, for it subordinates interpretation to an extraneous end that improperly constrains and distorts it.[7] But it is important to establish whether or not Lowes settled the issue, for suppositions deriving mainly from Lowes about the priority and probable dates of the Prologues have had a considerable impact upon our understanding of the chronology and development of Chaucer's work and upon our inability to conceive of the *Legend* as an accomplished work.[8] Assuming it to be a fact that Chaucer rewrote the Prologue to the *Legend* after the death of Anne in a way that radically diminished the earlier Prologue's courtliness inevitably buttresses the view that the *Legend* is not only an unsatisfying work but also one forced upon him against his genius; our contemporary distaste is warranted by Chaucer's supposed dissatisfaction. Thus we need neither take it seriously nor adjust our idea of Chaucer as a poet to it, but it to our idea of Chaucer. Besides unsettling the prematurely settled, a comparison that does not seek to establish which was the chicken, which the egg, can perhaps advance the more modest goal of understanding the characteristics of each.

Efforts to read the text as historical or biographical allegory have also done little to illuminate it or to clarify its relatedness to the "real world." The suppositions that lie behind much of this criticism, that the poem's particulars have their justification in contemporary events and that the critic's task is to discover this historical reality—the real subject of the poem—have all too often produced a criticism that wrenches these particulars out of context (that it may use them as allegorical pointers) and neglects the internal "logic" of the poem.[9] Thus, assuming that the justification for the god of Love's sun-crown lay in the history supposedly being represented—in Richard's use of the sun as a sign of his royalty or in the Black Prince's death, which made the halo an appropriate symbol for him—caused its perfectly adequate internal justification to be ignored: together, the sun-crown and the daisy-crown establish a correspondence between the god and queen of the narrator's dream and the sun and daisy of his waking experience.[10] While the possibility of historical allegory cannot be denied, when the reality supposedly being represented makes the text less intelligible, we must doubt either the relevancy of the alleged reality or the immediacy and closeness of the assumed representation. (A text need not allegorize an event to recall it.) Such is the apparent consequence of the legend that Chaucer wrote the *Legend* at the command of Queen Anne,[11] for assuming that the Prologue recreates Anne's reaction to the *Troilus* precludes recognizing the ironic comedy inherent in Alceste's characterization. Yet it would appear impossible to read the *Legend* as an even broadly coherent and consistent whole without seeing significant irony both in Alceste's defense of the poet and in the penance she assigns.

The problems inherent in such allegorizations of the poem now seem in large part the consequence of assuming too simplistic a relationship between text and life. After all, reading the Prologue as a virtual transcription of the court's hostile reaction to the *Troilus* is repudiated simply by Chaucer's anticipation of just such a reaction near the end of the *Troilus*—that is, before it was ever read at court. That Chaucer's protestation of innocence in the guilt of Criseyde occurs in conjunction with an expressed preference for Alceste's story to Criseyde's raises the possibility that Chaucer already had the idea of the *Legend* as palinode in mind. Indeed, R. F. Green suggests that this anticipation of criticism was a deliberate effort to provoke it and make the *Troilus* "a subject of fashionable debate," as though Chaucer were creating a demand for the *Legend* to satisfy.[12] There may be little reason to doubt that the Prologue expresses the attitude and thinking of some at court, whether provoked or not, but the evidence hardly justifies assuming either that the poem's source was Anne's feminist zeal or that the events expressing this attitude in the Prologue are thinly veiled history. For better or worse, the poem is Chaucer's creation.

Other characteristics of the poem further demonstrate the distance and obliquity of whatever topical and historical reference there may be. It has often been assumed, for instance, that Chaucer's depiction of the narrator's passion for the daisy was autobiographical.[13] While this is possible, what is undeniable is that Chaucer subordinated his representation of whatever reality existed outside the poem in this respect to the dictates of the dream vision and the conventions of *marguerite* poetry. The utterly conventional character of Chaucer's daisy worship (long ago established by Lowes)[14] and his completely self-conscious use of this tradition (established by his apology to his fellow poets—"loveres that kan make of sentement"—for borrowing their words) not only obviate seeking an autobiographical cause for the fiction but also require us to recognize that the dictates of literary tradition and the demands of the fiction have been given priority over history. Chaucer may have loved some lady, and this love may be expressed in the Prologue, but both the narrator and the objects of his passion are fictive personae in an imaginary world.

Such conclusions are strengthened by a consideration of the one poem by Chaucer almost universally supposed to memorialize historical events, the *Book of the Duchess*. Even it cannot be read simply as an allegorized representation of Blanche's death and John of Gaunt's grief, for this occasion has been subordinated to the demands of courtly convention (as in the representation of their re-

lationship as an instance of unmarried *fin amour*), to the forms of
poetry in general (as in establishing fundamental oppositions, like
that of black and white, and then treating this opposition metaphorically), and to the order of his own poem (as in the particular
metaphor of a chess game or in making the death of Blanche just
one of the narrator's many encounters with loss). The poem may
have arisen from an occasion, but Chaucer makes the occasion ultimately serve the poem. The evidence we have been considering
with respect to the *Legend* suggests that we must recognize in reading it a similar sequence of precedence: whatever occasion it may
have had has been submitted to the conventions and forms of literary tradition, and these in turn have been submitted to the demands of the poem's conception.

To argue at such length the tenuousness of the poem's connections with events in Chaucer's life may seem like denouncing Prohibition. After all, it is not occasional readings that are the day's academic fashion but formalist and structuralist readings that ignore
a text's relationship with anything but other texts. More and more
the individual text is subordinated to its antecedents, the muse replaced by the prisonhouse of cultural forms, the author's intention
judged irrelevant. The critic's task is to interpret the poem as a
product of literary tradition, as an expression of the laws of literature. Indeed, it is this depersonalization and historical dislocation
of the individual text that underscores the importance of privileg-
ing the author's conception, of insisting that a text as aesthetic object is an intentional product that manipulates the inherited, for the
only unity a work of literature can have that is not accidental is an
intentional one: an imposed design that, once recognized, functions to order and align, however imperfectly, the centrifugal plurality of culture and language.[15]

The importance of establishing, or at least of announcing, such
conclusions and assumptions is clear from the third traditional
question of *Legend* criticism, that of the relationship of the legends
to literary tradition on the one hand, to the Prologue on the other,
for this question confronts us directly not only with the issue of the
poem's textual relations but also with its manifest self-consciousness
in this regard. The immediate critical difficulty is that Chaucer's
versions of his heroines' lives often differ fundamentally from traditional accounts because of his accommodation of their lives to the

Prologue's requirements. These transformations have produced two opposed responses: an ironic reading and one that takes the legends at face value. The father of the ironic readings was H. C. Goddard.[16] Noting the apparent unsuitability of many of Chaucer's heroines for a legendary of good women and the consequent changes Chaucer made in his sources in order that his heroines might pass for good, he argued that Chaucer's intent was satire; his method, irony; and his expectation, that his audience would recognize and be amused by his alterations in his sources. From his point of view the legends can be read properly only in relation to their sources, for in his reading the crucial dimension of the legends is the altered or omitted, what isn't there. The great champion of the straight reading was John Livingstone Lowes.[17] He argued that the *Legend of Good Women* was written from within the tradition of courtly literature and that within this tradition the heroines in question were regarded as good inasmuch as they were devotees of the god of Love. From Lowes's point of view, the reader must forget what Chaucer's sources actually say, accept the perspective of the courtly tradition and the poem's apparent definition of itself in terms of that tradition, and attend to what Chaucer explicitly says.

While one need hardly subscribe fully to either point of view, the controversy raises important questions about the nature of this text and the character of its literary relations.[18] For one thing, the character of the poem's intertextuality as Lowes understands it differs fundamentally from its character as Goddard conceives it. In Goddard's reading, the incompatibility of the legends and their sources induces the reader to create a mental text as a sort of *tertium quid,* one compounded of Chaucer's written text and the divergent texts called to mind by his allusions. These allusions to works that are often distinctly other in their point of view require in effect a revisionist reading of Chaucer's text, one that rejects their explicit terms and conclusions in order to reformulate the issues at stake and the appropriate conclusions to draw. In Lowes's view, in contrast, Chaucer is not using his sources to expose the partiality of his courtly translations but incorporating the courtly tradition within the poem and the poem within that tradition. We are called not to rewrite the text on the page but to appreciate the traditional associations and significance of the conventional courtly elements that have been incorporated into the text in more or less conventional configurations. In the one case we sense disjunction; in the other, continuity.

Part of our difficulty as readers in determining Chaucer's intent derives from our uncertainty as to the kind of poem the *Legend* is. Genres are sets of reader expectations as well as sets of conventions, Culler reminds us, and we rely upon them to help us know how to take what we read.[19] Since Lowes appeals implicitly to this very principle, we might join his party and be done with the debate were it not for two textual facts. One is that Chaucer did not completely remove the objectionable matter from the legends, did not transform his versions wholeheartedly enough to sustain even the illusion that his heroines were faithful servants of the god of Love; the other is that the poem appeals to and draws upon traditions besides the courtly. Significantly, our uncertainty before Chaucer's text is analogous to the uncertainty of the medieval reader before the "Ovidian" sources of the legends, for if the courtly tradition had adopted them, so had the clerical.[20] Such facts do not dispense with the problematic character of the *Legend;* they do suggest that Chaucer is defining a complex intertextuality that deliberately places his poem and his reader betwixt and between.

That Chaucer desired us to read the legends with their narrative sources in mind is evident from his method of narrating several of them and from his manner of introducing them in the Prologue. Comparison with the way Gower narrates some of the same and numerous similar classical tales in his *Confessio Amantis* makes this intent perfectly clear. Though Gower begins the *Confessio* with a discussion of the value of books in keeping the past alive and often begins or ends a particular narrative with a reference to its source, he almost never makes his reader aware in the midst of his narratives that his stories have sources. He actually tells his tales as though he were their only inventor, their first and authoritative historian. Not so Chaucer, who repeatedly names his sources and refers his audience to them for additional information, even quarreling with them from time to time, so that one is repeatedly aware that Chaucer is providing a particularized version of an old story. Gower pretends to give us history, reality itself; Chaucer ensures that we see his legends as histories, versions of reality (trumpetings from the House of Fame, tidings from the House of Rumor, as it were). Thus, Chaucer would seem to be working at cross-purposes: even as he alters his sources to whitewash his heroines, he repeatedly refers the reader to his incompatible originals.

In addition, Chaucer often alludes to and intimates what he omits. Repeatedly, one is reminded of his technique in the *Troilus:* there, confronted with a text whose source was unknown to his audience, he invents an author and an original version of the story and incorporates them into his text at crucial moments, now appealing to their authority, now taking issue with them, now submitting. By presenting his text as the narrator's response to what "the storie telleth us," Chaucer undermines the text's claim to historical authenticity and makes the text itself a manifestation of the incompatibility of fact and desire. Similarly, given the repeated references to the legends' sources and the frequent allusions to their content, such as Hypsipyle's prayer that Medea may slay her own children, even the reader ignorant of these traditional narratives experiences the legends as individualized products of their narrator's point of view, his responses to his literary antecedents.

To conclude that Chaucer intends us to read the legends comparatively—as the precedent of the *Troilus* and the practice of the legends both imply—is to judge irony a fundamental, not just an incidental, aspect of them and what the text omits often a significant dimension of it. Such seemingly inescapable conclusions should leave the historical critic wary, however. At what point is one to stop before one arrives at the absurdity that a text is both itself and whatever is not itself, all it says and all it doesn't say? While Goddard limits the "other" incorporable in the text largely to earlier accounts of the heroines' lives and commonsense notions of what is good, his amused retellings of the legends with an eye to any difference that can be given a satiric twist still seems to play fast and loose—as though what Chaucer actually wrote were intended to exercise almost no restraint on the reader's freedom to fashion from the written text's ironies and omissions whatever mental text suits his or her fancy. Escape from such radical indeterminacy is possible only if restraints exist within the text, only if it defines the character and intent of its own textual relations. Since the Prologue authorizes the legends, presumably it is there that we should seek at least a preliminary idea of Chaucer's purposes.

The assumption that the legends were intended to be faithful executions of Alceste's and the god's demands requires a naive reading of the Prologue, for it supposes that the characters within the Prologue's drama express the poet's intention rather than that drama in its entirety. Few of us read any of the *Canterbury Tales* that naively, and indeed, to suppose that Alceste and the god speak for the poet in their prescriptions is to overlook numerous incongruities in the surface drama of the Prologue itself—for instance, the apparent incompatibility of Alceste's demand that the legends depict all male lovers as false and her simultaneous insistence that they portray love as good. The alternative is to entertain the hypothesis that the Prologue's explicit prescriptions do not express the poet's intent, any more than its criticisms of the *Troilus* express his views of that work; it is to suppose that Alceste's and the god's idea for the legends is not the poet's.

Such is the point of view of two important recent discussions of the relationship between Prologue and legends, those by John Fyler in *Chaucer and Ovid* and by Lisa Kiser in *Telling Classical Tales*. Like Goddard, both distinguish Chaucer's purposes from those decreed by the god and Alceste; but rather than viewing the legends with Goddard as primarily intended to satirize those it ostensibly praises, they read them as illustrations of the counterproductive character of the Prologue's explicit prescriptions, which deny the complexity of human experience. Fyler emphasizes the disparity of the legends and their sources to read them as "a comic exercise in censorship and distorted emphasis"; Kiser argues that the reductive character of the legends is intended to parody exemplary poetic forms in general, saints' lives in particular.[21] While their studies constitute significant advances in our perception of the incongruities inherent in the legends and of the ways in which these incongruities are the consequence of the imposed demands, the legends are hardly so many tales of Sir Thopas and cannot be reduced to deliberately bad art. The fact that so many critics have taken them at face value—only Harry Bailey ever missed the parody in Sir Thopas—suggests that they have a positive agenda, however inadequately it may have been apprehended. We must look beyond the Prologue's ironies, beyond its mere repudiation of the prescribed, to see if it does not contain another, more complex idea of the legends, an alternative program for them. If the *Legend* is a coherent and unified whole, presumably the Prologue contains an underlying idea that will account not only for the irony resulting

from Chaucer's contradictory practice of alluding to what he eliminates but also for aspects of the legends that seem in earnest.

Although an introduction is not the place to undertake such an
analysis of the Prologue, some preliminary consideration of what
this idea ought at least logically to entail is in order. If the Prologue
does anticipate the legends we have, then its underlying idea ought
to include the concept of their failed conformity; that is, the Prologue ought to anticipate that Alceste's and the god's demands will
require an untenable transformation of history. Further, if we have
to distinguish between the Prologue's explicit and implicit prescriptions for the legends, presumably we should distinguish more than
merely nominally between the poet and the narrator, who is a character in the explicit drama.[22] Alceste's and the god's demands are
applicable only to the narrator. The apparent effort in the legends
to make old books prove the goodness of women and the laudabil-
ity of love is his. He must be the author of the legends as partial
histories; Chaucer's poem depicts a narrator who translates old
books in order to satisfy Alceste and the god of Love. It is partly
this fact that accounts for Chaucer's representations of the legends
as an intertextuality and for the self-dramatizing character of so
much of their rhetoric: rather than seeing through the narrator's
eyes and sharing his feelings, we are distanced to the point where
the narrator enters our field of vision. (One is inevitably reminded
of those manuscript illuminations that depict not only the crucifix-
ion but also, half within and half without its frame, a solitary worshiper.) If such implications complicate the legends, they also provide a potential perspective on their relations to their antecedents,
for they suggest that Chaucer's presentation of his narrator in the
Prologue will exercise some control over the way Chaucer has him
effect the translations, and that part of Chaucer's purpose in con-
structing the legends as an intertextual event is to dramatize the
narrator's efforts to please his lady as lover and poet. The implication is that we should read the legends as a dramatic portrait of
an artist, even as we read any number of the *Canterbury Tales* as dramatic revelations of their narrators in relation to their estates.

The *Legend* has other literary relations besides those explicitly
dramatized in the legends, of course. The most explicit of these are
the Prologue's debts to the courtly tradition, in particular to *marguerite* poetry and the genre of the love vision. One must be wary

of oversimplifying this relationship, however. The employment of a set of conventions so as to make the reader aware of them as conventions—and that is the effect of Chaucer's acknowledgment of his debt to "lovers that kan make of sentiment"—is markedly different from a naive use of tradition. The reader's consciousness of the conventional character of the poetic elements being used inevitably alerts him to their arbitrary character and to the limitations of the perspective they define. We must also be wary of overstating the homogeneity of the courtly tradition. Though *marguerite* poetry is almost uniformly courtly, as a literary flower the *marguerite* descends from the rose; and though the perspective of Guillaume de Lorris's portion of the *Roman de la rose* has seemed to most readers naively and insistently courtly, Jean de Meun's continuation was clearly written from another and much broader perspective. This broader perspective includes both the antifeminist elements that have alienated the god of Love and a substantial inheritance from medieval philosophical poetry. As daughter of the *marguerite* and granddaughter of the rose, Chaucer's "flower of flowers" possesses a rich and diverse inheritance.

Critics have lamented Chaucer's return to the French tradition in the Prologue, but his adoption of the courtly manner there is, Lowes to the contrary, no proof that he also adopted its point of view. Indeed, by representing the *Legend* as a palinode for the *Troilus* and the *Roman* and by incorporating into Alceste's defense a review of his poetic history, Chaucer implies that it is a retrospective apologia, a reengagement with the philosophical themes and literary traditions that inform his literary corpus. To read the *Legend* properly, he implies, we must look beyond the courtly and the Ovidian to the monuments that have informed his poetic development. The *House of Fame* brings to mind particularly the *Commedia;* the *Parliament,* Macrobius's *Commentarii in Somnium Scipionis* and Alain de Lille's *De planctu Naturae;* the *Troilus* and "Palamon and Arcite," Boccaccio's romances and Boethius's *De consolatione philosophiae*. Robinson's notes reveal the incidental verbal impact on the *Legend* of such texts from the medieval tradition of philosophical literature. Our concern is more fundamental: to determine what these traditions may have contributed first to the conception of the poem and then to its realization of that conception. If the *Legend* is something more than a courtly piety, an antifeminist *jeu,* or a burlesque; if it continues the philosophical and literary seriousness of his earlier poetry, including those texts it pretends to repudiate, this is presumably because Chaucer has incorporated in it elements from the traditions that inform those earlier texts.

One other work has an a priori claim on the attention of the student of the *Legend:* Gower's *Confessio Amantis.* Gower's apparent reference to the *Legend* near the end of the *Confessio* (when Venus directs him to tell her poet to finish his "testement of love") and Chaucer's allusions to the *Confessio* that conclude the Man of Law's erroneous enumeration of the contents of the *Legend* imply that they themselves saw the two poems as in some ways of a kind. And indeed, the affinity of the two is obvious: both are framed collections of classical tales with lovers as fictive narrators; both tell some of the same stories and rather similarly; both dramatize their own inception and treat the state of the nation. At the same time, however, critics who have compared the narratives they share have concluded, as John H. Fisher notes, that neither was source for the other; and what the Man of Law actually points out—Chaucer's irony notwithstanding—is that Gower included materials of a kind Chaucer did not.[23] The two texts provide a perspective on each other; neither can be legitimately treated as a influence on the other.

The case of the *Confessio* reminds us that we must observe some fundamental distinctions when reading the *Legend* intertextually. We must distinguish between those textual comparisons that we ourselves authorize and those that the poet authorizes. Chaucer and Gower's "closeness" as poets working within much the same traditions and writing for much the same audience may validate our comparing the two; it cannot justify subordinating either to the other. Further, as the *Legend* itself reminds us, we must attend to the ways in which a text establishes and defines its own textual relations. It is one thing for an author to employ some unacknowledged antecedent in fashioning his text, quite another for him to imbue it with well-recognized conventions and readily apparent allusions, and yet another for him to make some aspect of its textual relations an explicit issue in the text: that is, to create a text whose subject is its own intertextuality, as Chaucer has apparently done with the legends and their narrative sources. Similarly, it is one thing for a critic to use antecedent texts and traditions to provide a range of definition for a text's terms (its language, its images, its motifs, its structures), quite another for him to use antecedent texts and traditions to construct a revisionary rewriting of a text.[24] Insofar as we are interested in texts as intentional structures, as the authors' realizations of their own ideas for them, we must attend to the ways in which and the diverse degrees to which a text empowers its antecedents. We must permit a text to establish and define the intertextuality that establishes and defines it. To empower the received willy-nilly over its user is indeed to place the author in a prison-house and deny him his own, but it is the critic who has placed him there.

The goals and methodology of this critical study, then, are largely conservative. Its background is the tradition of *Legend* scholarship. It intends to place the *Legend* and the *Legend*'s backgrounds against this background. Its goal is a reading of the *Legend of Good Women* that will reconcile its surface contradictions under the assumption that such an understanding will essentially accord with the poet's intent. It further assumes that modern critical divisions about how the poem should be read are at least in part the consequence of these surface contradictions; thus, the study hopes that reconciling the poem's contradictions will effect at least a measure of critical reconciliation. The results should contribute to our conception of Chaucer's poetry and thus make the *Legend* more recognizably Chaucer's.

Loving the
Alceste-Daisy

II

Though the manner of the Prologue is almost invariably courtly, its point of view is manifold. This multiplicity of perspectives results from its participation in a variety of literary and cultural traditions and is reflected in its pervasive ambiguity. As a prologue it is not suitable preparation for the simplistic.

One source of the poem's persistent ambiguity is its tone. The Prologue is narrated with wide-eyed enthusiasm, the legends with an almost equally exaggerated distaste. In the Prologue, unquestioning wonder and awe dominate the surface and create an apparent attitude of hyperbolic enthusiasm and affirmation. The manner is sustained "description of the Prioress." No narrator in Chaucer so reminds one of Guillaume de Lorris—not even the Squire—or so deserves the appellation "naive." One would think this daisy-eyed dreamer had never even met a comptroller of the customs.

The opening lines exemplify the narrator's attitude and the ambiguity inherent in its simplicity:

A thousand tymes have I herd men telle
That ther ys joy in hevene and peyne in helle,
And I acorde wel that it ys so;
But, natheles, yet wot I wel also
That ther nis noon dwellyng in this contree,
That eyther hath in hevene or helle ybe,
Ne may of hit noon other weyes witen,
But as he hath herd seyd, or founde it writen;
For by assay ther may no man it preve.
But God forbede but men shulde leve

> Wel more thing then men han seen with ye!
> Men shal not wenen every thing a lye
> But yf himself yt seeth, or elles dooth;
> For, God wot, thing is never the lasse sooth,
> Thogh every wight ne may it nat ysee.
> Bernard the monk ne saugh nat all, pardee! (F, 1–16)

Though these lines ask for belief, they evoke skepticism.[1] Such is the inevitable result of exclaiming the obvious. The progress of the argument by a series of "buts" also seems calculated to raise doubts. The tone is full throttle and straight ahead, but the argument keeps doubling back.

Much that comes later confirms the ironic implications of these lines. Such, for instance, is the narrator's insistence that he saw in his vision

> of wymen swich a traas
> That, syn that God Adam hadde mad of erthe,
> The thridde part, of mankynde, or the ferthe,
> Ne wende I not by possibilitee
> Had ever in this wide world ybee;
> And trewe of love thise women were echon. (F, 285–90)

These lines are of course a joke, a fact announced not only by the impossible number of ladies, to say nothing of the allusion to Dante's "io non averei creduto / che morte tanta n'avesse disfatta,"[2] but also by the rhetorical strategy of saving until last the even greater absurdity that they were true in love every single one. When we consider the opening lines in such a context, they become an old joke from the antifeminist tradition: if you wish me to believe in good women, you'll have to persuade me to believe in what neither I nor St. Bernard has ever seen. In this context, the request for credence becomes another invitation to go and catch a falling star.

Nonetheless, we cannot dismiss out of hand this appeal for belief. These lines are prefatory to the narrator's discussion of the necessity of believing in old books—the key of remembrance—where there is no other proof; they are part of the poet's effort, as Frank argues, to make his audience receptive to a less courtly poetic matter in the legends.[3] The inescapable conclusion to be drawn from the opening lines, that one's trust should be skeptical, is confirmed by the subsequent contrast between the narrator's argument that we should trust in books where we lack other evidence "in every skilful wyse" and his insistence that he himself gives them "feyth and ful credence." Throughout the Prologue, Chaucer will use his narrator's excessive enthusiasm in this way—simultaneously to affirm and to deny. The enthusiasm carries us forward, as it were, by its pell-mell momentum until its simplistic excess causes us to draw back skeptically.

The opening *sententia* on the joys of heaven and the pains of hell has other important functions. It places the poem within the framework of these ultimate opposites and, like the poem's irony, contributes to its manifold perspective. An appropriate gloss is Arcite's lament on the hell of being released from prison and Palamon's simultaneous lament on the hell of remaining jailed, for they demonstrate that what is prison, what garden, what hell, what heaven often depends on the eye and prospect of the beholder. The opening *sententia* also reminds us that the world is intermediate between these contraries and compounded of them, and thus a means of knowing them now and achieving one or the other ultimately. By thus locating his poem between heaven and hell, Chaucer implies that his fictive world is an analogous revelation of these ultimates. To call the Prologue "heavenly," the legends "hellish," is to borrow the poet's implicit metaphor.[4] Rather like the double message over the gates through which the dreamer enters the garden in the *Parliament of Fowls,* the opening lines cast a light simultaneously defining and ambiguous over the whole poem. They are the gate through which the reader enters the poem, and they suggest that poetry as well as love may lead to heaven or hell.

The duality referred to in the opening lines is only the first in a series of oppositions that defines the world depicted in the poem. Though this definition by contraries pervades the whole, it is most insistently used in depicting the activity of the birds upon the return of spring. The rich warmth of spring replaces the impoverished cold of winter. The birds rejoice to have escaped the snares of the fowler, who destroyed their brood in winter through his sophistry. Now they defy the fowler and rejoice in the season, leave hate and accord in love as "Daunger" gives way to "Pitee," "Ryght" to "Mercy." This conventional picture of spring and summer as a time of renewal and life, winter as a time of stagnation and death, is similarly multidimensional, for Chaucer has incorporated in it elements from different literary traditions that bring to it different perspectives and values.

Consistent with the polite surface of the Prologue, the courtly mode dominates. The coming of spring is pictured in the stylized fashion traditional in the love-dream vision: the setting is a garden; the main actors are singing birds and personified abstractions; all manifest a love seemingly ethereal. The whole picture is generalized and idealized. We do not see animals rutting, or smell the mephitic earth. Rather we watch birds do "observaunces." Like the behavior of the birds, the passage is ritualized, a stylized "observaunce." Thus the presentation of the birds' courtship culminates in the quintessential courtly manner, elaboration through personification. Spring is, it would seem, "Daunger" demurring to "Pitee." The assumption is that no one does or says any "vilenye" because there is no villainy in anyone. Here there are only "gentil" hearts, not least of all the narrator's, for the manner of the passage is itself an act of courtesy.

Simultaneously, however, Chaucer intimates a more naturalistic perspective:

> Forgeten hadde the erthe his pore estat
> Of wynter, that hym naked made and mat,
> And with his swerd of cold so sore greved;
> Now hath th'atempre sonne all that releved,
> That naked was, and clad him new agayn. (F, 125–29)

The courtly abstractness of this picture is relieved by the concreteness of the pun implicit in "releved." It is the season, we are gently reminded, that moves the birds. Indeed, the courtesy itself is apparently seasonal: it comes and goes with the summer. The naturalistic dimension of this revival is suggested particularly by the narrator's observation that the birds, besides honoring love,

> diden hire other observaunces
> That longeth onto love and to nature;
> Construeth that as yow lyst, I do no cure. (F, 150–51)

Though the disruption of the surface politeness is only momentary, the innuendo reveals that both spring and the narrator have other, less courtly dimensions.

Besides being informed with the values of courtly idealism and, obliquely, naturalism, this passage draws significant content and meaning from the philosophical and theological traditions of the Middle Ages. Such is the reference to the classical notion that virtue is the mean, "as Etik seith" (whether that means "according to Horace" or "according to Aristotle" or merely, as Norton-Smith suggests, "as moral philosophy instructs").[5] More important is the "Boethian" diction and ideology that pervade the passage, especially the repeated insistence that the birds leave hate and accord in love. The harmony of the birds' song recalls Boethius's celebration in the *Consolation* (2, m. 8) of the harmony that love produces throughout the cosmos by reconciling the contraries from which the world is compounded, contraries that would tear the cosmos asunder in their inherent antipathy were it not for this according love.[6] The union of the birds is here seen as part of this universal accord, a union which is itself harmonious song. The Boethian philosophical blends into the Christian theological. The latter is particularly evident in the traditional Christian imagery of the fowler, who would fiendishly ensnare the birds with his "sophistrye" born of "coveytise," and in the Christian diction of the birds' repentance for their past infidelities, their renewed vows of truth, and the ultimate forgiveness they receive, as "Mercy" replaces "Ryght."[7]

Thus Chaucer's picture of the revival of spring requires that we view it simultaneously as a celebration of courtly idealism, natural vitality, cosmic order, and divine redemption. Yet equally important to the passage are the ironies and ambiguities that reveal its own dimension of sophistry, the *faux semblant* inherent in it. Such things as the narrator's innuendo and the suggestion of the seasonal nature of the peace here established reveal limitations inherent in nature and potentially destructive of courtesy. While Boethius argues that the love which binds all in one accord binds together such contraries as summer and winter, nature's order being the source of death as of life, the birds are engaged only in defying winter and repenting for the time being. The *Legend* opens by celebrating books as the key of remembrance; this passage begins with the word "forgeten." One must doubt that either old books or the "ruled Curtesye" here being celebrated can eradicate man's capacity for forgetting.

Such contraries as are alluded to in the opening lines and catalogued in the picture of summer and winter are duplicated in the narrator. Like the birds, the narrator revives with the coming of spring: every May he abandons his books and rushes forth to worship the daisy. For all the narrator's opening praise of books, the attribution of his forgetful abandonment of them to his participation in the universal revival of spring inevitably associates books in their oldness with winter's death and stagnation, with its sophistries. And indeed, when the narrator returns to his books to write the legends, the world he will encounter there will seem wintry and sophistical. The narrator's dual devotion—to the fresh daisy in May, to his old books the rest of the year—suggests that he partakes of the same duality. Microcosm and macrocosm are one in their doubleness.

We should not conclude from this association of books with winter that Chaucer is rejecting art and affirming nature, as some critics conclude from the *Parliament*. The fact that the daisy from the natural realm is one with Alceste from the world of art, that nature and poetry can be analogous manifestations of truth, is an unmistakable revelation of the vision, though one as yet largely invisible to the narrator and to the reader. At this point it is sufficient to see that Chaucer structured the fictive world of his poem in terms of a series of parallel oppositions in imitation of the order of the cosmos, that he represents his narrator as participating in these contraries as microcosm, and that his presentation of this order of oppositions is pervaded with irony and ambiguity, an irony and ambiguity that themselves express this represented duality. This correspondence between the packaging and the packaged, between the *integumentum* and the truths represented, is nowhere more evident than in the courtly manner, for it is spring and love that make the world seem a courtly garden, and one of the truths revealed is that this is a sophistry and a false seeming.[8] In the *Legend*, style is indeed a dimension of meaning, being itself symptomatic and synecdochic. We should not conclude that the poem's many voices and multiple perspectives exist to overwhelm us in relativity and skepticism, however, for here also the vision of the oneness of the daisy and Alceste challenges us to discover unity in diversity. But that also is vision that lies ahead.

RATHER LIKE some contemporary critics who deny that the *Legend* is really about love, Alceste refuses to recognize that the narrator is a lover or at least a willing one.[9] In the narrator's own judgment, however, "ther loved no wight hotter in his lyve." In the *marguerite* tradition to which Chaucer pays tribute, daisies are transparently symbolic: in *marguerites,* poets celebrate their ladies, real or imagined.[10] At one level the narrator's flower is equally transparent: it represents Alceste, a classical heroine and the apparent focus of the narrator's other passion, his love of books. Assuming that the narrator's passion was Chaucer's own, an earlier generation of critics all too frequently abandoned the poem in quest of the historical object of the poet's supposed passion.[11] More recent critics have sometimes gone to the opposite extreme. They have judged that the narrator loves a mere daisy—at least until he belatedly learns that it is also Alceste—with all the passion the *marguerite* poets felt for their ladies.[12] From such a point of view, the more meaningless the daisy, the more delightful Chaucer's supposed parody of the *marguerite* tradition.

It has long been recognized that Chaucer's daisy imitates literature, not nature. Witness, for instance, the flower's sweet smell, whereas the *Bellis perennis* is in fact odorless. This bit of unnatural natural history derives from the *marguerite* poetry of Machaut, Froissart, and Deschamps—all Chaucer's contemporaries—and reveals that their flower was modeled on the literary rose.[13] As daughter of the *marguerite* and granddaughter of the rose, Chaucer's daisy is heir to an ancient and rich tradition. It is also a varied one, for not all the daisies and roses flowering in the fields of medieval poetry are the same: some are red, some white; some are naturalistic, some courtly; some are sacred, some secular. Chaucer's insistent use of the conventions of the *marguerite*-rose tradition inevitably informs his daisy with the varied riches of that tradition.

This allusiveness would seem to have been Chaucer's intention, for he makes the fact that daisies flower in literature as well as in fields a significant factor within the total drama of the poem. When the narrator wishes to praise the flower for which he has abandoned his books, he returns to the books seeking the help of "lovers that kan make of sentement." As Payne has observed, the narrator's use of books to celebrate his daisy denies by implication the opposition established at the beginning of the poem between literature and experience; it suggests that literature contributes to humanity's—and particularly to the poet's—understanding and ordering of experience.[14] In their ambiguity the lines that follow the narrator's address to his fellow poet-lovers continue this reconciliation. His address itself is in the second person. He concludes it by apologizing for rehearsing their phraseology in praising his flower and then adds of the flower, "She is the clernesse and the verray lyght / That in this derke world me wynt and ledeth" (84–85). He immediately returns to the second person:

> The hert in-with my sorwfull brest yow dredeth
> And loveth so sore that ye ben verrayly
> The maistresse of my wit, and nothing I.
> My word, my werk ys knyt so in youre bond
> That, as an harpe obeieth to the hond
> And maketh it soune after his fyngerynge,
> Ryght so mowe ye oute of myn herte bringe
> Swich vois, ryght as yow lyst, to laughe or pleyne.
> Be ye my gide and lady sovereyne!
> As to myn erthly god to yow I calle,
> Bothe in this werk and in my sorwes alle. (F, 86–96)

Even if these lines were not addressed to a daisy who represents a heroine from an old book, their metaphors would deny the apparent change of subject. The sudden return to the second person continues in effect the narrator's address to his fellow poet-lovers. Certainly much of the passage is applicable to these poets and their works. Throughout the poem the narrator's word and work is "knyt" to books both old and new. They are among the "maistresse[s] of his wit." In praising the daisy with their "fressh" words, he is a harp singing to their fingering. Chaucer is a medium through which the continental traditions sing in English. Besides looking forward to the reconciliation of nature and art in the union of the daisy and Alceste, the whole passage of apology and praise openly declares that the narrator's daisy must be understood in relation to literary tradition.

Both in manner and in matter, *marguerite* poetry belongs to the courtly tradition. The *marguerite* descends from Guillaume's rose, not Jean de Meun's.[15] The presentation is stylized in accord with the conventions of the allegorical romance. The mode is predominantly nonrepresentational.[16] The central poetic fact, that women are being celebrated in the guise of flowers, inhibits particularity and realism. Consistent with this are Machaut's use of personifica-

tion in the "Dit de la marguerite," Froissart's invention of a mythology for the daisy in the "Dittié," both Deschamps's and Froissart's incorporation of typical *marguerite* celebrations into full-dress
allegorical visions.[17] The daisy is perfectly at home among the singing birds and catalogued personifications of the allegorical dream
garden. The subject of *marguerite* poetry is romantic love, but there
is little eroticism. Perhaps the most undeniably erotic moment in
the *marguerite* poems is the assertion of Machaut's narrator in the
"Dit de la marguerite" that he is perfectly content when he can "bais-
ier, touchier, oudeurer, et sentir" his flower, and even here the sequence of the verbs leaves us as aware of the flower as of the lady,
to say nothing of the subsequent assertion that everyone who smells
it loves it, that whoever holds it can have no "mal."[18] The flowers
and the ladies they represent are largely generalized ideals. The
poets celebrate their *marguerites* as sovereign "en bonte, en doucour,
en honour, / Et en tous biens," to use Deschamps' phraseology.[19]

   Worthy of note in this regard is the significance attributed to the
flower's most singular trait, its habit of opening to the rising sun, of
following it all day, of closing upon its setting.[20] This worthy "vertu," as Froissart calls it in the "Dittié," signifies in Machaut's "Dit de
la marguerite" that the flower lacks pride, is humble, and possesses
a polite openness and receptivity ("courtois accueil"); in Deschamps's "Lay" that it is humble and "humaine," true and "cer-
taine," and that it wishes to show its "atour," its array, in the light,
to ensure that neither insult ("mesdis") nor anything else brutish
("villaine") may hinder it in the dark. In Froissart's "Dittié," the
flower thus shows its goodness and its "doctrine." This celebration
of the flower in terms of courtly virtues and values is one with the
attitude toward love accompanying it, the insistence that love is a
good and a source of good in man.[21] The very goodness of the beloved causes all to love her, making loving virtually an obligation.

   Though generalizing about attitudes even in a set of interrelated
literary texts inevitably involves reduction, the point of view in the
fourteenth-century courtly French poetry being imitated in the
Prologue is sufficiently similar to warrant treating this literature as
a unified cultural influence, a distinctive voice. Significantly, these
texts do not provide much scope for the Robertsonian revision that
turns praise into condemnation, for they are themselves revisionary. Their rhetoric may be largely continuous with that of the trou-

badours, but the love being celebrated is generally, albeit naively, assumed to be reconcilable with orthodox values as they apply to the aristocracy. The distinction Moshé Lazar draws between the *fin amour* of the troubadours, the radical doctrine that makes love the root of all aristocratic virtue, and the good of "courteous love" gradually defined in the north of France, which locates love within the ethical system of chivalry, suggests something of the accommodation taking place.[22]

An instructive example is the Boucicault biographer's defense of love as a good, a source of "gentilesse," of courage, of graciousness, provided one intends love for the sake of growing worthy rather than for the sake of sexual pleasure.[23] Consistent with this emphasis on intention, the courtly allegories of Machaut, Froissart, Deschamps usually anatomize the psychology of the lover not in possession of his beloved (either the love is as yet unrequited, or the lovers are separated) to confirm that, properly controlled, the passion of love can be both an individual and a social good. Ordinarily, the question of the social form that the relationship is to take— whether a marriage, a liaison, or a chaste devotion—is not raised; perhaps there is an element of bad faith in this silence, but one need not suppose insincere either the effort to locate the moral issue primarily at the level of intention rather than action or the conviction that love ameliorates the behavior of the powerful.[24] If the irony accompanying Chaucer's presentations of the good of love indicates his personal awareness of the evasions inherent in this ideology, the fact that the critique is conducted with irony suggests that the moral intelligence at work in the poetry is both complex and tolerant.

Given the disagreement among critics of the *Legend* as to whether or not the narrator's daisy represents a lady, we should note that in *marguerite* poetry the daisy and the lady are not always simultaneously present. At times the flower disappears altogether. Such is the case when human attributes are foregrounded or when the central metaphor of flower for lady is replaced by other metaphors. The next to the last stanza of Machaut's "Dit de la marguerite," for instance, provides ten new metaphors that completely obscure any flower: the beloved is suddenly sun, moon, star, oar, sail, water, and so on. At other times the lady seems to disappear completely. For example, Deschamps offers as evidence that all love the daisy—

presumably his lady—the fact that he sees daisies everywhere painted on walls, windows, dishes. Froissart in particular gives the daisy its own independent life in ways that anticipated and no doubt influenced Chaucer's treatment of the flower. Froissart informs us first that the daisy originated from the tears Heres shed in loyal love over the tomb of her husband Cephei, tears that the earth received in pity and that Jupiter, moved, caused the sun to nourish. Next he recounts how Mercury discovered these flowers blooming one winter and sent a "chapelet" of them to his beloved, the disdainful Seres. She was so pleased with the gift that she felt obliged to recompense the "courtesie" of the giver. Clearly, at such times there is no lady present in the daisy; nonetheless, the daisy is symbolic—of such things as the power of love, loyalty, and courtesy to call forth love. Having invested the flower with meaning in its own right, Froissart associates that significance with his lady by observing that the flower born of Heres's tears is of the same nature as the flower he loves. The lady and the flower embody the same ideals.

Chaucer's picture of the daisy is first of all a distillation of the essentials of the *marguerite* tradition. It is red and white, ever fair and fresh, filled with virtue and honor, the flower of flowers. He repeatedly describes its opening and closing to the rising and setting of the sun, and explains that it hates the dark and fears the night. The lowly daisy has been elevated to a position of preeminence. It is the summit of created things, the paragon of beauty and "al vertu," that in which all beautiful and good things unite. Even without looking ahead to Alceste, we recognize in the response of the daisy to the sun values similar to those the *marguerite* poets celebrated: humility, certainty, truth in loving. In the image of its unfolding to the sun we see "Daunger" accede to "Pitee," the "courtois accueil" that Machaut praised, even as Guillaume de Lorris had celebrated the "Bel Accueil" of the rose. Its closing at night indicates that its receptivity is not indiscriminate, that it responds to virtue, is disdainful of vice. Consistent with this idealization and with the *marguerite* tradition is Chaucer's characterization of his narrator's passion as "affeccioun," "reverence," "devocioun." His efforts to express his veneration culminate in the lines in which he addresses the flower as his sovereign lady. Here the flower is replaced by a series of new metaphors: she is the light that guides him in this dark world, the mistress of his wit, his earthly god; he is the harp upon which she plays. While the momentary disappearance of the flower does not ensure that the narrator's eye is on a lady or even necessarily on Alceste, it does help the reader to remember that traditionally the flower betokens a lady and to recognize in the narrator's daisy the values and ideology of "fyn lovynge."

While these lines celebrate the daisy as the light of the narrator's life with courtly decorum, aspects of Chaucer's description of his passion for it reveal that it is also the fire of his loins. Chaucer's flower reaches out beyond the courtly confines of the *marguerite* tradition. Beside such rarified terminology as affection, reverence, devotion, we find "Ther loved no wight hotter in his lyve" (F, 59). The down-to-earth connotations of "hotter" are echoed in the uncourtly bluntness of the assertion. Particularly suggestive of sexuality is the picture of the narrator watching the flower

> whan that yt shulde unclos
> Agayn the sonne, that roos as red as rose,
> That in the brest was of the beste, that day,
> That Agnores doghtre ladde away. (F, 111–14)

The allusion to Jove's ravishing of Europa and the characterization of the sun "as red as rose" are of a kind with the narrator's description of himself as "constreyned" to see the flower unclose with "so gledy desir" that he still feels the "fir" within his heart. The fire that ravished Europa and opens the daisy burns in the narrator's breast as well. We should perhaps remember the god of Love's anger at the narrator for translating the *Roman de la rose* and just what the rose symbolizes in Jean's continuation. The image of the daisy opening to the fiery sun permits a narrowly sexual explication that renders the sensual picture of the narrator kneeling to watch it unclose on the "smale, softe, swote gras" akin to fabliau comedy. Unwittingly, no doubt, the narrator in his penance for being so uncourtly as to translate the *Roman* is repeating the offense, for his daisy is in part a translation of Jean's rose. Like the narrator's momentary breach of courtly decorum in his observation that the birds did what belonged to nature, such imagery recalls aspects of nature that must be known and remembered even if they cannot be explicitly mentioned in a courtly poem.

NOW THAT we have witnessed Chaucer's simultaneous incorporation of the *marguerite* tradition in his daisy and his qualification of that tradition through the introduction of a biological naturalism largely foreign to it, we need to direct our attention to the way in which he further enriches both the flower and the heroine it represents by investing them with philosophical and theological dimensions.

That Chaucer's daisy seems more real than the French *marguerites* is partly due to his stress on the actual behavior of the flower with respect to the sun. Whatever the courtly implications of its adherence to the sun, first and last it is a fact of nature, one to be understood in the light of literary traditions little reflected in *marguerite* poetry though evident in Jean's *Rose*. In the daisy's relationship to the sun Chaucer strikingly dramatizes the medieval commonplace that nature is both a system of laws, an order uniting all in an harmonious accord, and a vital force, the mother of generation. The relationship of daisy and sun is an instance and a representation of "the faire cheyne of love" that binds all together in a hierarchy and connects the created with its stable source. At the heart of this representation is the characterization of the daisy as itself a sun, which Chaucer accomplishes primarily by his use of a traditional medieval technique for discovering the essential nature of a thing: he explains that etymologically the daisy is the "ye of day." Kiser rightly stresses this central fact in her examination of the Prologue as an epistemological statement. Her demonstration that things of the world and poetry are analogous revelations, analogous reflections or images of divine truth, needs a physical and metaphysical grounding.[25]

When Chaucer pictures the daisy opening to the fiery sun when it rises "red as rose" in Taurus, he intimates the sexual power of the sun to generate daisies. Pouring forth its light and warmth, its love, the sun is the efficient cause of the daisy.[26] The daily "resureccioun" of the flower is seen in turn as only an instance of the spring sun's general revivification of a world slain by winter.

To appreciate the implications of this picture of the sun's generation of the world in spring, we need to remember that according to the science of the age it is the "atempraunce" of the heavens—the heat and motion of the celestial spheres—which is the source of the sublunar world's vitality.[27] This celestial "atempraunce" reconciles the antithetical elements from which things are compounded and—in the language of Chaucer's Boece—"norysscheth and bryngeth forth alle thinges that brethith lif," including the "swote

smelles of the first somer sesoun warmynge" (4, m. 6).[28] In its perennial animation of a dead nature, "th'atempre sonne" reenacts
the role of celestial fire in the original creation—at least as that creation was explained in the platonic science elaborated at Chartres
in the twelfth century.[29] According to the theorizing of this tradition, God directly created only the four elements; the orderly unfolding of the rest of the cosmos (except soul) was the work of these
secondary causes, the effect of artifacting fire upon the other elements. It is this physics that informs Chaucer's celebration of spring's
regeneration in the General Prologue to the *Canterbury Tales* as an
interaction of the four elements—April's showers, March's drought,
the West Wind, and the young Sun—and makes its picture of annual regeneration in effect a recapitulation of creation. Similarly
here, in the sun's regeneration of a dead world and in its daily "resureccioun" of the daisy, we see creation reenacted. If the prologues
to both works picture this generation as a natural event, a consequence of secondary, physical causes, both reveal that the secondary order of nature is an expression of a primary power that is spiritual: the sun vivifies the daisy because love vivifies the sun.

As the sun is the daisy's efficient cause, so it is its formal cause:
it is the sun that makes the daisy a day's eye.[30] Again Chaucer's poetry is expressing the age's science, which assumed not only that the
heavens vivify the world but also that the stars order and inform
it.[31] The celestial spheres are intermediaries between this transient
world and the eternal *mundus* and function intermediarily both as
substantific genii and as fatal agencies.[32] As genii, they confer natures, transmit substantial form. It is their task to generate the many
from the One and to ensure that what is generated conforms to the
archetypes in the mind of God, even as they ensure as fatal agencies
that what transpires conforms to Providence. Accompanying
Chaucer's presentation of "th'atempre sunne" as reanimating a dead
world is the picture of it as reclothing a naked one. The image of
clothing the naked is a conventional one for the imposition of form.[33]
Chaucer's dramatization of spring's redressing seemingly derives
from the description of the coming of May at the beginning of the
Roman de la rose (45–66); both in turn are reminiscent of Alain de
Lille's depiction in the *Complaint* of the created's reaction to the appearance of the goddess Natura: all of nature is revivified and reclothed (except the swooning poet) in an *integumentum* that is de-

signed to recall Nature's annual regeneration of the created in spring and the original generation of the cosmos through her imposition of the cloak of form upon primordial matter.[34] Similarly here, the sun's revivification of the dead and its reclothing of the naked in spring reenacts the original beautification of chaos into cosmos. If the informing role of the heavens is visually evident in the daisy's form, in the fact that its petals around a golden center make it an image of the sun, this informing is also evident in the flower's activity—in its daily imitation of the sun's circular course. As the heavens are themselves simulacra of the eternal *mundus,* a moving image of eternity, so their agency ensures that the individual natures and the resulting activities of the things of this world are similar mirrors and images.

The love poured forth is returned. The daisy follows the sun as its final cause, the source of its fulfillment and perfection, its actualization as a daisy. Boethius's celebration (in *Consolation* 3, m. 9) of the way in which the Creator of all things calls them back to him with a "reduci igne," an "ayenledynge fyer," finds its perfect image in the burning desire of the day's eye for the sun. This is the love, flowing and returning, that Boethius depicts as ordering the whole cosmos and preventing the return of chaos through its union of contraries in that meter (2, m. 8) which *Troilus* appropriates to characterize his and Crisyede's union.[35] Love accomplishes this order, Boethius goes on to explain, by moving all of nature in stable circles through the desire of each created thing to fulfill itself by uniting its beginning to its end. The providential rudder, the *lex benigna,* that steers creation is this infused desire of everything to possess the good according to its nature.[36] Thus it is that the daisy's returning love, its desire to realize itself as the day's eye, turns it in the stable circling course of the sun, making it an instance and a representation of the universal order that results from the universal appetite for the good. Chaucer's image rivals any in Dante and is Dantesque—as though reality were nothing but light poured forth by God and returned to him in an endless circle.[37]

Even the picture of the accord of the sun and the daisy has its dark side, however. The sun sets, and the daisy must close against the dark; when the sun calls it forth again in what the narrator terms a "resureccioun," it shines out of Taurus. The allusion to Europa's ravishing recalls the allusions with which Chaucer surrounded Pandarus's initial calling forth of Criseyde. There the sun also arose shining from the white bull, and the swallow "Procne" was singing, even as the song of her sister the nightingale closed the day. These allusions to ravishing express in both poems the constraint, the brutal necessity, which is an inevitable part of nature's law. Boethius stresses that the same "atempraunce" that brings forth and nourishes all things also "ravysschynge, hideth and bynymeth, and drencheth undir the laste deth, alle thinges iborn."[38] The inevitable dark, the "cold swerd" of Winter, the ravishing constraint of Taurus—all intimate an ineluctable and malignant element in the created. Although recognizing a necessary source of imperfection in the original creation was unacceptable to medieval Christianity, the tradition of philosophic poetry informing Chaucer's Prologue repeatedly represented the postlapsarian world as inherently resistant to the light and associated this resistance with the material element in man and nature.[39] These limiting constraints were associated particularly with the fatalistic influence of the stars in determining individual natures and destinies.[40] Consistent with the medieval refusal to posit an absolutely alien necessity in creation, Chaucer does not quite present astrological influence as brute necessity. The fire that burns in Taurus may impose a necessary order on sublunar nature—the daisy having no choice as a daisy—and may bear some responsibility for the fact that the lion no longer lies down with the lamb, but its constraints seem to impel rather than compel humanity. If the responsive fire it generates often rages out of control to produce the tragedy of seasonal loving, the "reduci igne" burning in the narrator's breast produces the seasonal comedy of his spending whole days kneeling in front of a flower.

Chaucer's use of the tradition of philosophical poetry in his representation of the nature and order of the created in the daisy is also evident in this treatment of its colors. Instead of describing its green stalk, its yellow center, its red and white petals, as both Machaut and Deschamps do, he follows Froissart in stressing that it is red and white.[41] That the daisy unites the red of the rose and the white of the lily and thus deserves the appellation "flower of flowers" is evident from the G Prologue, where the harmony between Alceste and the god of Love is revealed by the parallel between her red and white crown and his crowning garland of roses and lilies.[42] Courtly heroines are conventionally complexioned to rival the lily and the rose, of course, suggesting the heroine's union of passion and purity. Other associations of the red and white are equally important. The assertion that Mars gave the daisy its red assigns the white to Venus and makes the daisy a flower like Emelye in the "Knight's Tale."[43] Emelye's union of the red and white is associated with the goddess Diana's similar harmonization of these contraries: that union expresses the chastening of the red associated with Arcite and Mars, the white associated with Palamon and Venus, and their consequent reconciliation. Similarly, love and war, the dove and the sword, meet in the daisy—in a reconciliation effected by "l'amor che move il sole e l'altre stelle," and through them, so much of what transpires beneath the moon.

Further implications of this reconciliation of contraries are suggested by the gloss Boccaccio wrote to the *Teseida*, in which he explains "myghtly Mars the rede" and his temple as a representation of the irascible appetite, Venus and her temple as a representation of the concupiscible.[44] That the daisy's red and white, its chaste union of Venus and Mars, is a similar manifestation of these two faculties cannot be doubted when one witnesses the irascibility and concupiscence evident in the two dream personae of the day's eye, the fiery god of Love and the piteous Alceste. In the "Knight's Tale" Chaucer locates the temples of Mars, Venus, and Diana within Theseus's circular amphitheater, adds a description of Diana's temple, one full of images of metamorphosis, and places it "intermediate" between Venus and Mars that we might see in Diana, the goddess of hunting and chastity, the kind of rational control that must be exercised on Venerean concupiscence and Martian irascibility if they are to be transformed and harmonized. In the process Chaucer transformed the "lists," that creation of Theseus which he liked "wonder weel," into an *imago mundi* significantly analogous to Boethius's picture (in 3, m. 9) of the soul of triple nature that moves all things—by conferring on each of the world's parts, the commentators explain, the life appropriate to it, whether vegetable, sensible, and intellectual or concupiscible, irascible, and rational.[45]

While some insistently referred Boethius's characterization of this soul to the human soul, others were prepared to recognize its true referent, Plato's World Soul, and even to identify it simultaneously with the World Soul and the Holy Spirit.[46] Increasingly, however, the philosophical poets of the later Middle Ages transferred the functions of the World Soul to the personification Natura, the secondary power established by God to invigorate and order the created.[47] Just as the *imago mundi* of the "lists," the *integumentum* of the philosopher-duke of Athens, depicts an order in macrocosm and microcosm like that philosophy associated with the World Soul and Natura, so the sun, that artifacting fire, and the responsive red and white daisy collectively express a similar order in the created and constitute an analogous *integumentum*.[48] Even as the heat, light, and motion of the sun, an expression of the rational order of the immutable heavens, invigorates and orders the life of the daisy, so in spring it animates flowers, birds, even humans—the whole hierarchy of being.

If we can see in the sun's animation and ordering of the daisy an instance of the universal natural order, one evident in both macrocosm and microcosm, we can see the same order in the daisy itself, especially given Chaucer's insistent treatment of it as a courtly *marguerite*. In its unwavering adherence to the sun, an adherence that might be said to perfect its innate likeness to the sun, we recognize an image of man properly ordered by love. Though we are accustomed to regard concupiscence and irascibility as vices, a view perhaps encouraged by the content of the temples of Venus and Mars in the "Knight's Tale," we should remember what Innocent tells us these appetites were created to be—in a text Chaucer claims (in the G Prologue) to have translated, the "Wreched Engendrynge of Mankynde"—the one a capacity to love the good, the other a capacity to hate the evil; it was, in turn, the responsibility of the rational faculty to distinguish between the two and guide these lower appetites.[49] If the daisy's red and white represent these two appetites, its adherence to the sun suggests the power of such things as reason, virtue, and love to order these conflicting passions. The proper gloss to the daisy's obedience to the sun in this respect is perhaps William of Conches's commentary on the "reduci igne" of the *Consolation*.[50] William explains that this fire is divine love; its splendor illuminates the mind that it may know the celestial, and its warmth fills it with a desire to imitate the heavenly, for love works in anyone who loves God to enlighten him and make him desire heaven. Thus, the love of God, his benign and providential law, the *lex benigna* of Boethius (3, m. 9), leads those God elects back to him through their adherence to the good and their rejection of vicious-

ness, even as the daisy loves the light and hates the dark. It is this
love, of course—a "faire cheyne" simultaneously infused and returning—that Boethius celebrates as harmonizing the cosmos and,
if it rules in the heart, as the source of true happiness; it is this love
that Dante declares at the end of the *Paradiso* to be moving his will
and desire along with the sun and the other stars; it is also this love
that Troilus discovers in and through his relationship with Criseyde—that joy which "thise clerkes wise / Commenden so."

Chaucer also draws on the narrowly theological to inform the
daisy with the sacred. This is suggested by much of the diction. For
instance, the narrator's love is "devocioun"; the flower's rising, a
"resureccioun." While such diction is traditional in courtly literature
and typical of the narrator's extravagance, an extravagance tinged
with irony, it points to an important dimension of the daisy's meaning. Especially noteworthy in this regard is the characterization of
the daisy as "of all floures flour, / Fulfilled of al vertu and honour"
(F, 53–54). As the first in the hierarchy of flowers, it contains all
flowers.[51] Its union of the lily and the rose expresses its capacity to
make the many one. As an image that returns multiplicity to unity,
it is a reflection of the *forma formarum,* of God as the idea of ideas.[52]
As an intercessor and bearer of light, the daisy recalls the Virgin,
the conventional flower of flowers, the immaculate rose.[53] Applied
to the Virgin, the phrase meant that she unites, to quote Dante's
expression of the idea, "quantunque in creatura e di bontate"
(whatever there is of goodness in any creature).[54] It is as a *summa* of
created things, a *forma formarum,* that Dante is celebrating her in
that final Canto of the *Paradiso.* If Chaucer verbally echoes that passage in Troilus's praise of "Benigne Love" as the "holy bond of
thynges," here he expresses its thought in his own images. The daisy is a similar *summa*—in the god of Love's imperium. All the ladies
in the god's company, having come forth from paradise into the
English countryside, kneel about the daisy, and sing "with o vois":

> Heel and honour
> To trouthe of womanhede, and to the flour
> That bereth our alder pris in figurynge!
> Hire white corowne bereth the witnessynge. (F, 296–99)

As the image of all the ladies kneeling about the daisy recalls the
Paradiso, even its final image of the white rose, so the words could

be sung of the Virgin. Of course, our knowledge of the identities of some of the singing women whose goodness is summed up in the Alceste-daisy brings us back down, closer to earth. This is Chaucer's dream, not Dante's, and it is an English daisy, not the white rose—though it does bear the prize as a figure.

Lilies and roses have other sacred associations that Chaucer has incorporated;[55] particularly relevant here are the lilies of chastity and the roses of martyrdom. The appropriateness of such associations is suggested by the fact that the *Legend* is cast in the form of a legendary and that symbolic flowers are common in the iconography of the saints. Indeed, there is some evidence that the *marguerite*-daisy occasionally joined the *marguerite*-pearl in the later Middle Ages in the iconography of the various saints named Margaret.[56] Though written after Chaucer's death, Lydgate's exemplification of Margaret of Antioch by the daisy (in language that seems to echo the *Legend*) perfectly illustrates the potentiality of the red and white daisy as saint's icon:

> This daysye, with leves rede and white,
> > Purpul hewed, as maked in memorye
> > Whan that hir blode was shad oute by victorye,
> The chaste lely of whos maydenhede
> Through martyrdam was spreynt with roses rede.[57]

Associated with Alceste—who is a "natural saint" in the chaste purity of her marriage, we may suppose, and in her martyrdom to truth in loving—and depicted as undergoing a daily death and "resureccioun," Chaucer's daisy is another Margaret: that is, another heavenly union of the lily of chastity and the rose of martyrdom.

Though we have by no means exhausted Chaucer's daisy as a figure, it is time to turn to its other half, the representative focus of the narrator's other devotion, the literary heroine Alceste. Though the narrator is slow to recognize her in his vision, he does apparently know her, associate her with the daisy, and reverence her (see F, 518–19): when the god of Love asks him if he does not have a book telling how Alceste was turned into a daisy, the narrator remembers that Jove stellified her, that "Cibella" made the daisy "in remembraunce of hire," and that Mars gave her crown its red, the rubies among the pearls. This union of the daisy and Alceste not only demonstrates that nature and art can manifest the same truth

in similar ways, as Kiser argues[58] but also furthers Chaucer's demonstration in the Prologue of the way in which the stable source returns all multiplicity to oneness. What we are told about Alceste
confirms and amplifies the truth we have seen in the daisy and thus
proves their oneness.

She is a similar model for lovers, one that apparently reconciles
courtly love and marriage:

> kalendar ys she
> To any woman that wol lover bee.
> For she taught al the craft of fyn lovynge,
> And namely of wyfhod the lyvynge,
> And al the boundes that she oghte kepe. (F, 542–46)

As queen in the god of Love's court she is the supreme embodiment of the courtly virtues and a mirror, in her relationship to
the god, of "wifely" counsel and obedience. There can be few better examples in all of literature of the manner of "ruled Curtesye"
than her deferential and faintly flattering yet firm insistence that the
god should be merciful as well as just. However temporarily, she
demonstrates that "fyn lovynge" and courtesy can reconcile the
concupiscible and the irascible so that they do express a love of the
good and a hatred of evil. She is the lady of ladies in the god's court
and every bit as much a "pris in figurynge" as the daisy. Something of what ideal love entails is clear from her history as the god
recounts it:

> She that for hire housbonde chees to dye,
> And eke to goon to helle, rather than he,
> And Ercules rescowed hire, parde,
> And brought hir out of helle agayn to blys. (F, 513–16)

As Hercules' rescue of her recalls Christ's harrowing of Hell, so her
own death and descent into Hades that her husband might live presumably manifests a love like that which moved Christ to die and
descend to Hell that his spouse might ascend to bliss.[59] It is this similar *caritas* that explains and justifies her own rescue and translation.

Alceste's capacity as a multidimensional figure confirming and
amplifying the daisy is particularly evident in the implications
Chaucer gives to her crown. Here Kiser again points us in the right

direction. In her discussion of the close analogy in the Prologue between words and things as metaphors—"good" metaphoric words being those that point to corresponding metaphorical realities—and her demonstration that the daisy and Alceste are such metaphorical *res*,[60] Kiser observes that Alceste's white crown links her simultaneously with the daisy and the sun; she refers us in a footnote to the Latin term "corona," which designated both the martyr's crown and the sun's corona.[61] Chaucer's embodiments of the complexities of the word in the thing, of the idea of "corona" in Alceste's crown, needs to be further explored.

Alceste's crown is shaped like a daisy and made of pearl. By making it a pearl daisy, Chaucer in effect creates a visual pun, the French term *marguerite* meaning both pearl and daisy.[62] This "corona" is simultaneously daisy, *marguerite*, and *margaritum*, a unification suggesting the power of *res* as *signum* both to undo Babel and to intimate the One diversely manifested by the many. We are inevitably and rightly reminded by this union of flower and pearl of the *Pearl*, where the dreamer loses a pearl that was but a rose when he lost it, though it is now the heavenly pearl it was created to be.[63] Having experienced something of a sea change herself, Alceste is both daisy and pearl, an imperishable gem-flower "evere ilyke faire and fressh." If Alceste's "corona" reminds us that "coronatur" could be used simply as the antithesis of "damnatur" and its pearl constitution recalls more particularly the reward of the martyr, the red given to the flower by Mars "in stede of rubyes" (as though the pearl of Alceste's crown were intermixed with them) inevitably remembers the price of such translation—the crown of thorns and the blood shed in suffering.[64] As a heavenly crown, Alceste's also calls to mind—like the god of Love's sun-crown, his halo—the "coronae" worn both by the sun and by the saints.[65] The women who kneel in a circle about the daisy to sing its praises, like so many additional petals, also constitute a "corona," a circle of people being another of its definitions and another analogous image. In a sense the saints are God's "corona," the light he radiates about himself— not his white rose but his red and white rose, his daisy. Is it any wonder the poet contemplates (all day on his knees) and sings the Alceste-daisy?

When Chaucer tells us that Alceste was stellified for her goodness, he explains that

Hire white corowne berith of hyt witnesse;
For also many vertues hadde shee
As smale florouns in hire corowne bee. (F, 527–29)

While the crown bears immediate witness to her goodness, the first
of these lines suggests that Chaucer may also have envisioned Alceste stellified as a crown, as a stellar ring of light. Indeed, given his
subsequent mislocation of Ariadne's crown, the "Corona Borealis,"
in the sign of Taurus, we may even suspect that Chaucer was implicitly reassigning the Northern Crown to Alceste and imagining
her shining forth from the heavens adjacent to the constellation of
her rescuer, Hercules.[66] Whether we imagine Alceste stellified a "di-
minutive sun" (with Kiser) or a heavenly crown, in either case she
is a circle of light, that ultimate image of unity and eternity, of the
divine simplicity. To know the word, then, is to know the thing; to
know the thing is to know the word, even the Word, that in which
all the multiplicity of words and things have their simultaneous Al-
pha and Omega. In the narrator's visionary dream, the Alceste-
daisy is indeed a "mistico serto," a "mistico raggio di luce e fior."

In short, Chaucer has taken an object from the natural world,
the daisy, and a character from old books, one presumably assumed to have been "historical," and has shown them to be mutually confirming and amplifying manifestations of the nature of
the universe. Together they demonstrate the order of nature, the
vitality and law of the mutable. Chaucer makes their demonstration
of that order simultaneously a revelation of the character of nature's transcendent source and end and an intimation of the life of
those who attain to that transcendent immutability. He further
demonstrates that at the heart of the order linking the mutable with
the immutable is a fiery chain of love, a constraining power that
mandates alike the revival of spring and winter's "swerd of cold"
but that can become for mankind a means of "transhumanization,"
whereby one can become a god by participation.[67] By presenting
the daisy as a *marguerite* and Alceste as a courtly heroine, he locates
that same order and power in his audience's here and now and thus
makes the Alceste-daisy an affirmation that the beloved can be the
lover's Beatrice, the object in and through which the "reduci igne"
descends to enable a reascent. This flower of flowers is a lyric and
a hymn celebrating the possibilities of the "craft of fyn-lovynge."

At the same time, however, the location of this possibility in the quotidian present, the domestication of the ideal, confronts us with the comedy of human fallibility, with the drama of humanity's manifold and mutable responses to the freedom that the constraining fire of love permits.

THE DRAMA that takes place in the narrator's dream, the trial of the narrator, appears to be a distanced, fictionalized recreation of Chaucer's relationship with his court audience and of certain political realities of the day. The distance is evident in the thoroughly conventional character of this drama. The god or goddess of Love angry at a reluctant servant is a familiar figure, as is the lady as intercessor. Two literary analogues from court poetry merit particular mention, either or both of which may have been sources of inspiration: Machaut's *Jugement dou Roy de Navarre,* in which the poet is accused of having defamed women in a previous poem and, found guilty after long debate, assigned the punishment of composing three short lyrics; and Froissart's *Trésor amoureux,* in which the god of Love accuses the poet of writing against him and of dissuading his followers, while two ladies, "Beau Parler" and "Congnoissance," speak in the poet's defense.[68] The presentation in the Prologue of the conflicting demands of justice and mercy also has important sacred analogues: most notably, of course, Mary's traditional role as mankind's advocate before her Son; somewhat less immediately, perhaps, the literary debates of the four daughters of God.[69] The power inherent in the conventional idea and image of lady as intercessor is suggested by the role apparently assigned Queen Anne in the ceremonies reconciling the king and the city of London, that of supplicating Richard on behalf of the city to restore its ancient rights and liberties, as though she alone in the two persons of wife and queen could overcome his righteous anger.[70]

Chaucer has personalized this stock situation. Much of the defense of the poet surveys his life's work with regard to its attitude toward love. At the same time, the persona on trial is a distinctly comic projection of self, and the trial is clearly marked as an event in the life of that fictive character; it is his dream, one induced by a day spent in the sun observing the daisy and a night sleeping on a couch strewn with flowers. By linking the narrator's dream so closely and so sensuously with his waking experience, Chaucer renders its revelation tentative, for these connections express the possibility that the dream is little more than a product of the narrator's memory and imagination running riot while his reason sleeps. The suggestion that the drama is at root a *psychomachia* is reinforced by the allegorical character of its nearest analogues.[71] Consistent with this subjectivism, the actual behavior of the personae of the dream, those simultaneous mirrors of the narrator's mind and of Richard and Anne's court, threatens to negate the affirmation of their prototypes.[72]

The action of the dream recalls the order of nature evident in the behavior of the birds, the universal clash of contraries. The conflict there of winter and summer, "Daunger" and "Pitee," irascibility and concupiscence, sin and repentance, justice and mercy, is here reenacted. Listing the narrator's sins against his law, the god of Love angrily threatens vengeance. Responding with magnificent "ruled Curtesye," Alceste pleads for mercy. Once again justice yields to mercy, and once again the yielding is temporary, for no sooner has Alceste won the narrator the god's forgiveness than she shows him her own frosty "daunger." The narrator's rapid movement from winter to summer to winter, as it were, reminds us, like Chaucer's characterization of spring as a forgetting of winter, that this clash of contraries produces an order of cyclical change in nature. In spite of the implicit recapitulation of the progress of the seasons, however, these changes are so sudden and so seemingly capricious (in the manner of Dame Fortune's cyclical whimsicality) that they seem anything but orderly.

Similarly, though the courtly manner dominates both the behavior of the characters in the dream and the narrator's account of it, Chaucer's irony suggests that for all the surface harmony, the "ruled Curtesye" of the dream may conceal rather than control chaos. While the god's charges, the queen's defense, and the penance assigned all make superficial sense, radical discontinuities throughout the trial in words, deeds, and apparent motives reveal the presence of considerable irrationality. As the god's complaints against the narrator indicate that he is a lord who prefers flattery and does not wish to hear the truth about the sublunary lovers over whom he rules, so they show him to be more concerned with maintaining his dominion than with the justice of his rule. Further, though we may understand Cupid's complaining that the *Troilus* makes the wise withdraw from his service, it hardly seems a just assessment of the poem's offense against his law to judge it an attack on women—as though the narrator, who is so fond of Criseyde and so insistent that he writes to warn women against false men, were deliberately and virulently antifeminist. If the god's initial attack seems an ill-conceived outburst of irascibility, his subsequent forgiveness appears almost totally capricious. The god's decision to be merciful apparently has nothing to do with the queen's largely hypothetical defense of the poet. He never investigates to see whether there is any truth in it. He never stops to ponder whether or not her assertion that the narrator's poetry has made "lewed folk" delight in serving him is an adequate answer to his charge that the narrator's poetry has discouraged the wise. Rather, he changes his mind because it aggrandizes his own image of himself to do so. Having been reminded that gods are merciful and that he should consider what befits his honor, he forgives the narrator that he may save his "degree" by showing himself a god.

There is as great a dissociation between his queen's words and deeds. Though she begins her intercession by observing that the god should listen to whatever the narrator can say in his own defense, her own response to his attempted defense shows no intention whatsoever to let him have his say:

> Let be thyn arguynge,
> For Love ne wol nat countrepleted be
> In ryght ne wrong; and lerne that at me! (F, 475–77)

She rescues him from the god's unjust wrath only to show him her own imperious disdain. Rather than the mercy she recommends to the god, it is "daunger" that "renneth soone in [her] gentil herte." Such, it would seem, are the effects of power. The absurdity of this action, in which she inflicts upon the narrator the same injustice from which she ostensibly rescues him, has a counterpart in her defense of him, for it proves an indictment. Having defended the narrator on the grounds that he may have been commanded to make the offending translations and that he may have made them unwittingly, unaware in his simplicity of their malice, she commands more translations;[73] if he is as heedless and as "nyce" as she says he is (in his defense), the result can only be a repetition of the offense. The ultimate irrationality is her antimasculine requirement that all the tales depict men as false, for if telling of false women defames love, tales of the seductions and ravishments that men carry out under its influence can scarcely glorify love. Her penance for a sin the narrator has not committed, defamation of love, imposes that sin upon him. The final irony is that when she has finished this "rescue," the god will call upon the narrator to confirm her goodness and express his gratitude for it.[74]

The narrator's trial would appear to demonstrate that the disorder of injustice rules in society as well as in individuals. Drawing upon medieval political philosophy, Chaucer has Alceste characterize a king as in effect an intermediary between society and God.[75] As society's head, it is his task to order its members according to the justice and mercy with which God orders the cosmos.[76] In a sense, a king is to his society what a lady is to her lover, a red and white mediator. The fate of the narrator in the hands of the god and his queen suggests that the lot of the subject in Richard and Anne's England, even those subjects who were "half-goddes" in their own right, was less than enviable. The frailty of kings evident in the god, like the frailty of women evident in the Alceste of the dream, would seem to distort beyond all recognition the descending love and justice of which they are the intermediaries. Not irascibility and concupiscence harmonized but the impulsive expression of now one, now the other, would seem to rule here.

Considered as a mirror of the narrator's mind, the dream appears an equivalent disorder, a manifestation of his own lack of psychological harmony. In the god's criticism we see the narrator's own irascibility turned against himself, perhaps the result of an uneasy conscience. Though he is hardly guilty in the *Troilus* of the blatant antifeminism the god attributes to him, in his case the bond between male and male is stronger than the love that unites the contraries male and female: he may be fond of Criseyde, but he identifies with Troilus; it may have been his intention to warn women against men, but his actual narration makes light of Pandarus's and Troilus's machinations. If the god's criticisms manifest guilt's self-accusations, the hostility to self inherent in humanity's divided and sinful nature, Alceste's defense expresses the self-justification that the elemental love of self concocts: it's not my fault. Indeed, one may well feel that the *Legend* dramatizes the very sins, the same divisions, in its narrator that it is supposed to be penance for: though the penance is to vindicate women and speak well of love, the poem the narrator writes has seemed to many antifeminist satire. As we shall see, viewed as an expression of the narrator, the *Legend* dramatizes his concupiscence and irascibility loving and satirizing in an imperfect apprehension of what is good and lovable, what evil and contemptible. As a projection of the narrator's feelings, as a creation of his memory and desire, the dream reveals him to be a disorder in need of a harmonizing sun. In short, the fires of spring and the cold sword of winter in the little world that is the man seem anything but concordant.

For all its confusions, the narrator's dream is the poet's vision of the love that unites justice and mercy and orders all things according to the demands of these expressions of God's nature. Just as the narrator discovers that his two loves, the daisy and Alceste, are one, so the reader comes to realize that all the contraries which seem to disorder life are reconciled in an all-embracing and harmonizing love. We come to see that the god, Alceste, and the daisy all reflect, however distortedly, the love that unites justice and mercy. The daisy is both red and white; the god demands justice yet forgives; Alceste expresses both "daunger" and pity. For all the capricious forgetfulness of Alceste's actions, they are both merciful and just. However comic her behavior, its effect is to forgive and not forget—even though that behavior is itself a product of forgetting. Thus it is that divine love orders human divisions and makes them serve the good. Or such would seem to be the faith of the vision.

It is not enough to see in these changes the pattern of summer and winter and in both the eternal oneness of God's justice and mercy mirrored in time in alternating contraries. The daisy is simultaneously red and white, true love simultaneously just and merciful, the summer justly merciful, the winter mercifully just. Chaucer's poem would teach the ladies at Richard's court (and Richard) that to be true and to be loved truly they must join pity and "daunger." The legends are full of the tragedy that results when women are at first all self-indulgent pity and then, when their too freely given love is betrayed by faithless men, all remorse, recrimination, and desire for revenge—a revenge they ultimately visit upon themselves. Neither justice nor mercy alone can reform either man the ravisher or the self. The union of the two in the Alceste of the narrator's dream is evident in her demand for penance, however absurd the actual penance assigned, for penance unites the demands of justice and mercy and reconciles these two daughters of God. It simultaneously satisfies the demand of justice that sin be punished and the contrary demand of mercy that there be a means of redemption. The very antagonism to self expressed by the narrator's dream, the consequence of his divided nature, is necessary for him to regain unity, for the self-flagellations of contrition are both a product of man's division and a means of purging the self of divisive sin; consequently, and paradoxically, contrition is simultaneously an expression of love, a desire for unity. Penance perfectly expresses the divine economy, the *ordinatio,* that makes the consequences of the Fall the very means of redemption. Divine justice and mercy are one. They inform and order all multiplicity and every moment in time, insuring, the *Legend* implies, that all things are red and white flowers, whether freely, through a rationally willed participation like Alceste's, or necessarily, like the daisy.

THOUGH THE humanization of the Alceste-daisy in the lady of the narrator's dreams makes her a less than perfect mirror of the good, or rather a less perfectly free mirror of the good, clearly the love of such a creature, especially as rectified by God, can be potentially ennobling and redemptive. In the *marguerite* tradition, as in courtly love in general, the beneficent effects of love derive in part from the nature of the beloved, in part from the experience of love itself. Chaucer's most significant reiteration of this assumption in the *Legend* is not explicit but dramatic: his dramatization of the narrator's obedience to the flower in the Prologue, to Alceste in the legends. Chaucer pictures his narrator as so constrained by love that he arises before day to watch the daisy rise to the sun's rising; that he spends the whole day following the daisy as it follows the sun; that he goes home to bed when it closes upon the setting of the sun so that he may rise early the next day to begin the cycle anew. His love of the daisy causes him to imitate its imitation of the sun. One potential result of his adherence to it and his participation in its circular course is that he too may become an eye of day, a daisy and a sun. If the responsive fire that burns in his heart when the sun is in the breast of Taurus, constraining him to kneel all day before the daisy, is potentially a disordering passion, a source of seasonal ravishing, it is also possible that the love of one who so manifests the truth as the Alceste-daisy may transform the narrator into a similar source of light and truth. To imitate the daisy is to love the light, to hate the dark, to be faithful to the light even in the night's darkness. If the distance between the narrator's love and such perfect truth in loving is suggested by the sensuality of his going to bed on a couch strewn with flowers, his innate hunger for the good is evident in the fact that he dreams during the night of the Alceste-daisy.

What is entailed in journeying through the night while mindful of the good is clear from the fact that Alceste travels a circular course analogous to the daisy's: she too descended into darkness, into the very darkness of hell, until Hercules "brought hir out of helle agayn to blys." The significance of Alceste's infernal descent is clear from Chaucer's definition of it in the *Troilus,* where he implicitly contrasts her successful infernal descent with the unsuccessful descents of Orpheus and Eurydice and of Proserpina.[77] As Boethius presented the Orpheus myth and his commentators interpreted it, Eurydice's death and descent into hell represents the way in which man's concupiscence, his innate appetite for the good, goes astray and "dies" when it becomes enamored of the false goods of the infernal—that is, the sublunar—world; and Orpheus's attempted rescue, the effort of man's rational faculties to return the appetite "wandrynge by the weye" to the true good.[78] The poet-philosopher fails, in the rescue he attempts through the power of his song, to harmonize the infernal world's discord because he breaks the prohibition against looking back as he leads Eurydice out of hell; that is, he fails to keep his thoughts from turning from the "cleernesse of sovereyn good" to the darkness of "erthly thinges." His failure is due, of course, to the fact that "the moste ardaunt love of his wif brende the entrayles of his brest" and constrained him to look back in desire, for no one "may yeven a lawe unto lovers."

Alceste's successful adherence to the light of the good is also implicitly contrasted in the *Troilus* with Proserpina's (and Criseyde's) analogous violation of a prohibition, her failure to abstain from eating the fruits of the underworld when she was "as out of the world agon." Thus Alceste does not have to spend half of each year in Hades; more accurately, though she has to experience the world's seasonal changes, endure its nights and winters, she is not of them, is not their mythic source, as is Proserpina (and Criseyde). If Al-

ceste is a successful Orpheus who did not forget the good while in
the land of the false and thus is herself heroically self-sufficient—
the master of her own concupiscence and irascibility—from another point of view, the role of the succcessful Orpheus, of Hercules,
is played by the sun.[79] To adhere to the sun is inevitably to be res-
cued from the darkness with the morning's "resureccioun." Ultimately, for a medieval Christian, salvation waits upon grace, upon
the infusion of light. If the failures of Orpheus and of Proserpina
make them mythic sources of the world's duplicity and division, Alceste's success makes her a mythic source of the heavenly crown and
translates her to the world beyond change.

That the narrator's love of the Alceste-daisy turns him in analogous circles is evident not only from his imitation of the daisy but
also from Chaucer's dramatization of the origins of the legends.
Moved in spring to abandon his "olde bokes" and go forth to spend
the day with the fresh daisy, the narrator returns at night to have
a dream that returns him in its turn to his wintry books. In this descent into winter and darkness he is guided by "the clernesse and
the verray lyght" of the Alceste-daisy; she is his "gide," his "sover-
eyne," and his "erthly god" "both in this werk and in [his] sorwes
alle." By associating the creation of the legends with the daisy's en-
durance of the night and Alceste's descent into hell, Chaucer implicitly declares his narrator a poet-philosopher and makes his quest
through the *inferna* of old books in search of truth in loving an image of man's efforts to discover and adhere to the true light as he
journeys through this world. Any expectations that the narrator will
succeed in this quest, expectations presumably encouraged by the
fact that his guides have successfully made the journey before, are
dampened somewhat both by the fact that the entrayles" of his breast
are also on fire with an ardent love and by the actual guidance his
lights provide him. The penance, the "sorwe," that Alceste assigns—to promote truth in loving by celebrating the goodness of
women and exposing the falseness of men—hardly seems the means
to lead the narrator to a heavenly crown. Indeed, it seems decidedly unheroic and a distinctly unlikely way to discover truth.

Chaucer's simultaneous elevation and denigration of the present undertaking, writing a *Legend of Good Women*, recalls Gower's
simultaneous wish at the end of the Prologue to the *Confessio Amantis* that another Arion might arise to heal the divisions in England,

followed by his personal disavowal of any such capacity.[80] Like Orpheus, Arion was a harper whose music could reconcile the hare and the hound and make the hind live "in pes with the Leoun." Declaring himself no Arion, Gower goes off to heal the divisions within himself—or such is the implications of the confessional form of his collection of love stories and of his apparent recovery from the sickness of love at the end of the work. Chaucer expresses a similar humility in the face of the high calling of philosophical poet, simultaneously embracing it and disavowing it, by casting himself in the Christlike role of Alceste and by giving himself the Herculean labor of vindicating an irate Cupid. If Dante protested that he was no Aeneas, no Paul, no one suited for the journey Virgil was confronting him with, Chaucer protests in effect that he is no Hercules, no Dante.[81] In response to the ardent fire burning in his breast, his harp sings only of daisies (in borrowed words at that) and tells unlikely stories, mere fables ("Leveth hem if yow leste!"), of women true in loving. Yet if the very undertaking of the narrator seems a "looking back," it is also a penance and thus a potential means of redemption.

Perhaps we should end this discussion of the Prologue by remembering one thing Bernard the Monk did see: that the Word was made flesh because carnal man cannot know the Word itself, at least not initially.[82] The Word became flesh that Christ might move humanity to love him first in the flesh and afterward in his divinity. Similarly, the eyes of carnal man cannot look directly at the sun. The implication is that it is through contemplating daisies and engaging in such exercises as the present poem that one can learn to see the light itself. As a lover and poet, a harp singing to the fingering of the Alceste-daisy—those dissimilar similitudes to the sun—perhaps he can become himself a revelation of truth in loving, make himself and his poetry Alceste-daisies by which we can learn to look at the sun. That is the hope and promise implicit in his characterization of the Alceste-daisy and in his dramatization of the genesis of the poem.

The Narrator as Translator

III

The fundamental problem confronting the reader of the legends is to determine the point of view from which they ought to be read or—to phrase the question another way—to determine their relationship to the Prologue, for one's view of this relationship is bound to govern one's perception of how Chaucer's narratives relate to their sources. Having been commanded in the Prologue to "speke wel of love" by writing of good and faithful wives and of false men, Chaucer's narrator produces a sequence of legends whose heroines and villains seem highly unsatisfactory. Some critics have chosen to minimize the apparent discrepancies between the demanded and the delivered: Lowes, for example, argues that the heroines are all "stock *exempla of fidelity in love*," and Robinson declares them "good in the only sense that counted for the purpose at hand."[1] Others have emphasized the discrepancies to read the legends ironically: Goddard, for example, declares them "a most unmerciful satire upon women"; Garrett, "a masterly set of humorous sketches."[2] While Chaucer must have known that these "stock *exempla*" were far from ideal representatives of truth in loving, the critical question is whether or not he intended the discrepancies in his versions to be recognized as such, a question that directs us first to the Prologue to see what guidelines it provides.[3] If Chaucer's intent was "unmerciful satire," the critical history of the legends suggests that he was as unsuccessful as he was if he wished us to respond to his heroines with heartfelt sympathy and unqualified respect.

When Alceste and the god of Love lay down the law, they impose it on the narrator: that is, not on the poet but on the fictive representation of himself that Chaucer creates in the poem. What they impose is the manner and matter of the courtly tradition. The narrator proves an intrusive teller of tales, and though he begins reluctantly, apparently still convinced that men as well as women can be true in love, and admits near the end that he is "agroted" from telling of false men, his intrusions overwhelmingly reinforce the prescribed attitude. He pities his heroines as innocent victims and denounces their lovers as faithless. Time and again he addresses his audience directly, urging the women in it not to trust men and implicitly indicting the men in it as false. Indeed, the narrator's reactions are so frequent and so frequently extreme that they prove self-dramatizing, even comically so. This fact reinforces our sense from the Prologue that we must distinguish not only technically between the poet and the narrator—the one being inside the poem, the other outside it—but also ideologically. They speak with different voices and represent different points of view. Thus, to address again the old question of the point of view appropriate to the legends is to confront another of the perennial problems of Chaucer criticism: the relationship of Chaucer to his narrator.[4]

R. W. Frank has argued that the question of the goodness of the legends' heroines is in effect a red herring. He contends that Chaucer's purpose in the *Legend* was to introduce his audience to a new and essentially uncourtly subject matter and that the Prologue was his strategy for achieving this end. By making the legends penance for his past sins against the god of Love, even written at the command of the god and his queen, Chaucer "lends an illusion of orthodoxy to the new kind of story he is introducing" and thus frees himself to "do almost anything he wishes":[5] namely, to tell stories simply for their own sake.[6] While Frank's approach ignores the crucial fact that these stories have been altered to increase their agreement with the letter of Alceste's demands (often to the detriment of the story) so that they seem anything but free performances, it does implicitly recognize that the problem of the relationship of the legends to the Prologue is not simply a question of whether or not they satisfy Alceste's and the god's requirements. Before we can read the *Legend* as a poetic whole, we must distinguish between what Alceste and the god require the legends to be and the purposes the Prologue as a whole assigns to them. We must distinguish between Alceste's idea for the legends and the poet's.

The first thing the Prologue as a whole indicates is that the legends will not satisfy the demands of the god and his queen. The shallowness of the god's criticisms, the absurdity of much of Alceste's defense, and the contradictory nature of their prescriptions all indicate that the legends must inevitably fail to meet their desires. The god's complaint reveals that what he wants from Chaucer's art is flattery for himself and his servants. If Chaucer intended the legends to be taken at face value, presumably he would not have implied that the desire for such legends was a self-serving denial both of the complexity of reality and the profundity of old books. While each of Alceste's defenses makes good enough sense in itself—that Chaucer may have been falsely accused, there being many liars and flatterers in the god's court; that he may have been translating heedlessly; that he may have been ordered to make the offending translations; that he may have repented; that he was only translating others' words—collectively, they do not augur well for any future efforts. If Chaucer is as simple-minded, as "nyce," as she implies, this fact can only be a recipe for further trouble. The difficulties it predicts are guaranteed when the god orders the narrator to begin with Cleopatra, for Cleopatra is impossible in the role of a woman true in loving all her life. Even without this stipulation the narrator's task is impossible, for the requirement that he speak well of love is in conflict with the demand that he depict all men as false lovers. How is one to speak well of a love that has no beneficent effects upon its servants? In defense of love, the narrator has been ordered to deny, at least by implication, that which was thought to prove its worth: its ennobling power, a proof of the value of love repeatedly appealed to in the *Troilus*, we recall.

The fact that Chaucer dramatizes the irrationality of the program he nonetheless has the narrator execute not only predicts inevitable failure but also indicates that this failure is part of his true subject. In effect, the narrator is the author of the legends as courtly poems; he writes the poem Lowes reads. Chaucer wrote the rather more elusive poem that those who read the legends as an ironic intertextuality have been trying to define. What has not been sufficiently realized by those whose footsteps this chapter follows is that the poet's poem is not merely the ironic inversion of the narrator's poem but contains it, is about those translations. By reading the legends as illustrations of Alceste's and the god's inadequate idea, Fy-

ler and Kiser take the first step toward appreciating the significance
of this fact. The next step is to realize the importance of the visibility of the narrator, for it implies that the second poem dramatizes
his writing of the first poem. Thus the Prologue not only narrates
the events that account for the narrator's translations but also presents itself as the narrator's response to those events. The apostrophe to the daisy, invoking its help; the inclusion of the *balade;*
the speculations about the value of old books, with the subsequent
comment that he will tell us why he spoke of old books when he has
time—all these belong to the time of the writing and dramatize that
writing. The same must be said of the narrator's apostrophes to his
characters and his direct address to his audience in the legends.
They dramatize the writing. One implication of this fact is that the
conventional problem of the reader, how to reconcile the Ovidian
sources with Alceste's and the god's prescriptions, is inside the poem;
it is the narrator's problem. Chaucer's legends are about his efforts
to deal with this difficulty.

Much of Chaucer's characterization of his narrator in the *Legend*
is familiar. While we may hear "Chaucer the man" protesting in the
narrator's insistence in the Prologue that it was always his intention
to further truth in loving in his poetry, we also recognize that familiar persona of the affable bumbler by which Chaucer time and
again represents himself in his poetry. His denigrating dramatization of himself in the Prologue is evident in the apparent literal-
mindedness of the narrator's veneration of the daisy, in the naive
credulity of his declaration that he himself gives his old books "ful
credence," in the obtuse forgetfulness with which he fails to recognize his own Alceste in the dream, in the ineffectuality of his pro-
testations of innocence. When Alceste defends the narrator on the
grounds that he is "nyce" and, hence, may have translated the offending works not from malice but from carelessness simply because "he useth thynges for to make" (F 364), as though he translated mindlessly and compulsively, she describes precisely what we
find in the legends from the point of view of her demands, stories
rather carelessly chosen and dubiously interpreted. The narrator is
a man who gets little right, and that little is misunderstood. This
accord between Alceste's characterization of the narrator and the
legends he produces indicates that the lack of accord between the
demanded and the delivered is no accident but an integral part of

Chaucer's idea. While the Prologue does not require so many tales of Sir Thopas, this accord indicates that the unsatisfactory character of the legends reflects the narrator's comic limitations as well as the artistically counterproductive character of the demands imposed upon him.[7]

All is not comedy, however. The Prologue anticipates a drama of considerable import and poignancy. First, the narrator has two loves: he loves the daisy from the natural world; he loves Alceste, a heroine from old books, and more generally, old books themselves. While his vision reveals that his diverse loves manifest the same truth, the initial presentation of them in opposition implies at least some conflict between authority and experience, between the "doctrine of these olde wyse" and the way things seem to be in the here and now of fourteenth-century London. Further difficulty is implied by the disparity between the narrator's ideal loves, the daisy and the historical Alceste, and the humanized counterparts that people his dream. The latter are the source of the Prologue's contradictory prescriptions. By depicting their imposition of the courtly ideology as an irrational comedy, one that places the lady of the narrator's dream at odds with her ideal prototypes, Chaucer further intimates the irrationality of that ideology—its commitment to illusion rather than to reality—and implies that the imposed perspective will contradict both experience and the "doctrine" of old books. The narrator would indeed seem to be trapped among these irreconcilable loyalties and obligations.

It is equally clear that the narrator's drama enacts Chaucer's own dilemmas as poet. Behind him as courtly maker stands an enabling tradition, which—if the god and Alceste can be taken to speak accurately for it—threatens to frustrate his apparent ambition to be a philosophical poet. Before him stands an audience determined that his poetry should pamper its illusions and delusions. If he finds a way of surmounting these impediments, a way of transforming courtly making into philosophical poetry, all the hazards inherent in that high calling await him. "Storyal soth" is elusive and, discovered, but a dark mirror of transcendent "trouthe." As we shall see, the narrator and his courtly poem are both Chaucer's dramatized confession of his own inadequacy for this task and simultaneously his means of realizing it.

THOUGH ALL the possible sources discovered so far by modern scholarship for the "Legend of Cleopatra" require significant modification if her story is to satisfy Alceste's demands, the narrator judges it adequate for the purposes at hand.[8] He concludes it by extravagantly wishing that he may never have a headache before he finds a man "thus trewe and stable," one who will die for love "so frely" as Cleopatra did. Though the very next legend provides "thus trewe" a lover, indicating that Chaucer hardly undertook Alceste's penance in dead earnest, we cannot be certain that he assumed his audience would know the narrator's account to be less than the "storyal soth" he claimed it to be. What is demonstrably clear is that the narrator's account provides ample reason for doubting his interpretation of it. As is the case throughout the legends, much of the suppressed is intimated: though the narrator omits the fact that Cleopatra committed suicide to avoid the shame of being paraded by Caesar, the observation made in passing that she "coude of Cesar have no grace" reveals that she died for love somewhat less than "frely." Especially revelatory of the incompatibility of the narrator's old books and the prescribed interpretation is Cleopatra's jarring reminder, in the midst of her final, theatrical protestation of fidelity, that there have been others, when she specifies to whom she has sworn to be true: "I mene yow, Antonius, my knyght."[9]

The qualification of the assertion that Antony was the equal of any "wight"—"but if that bokes lye"—confronts directly the question of the reliability of books. Whether the "storyal" is "soth," written history, historical, is a question also raised in the Prologue, where we are told with admirable discretion that we should believe in the "doctrine" of old books "in every skilful wyse" when we have "noon other preve," and where the narrator simultaneously assures us that he himself gives books "feyth and ful credence." The folly of giving "ful credence" to any book, including this one, is confirmed by the systematic contradictions in the narrator's account. On the alleged authority of his books, the narrator praises Antony for his "gentillesse," though he characterizes him as a traitor to his wife and country; for his "discrecioun," though he tells us that love had brought him in a "rage"; for his "hardynesse," though his own account of the Battle of Actium clearly implies that Antony fled before Cleopatra. That the target of these systematic contradictions is not simply Alceste and the god—that is, those who would impose a priori truths upon the poet and historian—is evident from the fact that these contradictions undermine the narrator when he is resisting, apparently out of male vanity, Alceste's claim that all men are false.

Much of the narrator's difficulty in the legends derives from the requirement that he be brief, especially as he somewhat hastily and heedlessly obeys it. Chaucer's means of demonstrating this, one we will see time and again, is to establish parallels between the narrator and his dramatis personae. In Thisbe's story, with which Cleopatra's is paired, he links the narrator's desire to get on with the story to Pyramus and Thisbe's haste to run away together. After describing how they agreed to meet, the narrator concludes, "and, shortly of this tale for to telle. / This covenant was affermed wonder faste" (789–90). That "wonder faste" was too fast is clear from the assertion early in the legend, in an addition Chaucer made to Ovid, that maidens were closely watched in that country "lest they diden som folye."[10] By juxtaposing the narrator's haste with theirs, Chaucer implies that it too may well be foolish. If Thisbe's "so gret haste Piramus to se" leads to her death, the narrator's equivalent haste leads to the moral confusion that allows him to celebrate their folly.

Chaucer establishes a similar parallel between the narrator and his characters in the "Legend of Cleopatra." There, after describing the mutual love of Antony and Cleopatra, he adds,

> And, for to make shortly is the beste,
> She wax his wif, and hadde hym as hire leste.
>   The weddynge and the feste to devyse,
> To me, that have ytake swich empryse
> Of so many a story for to make,
> It were to longe, lest that I shulde slake
> Of thyng that bereth more effect and charge;
> For men may overlade a shipe or barge.
> And forthly to th'effect thanne wol I skyppe,
> And al the remenaunt, I wol lete it slippe. (614–23)

Though some of the force of "to make shortly" may attach to the wedding, especially given the uncourtly bluntness of "hadde hym as hire leste," it refers primarily to the narrator's need to be brief. While we may sympathize with the narrator's decision not to describe the wedding, in part because Antony already has a wife, its omission only leaves us to wonder how the battle subsequently described in such vivid detail can be more "to th'effect."[11] This was not his charge. In his haste, the narrator has only inadvertently revealed that the effects of this hasty bond-breaking love are not the harmony of marriage but the discord of war and death. Paradoxically, the god's injunction to be brief is overloading the narrator's ship, and the characterization of the narrator's account as a "shipe or barge" further underlines the parallels Chaucer is establishing between his narrator's situation and conduct and those depicted in his narratives, for the effect to which he skips is the sea battle at Actium.

The effects of the narrator's careless haste are especially evident in his account of how Cleopatra came to have Antony "as hire leste." He describes Antony's betrayal of his wife and country, giving us a false husband if not a false lover. He assures us that "natheles, for sothe," he was a "ful worthy, gentil werreyour." He then continues with what is in effect an explanation of how a "worthy, gentil" man could betray wife and country:

> But love hadde brought this man in swich a rage
> And hym so narwe bounden in his las,
> Al for the love of Cleopataras.
> That al the world he sette at no value.
> Hym thoughte ther nas nothyng to hym so due[12]
> As Cleopatras for to love and serve. (599–604)

"But," "swich a rage," and "hym thoughte" ensure that the narrator's justification of romance can as easily be viewed as a denigration of the basic principles of courtly love: that it is a lover's highest duty to serve his lady, and that lovers ought to sacrifice all the world for love. In hastily trying to make his old books conform to the courtly credo, the narrator inadvertently calls that credo into question.[13] Thus, the irony that results from the narrator's hasty and obedient oversimplification of life becomes Chaucer's means of reasserting the multiple perspectives that the complexity of life and old books requires.

Recognizing the analogies between the narrator's circumstances and the dramas recounted in his narratives enables us to perceive in Cleopatra's final act a comment on the narrator's present poetic situation. After having workmen build a shrine adorned with rubies and other precious stones and filled with "spicereye"—a giant reliquary, as it were—Cleopatra enshrines Antony's "dede cors" and proceeds to leap into an adjoining snake pit. Both Antony's past and the emphasis on the "cors" in the description of the enshrining, to say nothing of Alceste's claim that all men are false, call into question the appropriateness of Cleopatra's devotion to Antony as a saint. In spite of her inspiring farewell to Antony prior to leaping into the pit, in which she recalls the "covenaunt" she made with herself to share his fate for better or worse, Cleopatra's past and the suggestion that she committed suicide because she "coude of Cesar have no grace" also force us to question the narrator's treatment of her as a saint, his enshrinement of her in his legendary.[14] One suspects that in keeping his covenant by treating her like a saint, he is leaping into a snake pit himself—or rather, since he was ordered to begin with her, is being pushed into one, for as Garrett long ago observed, "If Cleopatra is to head the procession, who may not walk in it?"[15]

THE NEXT pair of legends continues Chaucer's dramatization of the narrator's efforts to satisfy Alceste's and the god's demands and his exploration of the difficulties that confront the poet who would know and tell the truth. In the stories both of Dido and of Hypsipyle and Medea the narrator indicates that he is compiling his account from more than one source. Like much else in these two legends, his references to his multiple sources are often self-dramatizing. Indeed, the narrator becomes positively assertive in his determination to uncover and publish the truth. Significantly, though, as the denunciation of false lovers grows more emphatic, the reader's sense of the unreliability of fame and the elusiveness of truth increases, to the point where the narrator's account of Jason's perfidy strikes the reader as well-nigh incredible. More authorities and more fervor do not always produce more certainty, it is clear.

Some of the difficulties of trying to determine the truth by multiplying sources are suggested by the opening of the "Legend of Dido."[16] The narrator declares that he will follow Virgil's "lanterne" and yet take the "tenor" and the "grete effectes" from Ovid; he subsequently tells us that he could "folwe, word for word, Virgile." But reconciling Virgil's account of Aeneas's pious obedience to his divinely decreed destiny, the founding of a new Troy, with Ovid's subject, his betrayal of Dido, is impossible—especially when one is following Alceste's light. It is the Prologue's requirements that dictate taking the "tenor" from Ovid, of course, since Dido's epistle provides the needed victimizing lover. And these requirements, this "tenor," necessitate suppressing the facts as Virgil presents them.

Much of Virgil is unsuitable for the narrator's purposes, and repeatedly we are reminded that he is adapting his primary source. After describing Aeneas's encounter with Venus, the narrator notes that Venus told Aeneas how "Dido cam into that regioun," but then he declines to tell *us*, assuring us that it would be but loss of time. Later, after reporting that Venus made Aeneas and Achates invisible, he questions whether such a thing is possible before affirming, "Thus seyth the bok." Later still, after declaring that he will not describe the feast with which Dido entertained Aeneas, he does so, including Venus's substitution of Cupid for Ascanius so that Dido would fall in love with Aeneas. Having told us what "oure authour telleth us," he dissociates himself from it: "But as of that scripture, / Be as be may, I take of it no cure" (1144–45). For all his faith in old books, the narrator distances himself from them when they contradict everyday experience or Alceste's demands. If one of the effects of such passages is to keep Virgil's rather different story in the reader's mind, another is to force the reader to see the narrator and the difficulties he is having with his authorities. His version is never allowed to appear a transparent account of the truth.

An especially crucial alteration is the reduction Shannon has noted in the importance of the gods in Chaucer's version. They must be transformed from the causes of Aeneas's departure into mere excuses for his desertion of Dido.[17] Thus, the narrator suppresses the role of the gods in the cave episode and declines to narrate the adventures at sea with which Virgil portrays Aeneas as both the victim of the warring wills of the gods and the instrument of Jupiter's determination to found Rome. As he himself says, it does not accord with his "matere."

The climax of the narrator's efforts to rewrite Virgil so as to please Alceste begins with his vilification of Aeneas as a false lover. After some two hundred lines devoted almost exclusively to depicting Dido falling in love, without the slightest suggestion of what Aeneas may be feeling, the narrator suddenly switches his focus: he rapidly pictures Aeneas vowing love and truth on his knees in the cave as only a "fals lover" can, cruelly laughing at Iarbus's sorrow at being rejected in love. This vilification culminates in his apostrophe to "sely" women not to trust men, using Aeneas to illustrate all the devices of the seducer. He pictures Aeneas as feigning truth, obedience, gentility, secrecy; as waiting upon Dido at "festes" and dances; as fasting, jousting, sending her "lettres, tokens, broches, rings." The repeated implication is that his purpose is seduction and that once he succeeds, his interests will wane.

This impassioned denunciation is followed by an account of Aeneas's desertion of Dido which is full of pity for her and adopts completely her point of view. Thus, instead of depicting Mercury's appearance to Aeneas to order him on to Italy, for instance, the narrator merely recounts Aeneas's claim to that effect—a claim accompanied, he tells us, by false tears. Finally, the narrator is so overcome with "routhe" for Dido that he is unable to "write" her complaint to her sister Anne. Though he may have initially adopted Ovid's tenor because of the Prologue's requirements, by the end his pity for Dido has converted him. His resistance (evident in the first two legends) to the notion that male perfidy is the root of love's tragedy has vanished. Now he sings with complete conviction Dido's double sorrow, her agony in love and her grief at being betrayed, and Aeneas's double perfidy, his seduction and desertion of Dido. Like Augustine before him he has been seduced by pity for Dido, and his translation bids fair to seduce us.[18]

At the same time Chaucer would limit our participation in this seduction. The sudden picture of Aeneas's labors as a false lover follows too abruptly the picture of Dido inflamed with passion to be credible, and the narrator's motivation is too readily apparent. The location of the detailed description of Aeneas's machinations as seducer after the consummation of the affair renders it even more suspect. There was not a whisper of it before the fact. (Before the fact it was Dido who was lavishing presents on Aeneas, as though she sought to seduce him.) That none of this is in Virgil is clearly implied: before the scene in the cave, the narrator tells us that his "authour" does not say whether anyone went in with them. The implication of this, a correct one, is that Virgil does not describe in detail what transpired there; consequently, he provides no authority for the narrator's picture of Aeneas playing the false lover in the cave. The suggestion that the narrator is inventing to suit his pur-

pose is confirmed by the subsequent description of how people re-
acted to the rumor that the two were in the cave together:

> The wikke fame upros, and that anon,
> How Eneas hath with the queen agon
> Into the cave; and demede as hem liste. (1242–44)

The fact that the narrator is one of those who "demede as hem liste"
reduces his subsequent picture of Aeneas the seducer to the status
of a self-serving rumor. Thus, the narrator's "Legend of Dido" becomes a dramatized expression of the unreliability of fame and of
the role poets play not only in upholding fame but also in fostering
its unreliability. What the *House of Fame* tells us allegorically, the
Legend of Good Women expresses dramatically.

Virgil does say of the episode in the cave that Dido hid her fault
by calling it marriage.[19] Here the narrator joins Dido in trying thus
to conceal her "culpa": he tells us that she "tok hym for housbonde,
and becom his wyf / For evermo" (1238–39). Just as the narrator's
efforts to blacken Aeneas's character are unsuccessful, however, so
are his efforts to redeem Dido's, for when Aeneas declares that he
must leave for Italy, Dido's response exposes the fraudulency of her
efforts—and the narrator's—to call it marriage.[20]

> Have ye nat sworn to wyve me to take?
> Allas! what woman wole ye of me make?
> I am a gentil woman and a queen. (1304–6)

When the truth comes out, it exposes both of them, for even as her
actions in the cave reveal the kind of woman she truly is—one foolish and weak enough to be mastered by her own passions—so the
narrator's readiness to submit Virgil's "objective" point of view to
Ovid's subjective one in order to please his lady and indulge sentiment suggests a similar weakness and folly. Though Alceste and the
god of Love may judge his account of Dido's double sorrow at the
hands of Aeneas appropriate penance for having written of Troilus's double sorrow at Criseyde's hand, in fact he has only reenacted his error there of ignoring the victim's complicity with his/her
own undoing. The penance recreates the sin.

Having warmed to the task of denouncing false men and having
at last found an unequivocally false lover, the narrator opens the
"Legend of Hypsipyle and Medea" with a rhetorical attack on Jason

as "sly devourere and confusion / Of gentil wemen, tendre creatures" (1369–70). For all the narrator's self-dramatizing enthusiasm, however, the matter in hand is hardly ideal for his purposes,
as anyone who will take his advice and read the several sources from
which he has compiled this narrative—Guido's *Historia destructionis
Troiae,* the *Argonautica* of Valerius Flaccus, and Ovid's *Heroides*—
cannot fail to realize.[21] Actually, one need not bother, for though
the narrator insists on treating even Medea as an innocent victim,
Hypsipyle lets the truth out when she prays

> That she, that hadde his [Jason's] herte yraft hire fro
> Moste fynden hym untrewe to hir also
> And that she moste bothe hire chyldren spylle. (1572–74)

It is a prayer that renders horrifyingly ominous the narrator's subsequent lament that when Jason deserted Medea, he left "his yonge
children two" with her.[22] Thus, one of the narrator's heroines undermines the other, and the narrator as well.

It is the person of Jason that accounts for the presence in this
legend of two martyrs, of course. Though the narrator assails him
as an archvillain, "devourere" and "dragon," Chaucer's actual treatment of Jason's quest borders on the farcical. After all, it is Medea
who saves Jason's life and honor, and wins him a name as a "con-
querour" by "the sleyght of hire enchauntment"; and as Frank observes, if she saved his life, she cannot have saved his honor—at
least not by any recognizably heroic code.[23] Jason's conquest of
Hypsipyle is equally unmanly. In an episode seemingly modeled on
Aeneas's stay at Carthage (or should we say on the previous legend?), Chaucer has Hypsipyle welcome the Argonauts with concern for their suffering at sea.[24] In fact, however, they have not been
suffering at sea; they have come ashore "to pley," being weary and
in need of a better wind. Jason is no storm-tossed, destiny-driven
Aeneas, but then neither was Chaucer's Aeneas. We proceed to
watch the ultimate male reduced to playing the customarily female
role of matchmaker: Hercules so praises Jason as to raise him to the
sun, especially by stressing how "agast" he is to love.[25] As for Jason
himself, he woos Hypsipyle by being "as coy as is a mayde: / He loketh pitously, but nought he sayde"(1548–49). What we are to make
of Jason is suggested by the elaborate comparison of false lovers to
foxes at the beginning of the legend:

> For evere as tendre a capoun et the fox,
> Thow he be false and hath the foul betrayed,
> As shal the good-man that therfore hath payed.
> Al have he to the capoun skille and ryght,
> The false fox wol have his part at nyght.
> On Jason this ensaumple is wel ysene
> By Isiphile and Medea the queene. (1389–95)

Though one naturally assumes that Jason is the fox—an assumption made all the easier by the fact that we have supposedly just watched the sly Aeneas steal the tender Dido from the deserving Iarbus—we do not actually see Jason steal anything from anyone, deserving or otherwise. We do see Medea steal Jason from Hypsipyle, or at least that is how Hypsipyle herself understands her loss of her husband. The suggestion that Medea is the fox, a comparison consistent with her traditional characterization, leaves Jason in the role of capon, of course.[26]

An equally interesting comparison is that of Jason's appetite for women to matter's appetite for form, as it passes "from forme into forme." Guido, we might note, used this comparison to characterize the lustfulness of women.[27] Though its transfer to Jason is consistent with the narrator's purposes, the implications of this transfer are not. If in the medieval view of marriage the man is the head and the wife is the body, the man the form and the wife the matter, in courtly love it is the beloved who forms the lover. He serves, suffers, and grows gradually worthy of her. Similarly, in medieval psychology it is the will that should control and form appetite, and, we should note, Chaucer subtly stresses that it is first Hypsipyle's and then Medea's will that is done, the heroines being the initiators like Dido before them (see 1400, 1617).[28] When Medea laments, "Whi lykede me thy yelwe her to see / More than the boundes of myn honeste" (1672–73), his yellow hair being her golden fleece, she all but explicitly admits that if she was devoured by Jason it was because she could not control her own appetite. Paradoxically, if Jason proves "of love devourer and dragon," he does so by being a formless creature, a capon, who takes his definition from others. Finally, from one point of view, Medea herself is the dragon who guards the golden fleece. Jason conquers her by submission, by accepting her terms and following her instructions.[29] In the process, he becomes the dragon he conquers.

Given such a radical denigration of Jason's stature, what are we to make of a narrator who presents himself as the champion of the ladies by defiantly challenging him and his kind?

> Yif that I live, thy name shal be shove
> In English that thy sekte shal be knowe!
> Have at thee, Jason! now thyn horn is blowe! (1381–83)

The dangers of translating into English hardly seem to require "yif that I live."[30] If the exaggerated rhetoric of this defiance and the insubstantiality of the defied make its heroism as bluff and hollow as Jason's, matters are only made worse when the narrator capitulates on the promised exposé:

> As wolde God I leyser hadde and tyme
> By process al his wowyng for to ryme!
> But in this hous if any false lovere be,
> Ryght as hymself now doth, ryght so dide he,
> With feynynge, and with every subtil dede.
> Ye gete namore of me, but ye wole rede
> Th'original, that telleth al the cas. (1551–58)

Having promised to thrash this "dragon" and his kind, he turns tail (like Sir Thopas?) and leaves it to the ladies to recognize and conquer the beast for themselves. Having set out to use his old books to help his audience understand their experience by providing an authoritative description of the seducer and his wiles, he now calls on his audience to use their experience to flesh out his "brief" translations. If Jason betrays both his ladies, the narrator would seem to betray both his loves—his old books and the ladies he is committed to championing.[31] The final irony is that much of the narrator's failure results from the conditions which the women in his audience have imposed upon him, for what he ought to tell them is that the only protection against hypocrites and confidence men is to look to the "boundes" of one's own "honeste," and they have forbidden him to say that.[32] Thus, like Hypsipyle and Medea, the women in the audience betray themselves. From one point of view at least, the narrator is little more than another Jason, an instrument in the betrayal, a means by which women satisfy their own appetites and vanities. The manly pose only underscores the capon's role.

If the legends of Dido and of Hypsipyle and Medea indict both art's patrons and their too compliant poets for fame's unreliability, they also reveal how difficult it can be to discover and express truth. Chaucer's reduction of the narrator's account of Aeneas's perfidy to a mere rumor inevitably reminds us that much of what a poet needs to know to give a true account takes place out of sight—in the imperfectly recorded past, the darkness of caves, the privacy of dreams, the secrecy of intentions. Similarly, by suggesting that Jason is dragon, fox, capon, golden fleece—depending on one's point of view—Chaucer implies that the truth behind the rumor may be so complex and so uncertain, however many one's sources and however ample one's experience, as to be scarcely expressible at all. If the hollowness of the narrator's rhetoric is partly attributable to the gap between the prescribed and "storyal" record, it also results from the insubstantiality of "storyal soth" itself.

HAVING DEMONSTRATED the frequent indeterminacy of historical truth through the multiple viewpoints that coexist in the narrator's account of Aeneas and Jason—multiple viewpoints resulting in part from his use of several, often conflicting authorities—in the next two legends Chaucer explores the problem of the inadequacy of human knowledge and language to grasp and present truth. One hypothetical poetic ideal, that expressed by Raison in the *Roman de la rose* when she insists that she must name things with names that would truly name them—making the word "cosyn to the dede"— would seem to produce a variety of literalism.[33] The text mirrors, even (with its use of the proper words) reproduces, history. Confounding this ideal is the fact that their images must pass through a distorting medium, human consciousness. This suggests another, less naive ideal, that of a text as a mirror of human consciousness. The age's (and the poem's) supposition that both historical reality and human consciousness are only shadowy images of a truer world implies in its turn that, willy-nilly, the poet's language is improper, metaphorical. Indeed, if the ultimate truth is beyond naming precisely, presumably the best anyone can do is create another shadowy manifestation of it, a yet dimmer mirror of these already dim mirrors.[34] Though the Prologue affirms the capacity of historical reality and "storyal" literature to manifest transcendent "trouthe," the legends are ordered not only to dramatize the impediments to human knowledge but also to reveal the distance between "soth" and "trouthe." Chaucer's ultimate demonstration in the legends of the otherness of perfect truth in loving and of the inadequacy of human efforts to know and name it is his story of Lucrece.

The "Legend of Lucrece" opens with a situation strikingly and significantly analogous to the narrator's, one that implicitly comments upon the nature and value of the task he is engaged in. As Alceste and the god of Love require him to praise good women, so Tarquin proposes to the men at the siege of Ardea that, being idle, they amuse themselves by praising their wives. When Colatyn responds by taking Tarquin to observe secretly what he insists is the very deed of "trouthe," Lucrece's "wifly chastite," and Tarquin responds by ravishing her and seemingly destroying her "trouthe," we are forced to question the wisdom of the narrator's assignment and his willing participation in it. For the parallel not only implicitly indicts those ladies in Chaucer's audience who would have him celebrate female goodness of a pride and folly similar to Colatyn's but also implies that a poetry which idly celebrates womanly goodness can destroy what it seeks to promote. Significant differences in the two situations, however, leave open the possibility that poetry can have a positive function as well. Unlike Colatyn, who insisted on showing his wife's beauty and virtue in the flesh, poets trust in words. Tarquin's original proposal—that the men at the siege "ese" their hearts with "speche"—reminds us both that words can at times be a desirable substitute for action and that poetry can have a purgative function, that it can defuse as well as inflame.

Central to Chaucer's dramatization of the artist's dilemma is the question of the relationship of word to deed. When Tarquin suggests that the men amuse themselves by praising their wives, Colatyn, apparently assuming that men do not always speak the truth (at least not when speaking of women as good), declares that "it is no nede / To trowen on the word, but on the dede" (1706–7) and takes Tarquin to see his wife "dischevele" in her chamber—in her naked virtue, as it were. They find her faithfully lamenting her husband's absence. The narrator observes, "Hyre contenance is to hire herte dygne, / For they acorde both in dede and signe" (1738–39). If Lucrece would seem to be precisely what she appears to be, a rare case of complete accord between sign and thing signified, the reverse is the case with Tarquin. When he sits on the edge of Lucrece's bed, she awakes to ask, "What beste is this?" Though Tar-

quin answers, "I am the kynges sone, Tarquinius" (1789), his subsequent behavior reveals that her characterization of him more
accurately names his actions and his nature.

Obviously, the poet's task, to name things properly, to make the
word "cosyn to the dede," is no easy one.[35] Even as the designation
of Lucrece's countenance as the sign, her heart as the deed, implies
that one must know what motivates an act if one is to name it correctly, so Colatyn's distrust in words reminds us of the need to know
the intentions of a speaker if we are to assess the truth of an assertion or narration. That the narrator is anxious to name things
properly is evident from his rhetorical questioning of Tarquin after
the rape:

> Tarquinius, that art a kynges eyr,
> And sholdest, as by lynage and by ryght,
> Don as a lord and as a verray knyght,
> Whi hastow don dispit to chivalry?
> Whi hastow don this lady vilanye?
> Allas! of the this was a vileyns dede. (1819–24)

The medieval commonplace that, properly understood, the term
"gentilesse" names virtuous behavior, not upper class behavior, implies that "vilanye" must similarly designate vicious behavior, not
lower-class behavior.[36] As the old hag puts it in the "Wife of Bath's
Tale," "vileyns sinful dedes make a cherl" (*CT* III, 1158). Thus the
narrator's insistence that Tarquin is acting like a peasant reveals not
only his naiveté about the consequences of being born a gentleman
but also his difficulty in understanding and employing words properly, according to their *proprietates.* Whether or not a particular act
deserves a particular name depends not on its customary designation but upon whether or not it shares the essential nature of the
deed the word properly names. Whatever the etymological facts,
according to this concept of naming, the property "lower class" has
nothing to do with the real meaning, the proper idea, of villainy.

Frequently this real meaning was explained with reference to a
word's (supposed) etymology, as though knowing the etymology of
a word would allow one to recover its meaning when it was first and
rightly used, prior to its corruption. A relevant example is the word
rex. As John of Salisbury—an appropriate authority, given his apparent influence on Chaucer's discussion of kingship in the Pro-

logue—informs us, a king is one who rules justly, for *rex dicatur a recto*.[37] He also explains that when the word is applied to tyrants, those who oppress the people by force, it is being abused, though he does not hesitate to so use it himself. The term the narrator most immediately associates with Tarquin is *king*. He terms him a "kynges eyr" in the process of protesting his ungentlemanly behavior; begins the legend with a reference to the "exylynge of kynges" that resulted in part from Tarquin's rape; and incorporates in the conclusion the observation that, father and son being banished, "never was ther kyng in Rome toun / Syn thilke day" (1869–70). We are reminded of the proper name for "the horrible dede of hire oppressyoun," however, when the narrator advises the women in his audience to observe what "tirannye" men "doon alday," for (according to John of Salisbury, at least) tyranny is the term for private as well as public acts of oppression.[38] (It is a term Gower uses in the *Confessio* to name Tarquin's rape, we should note.)[39]

The narrator has even less success in understanding and correctly naming Lucrece's behavior. Though he takes her to be a perfect expression of "wifly chastite," his account of her rape and suicide forces us to see that she is not quite the perfect truth she seems; as Kiser has observed, he must "feign" her sainthood.[40] Initially, Lucrece resists Tarquin's assault as best she can, but when he threatens to slay her knave, put him in bed with her, and cry adultery, she faints. The narrator attributes her fainting partly to fear of death, partly to the love of "name" and fear of slander and shame characteristic of the Roman wives of the time.[41]

We see this same concern with reputation when she resolves that her husband will never have a "foul name" on account of her "gilt" or "blame." Though her friends protest that they forgive her and that there is nothing to forgive because she is not guilty (a judgment in which we must concur, since Chaucer has her faint), she scorns forgiveness—" 'Be as be may,' quod she, 'of forgyvyng, / I wol not have noo forgyft for nothing.' " (1852–53)[42]—and commits suicide. The fact that her friends simultaneously declare her not guilty and forgive her dramatically reveals the imputed blame Lucrece faces. Her determination to die to establish her virtue, though she is innocent, reveals that being thought blameless is more important to her than being blameless. Like Gower's Lucrece, she apparently slays herself that none may "reproeven" her for what was done to her.[43] The irony is that her suicide to preserve her name as a good and true wife only violates her goodness and truth.

That the legend was designed to provoke such reflections is confirmed by what was actually said by the "grete Austyn," whose compassion for Lucrece the narrator invokes. After pondering why she committed suicide if she was innocent, Augustine finally concludes that she did so not from a love of purity but from a mistaken and exaggerated sense of shame, one deriving from an excessive desire for glory and a pride that was unwilling that anyone might ever think she consented.[44] He thus condemns her, in effect, for preferring the opinions of men to truth, the name of chastity to true purity, the word to the deed itself. In addition, he implicitly condemns her for failing to understand true chastity, which is of the will and not the body, and real sanctity, which desires only a clear conscience and the esteem of God.[45]

That the narrator himself is having an analogous difficulty understanding the good is evident from the almost embarrassingly inappropriate conclusions he draws: his praise that "in hir wille she chaunged for no newe" (inappropriate at the very least because in his version she had fainted), and his explanation of her dying care "lest that hir fet or suche thyng lay bare" as evidence of her love of "clennesse and eke trouthe."[46] Paradoxically, the narrator's misnaming, the product of his own imperfect apprehension of truth, makes his account "storyal soth," for his celebration of her goodness is grounded in the same misapprehension of the good and in the same overvaluing of appearances as her deed; it constitutes a similar, unwitting betrayal of the good. He and his tale do reproduce her history.

But all is not Chaucerian irony. If the narrator's legend reveals the limitations of the "lawe" that venerates Lucrece, whether that law is practiced in ancient Rome or in Richard's court, so it evokes in us both admiration for Lucrece's highmindedness and compassion for her suffering.[47] Though Lucrece is not the perfect incarnation of the good the narrator takes her to be, she does have a certain dissimilar similitude to that perfect good. Her deeds and the narrator's words engage us in the dialectic by which medieval man sought to approach the transcendent good. One affirms the transcendent good but then immediately affirms it not good, lest one betray "trouthe" by limiting it to our partial ideas of it. The best in this kind, whether deeds or words, are but shadows, mere metaphors. This is an emotional dialectic as well as an intellectual one. One learns to love the good by first loving such dark mirrors of it as Lucrece. If the legend dramatizes "our" law's critique of "hir lawe," it opens by appealing to Augustine's compassion for her and ends by implying (not without irony) Christ's approbation. For a medieval Christian the "doctrine" of history is the movement from "hir lawe" to "ours," from shadowy prefigurations such as Lucrece to Christ; similarly, the individual soul's intellectual and affective journey is from a less to a more adequate idea and love of the good. Lucrece and her "legend" are the necessary first steps on this road to Christ. In this process the narrator's pity is as important as Chaucer's justice. By participating in both Lucrece's glory and her folly, the narrator's legend is both "storyal" and psychological "soth."

The artistic principle that "the wordes moote be cosyn to the dede" requires the poet to find, besides the right generalizing word, a suitable style, an appropriate manner of treating his matter. There is no such decorum in the "Legend of Ariadne," for it repeatedly violates the ideal of proper naming and the related principle of decorum. Particularly expressive of the disparity between manner and matter is the clash between the romantic picture of the two young heroines listening in the moonlight to the supposedly innocent young Theseus lamenting his imminent death in the dungeon below, and the mundane fact that his lamentations ascend to their eager ears through the drain of their privy.[48] Similarly striking in their incompatibility with the requirements of romance are Theseus's assertion that he will serve Ariadne as a lowly page for the sake of her company and to save his life, and Ariadne's observation—after she tells Theseus that he would do better to marry her—"But what is that that man nyl don for drede?" Indeed, no other legend is so insistent as this in its inclusion of the incompatible.

In her determination to get what she wants, Ariadne dominates the action. Her assertion of self to the contempt of virtually all else in the scene in which she and her sister save Theseus is anything but the stuff of romance; indeed, both Garrett and Preston have characterized the scene as farce.[49] After Phaedra explains in detail to Ariadne how Theseus can save himself "if that he be a man," we are told in four lines that Theseus was called, that "thynges ben acorded thus" (that is, as Phaedra has spelled them out), and that

Theseus fell on his knees and addressed his "ryghte lady."[50] Though the logic of Chaucer's narrative requires the supposition that Theseus is addressing Phaedra, Ariadne answers. The suspicion that she thrust herself none too gently between Theseus and Phaedra is confirmed when, after claiming Theseus for a husband, she consigns Phaedra, her older sister, to Theseus's son (a consignment that inevitably reminds us of Phaedra's subsequent passion for Hippolytus).[51] That Theseus is only twenty-three and that any son he may have must consequently be the merest boy implies not, as Skeat suggested, that Ariadne is jesting but that she is putting everyone in his or her place.[52] Similarly assertive of her own interests is her assumption of the role of wife rather than beloved.[53] The price of her help is a present dukedom and a future kingdom. From one perspective at least, Ariadne holds the Minotaur to Theseus's throat as surely as Tarquin held a sword to Lucrece's, a perspective that perhaps explains why Chaucer placed her story between those of the ravishers Tarquin and Tereus. Ariadne's abrupt dismissal of the rituals of courtship lends considerable irony to Theseus's subsequent assertion that he has already loved Ariadne for seven years though he has not known her, even as the brutal way in which she arranged Theseus's salvation renders his acceptance of her terms sardonic: "Now have I yow, and also ye me, / My dere herte, of Athenes duchesse" (2121–22). Her manner of arranging things may also help account for why he ultimately takes Phaedra for his "ryghte lady." (The narrator says it was because she was prettier!)

However grasping Ariadne may be, much of her behavior is romantic in the extreme. Witness her, deserted, kissing "in al hire care, / The steppes of his fet, ther he hath fare" (2208–9) or her cry to Theseus's departed ship, "O turn ageyn for routhe and synne! / Thy barge hath nat al his meyne inne!" (2200–2201) How wistful and pathetic her momentary belief that she has been forgotten rather than betrayed! Her whispered remarks to Phaedra after Theseus has proclaimed her his duchess seem those of a child:

> "Now, syster myn," quod she,
> "Now be we duchesses, bothe I and ye,
> And sekered to the regals of Athenes,
> And bothe hereafter likly to ben quenes;

And saved from his deth a kynges sone,
As evere of gentyl women is the wone
To save a gentyl man, emforth hire myght,
In honest cause, and namely in his ryght.
Me thynketh no wight oughte herof us blame,
Ne beren us therfore an evil name." (2126–35)

There is, of course, an immense disparity between the character of Ariadne's actions and her characterization of them, whether or not she is aware of it. Word and reality have almost totally parted company here. Similarly, there is an immense disparity between the unintentional farce of the narrator's dramatization of the covenant scene and his pathetic portrayal of the deserted Ariadne, whether or not he is aware of it.

If one supposes Ariadne an innocent, as the narrator must, some of the responsibility for the monstrosity of her behavior must be placed on those who nurture such innocence: those who teach that it is ever the custom of gentle women to save gentle men,[54] no matter what the circumstances or means; or those who have given "daunger" such a bad name that Ariadne can believe that it would be a shame to her sex if a man as noble as Theseus should be her servant. That the narrator is such a romancer is clear from both the beginning and the end of the legend, those frames of its antiromantic middle: the final effort to milk pathos from Ariadne's deserted condition, and the seemingly irrelevant opening, Minos's conquest of the city of Alcathoe. The narrator tells us that when Scylla, the daughter of Alcathoe's king, saw Minos from the wall as he besieged the city, she became so enamored of him that she delivered the city into his hands. Though the reader may not know that Chaucer's source, Ovid, had judged Scylla's behavior monstrous and Minos's just when he rejected her love, he should recognize that the narrator's interpretation of this as another instance of how false men wickedly repay kindness is perversely romantic and morally blind.[55] It is just such nonsensical misnaming that enables Ariadne to pretend that no one could possibly blame her for duplicating Scylla's betrayal of father and country.

Though it may seem logically preposterous to make the narrator responsible for Ariadne's monstrous behavior, Chaucer denies the normal distance here between a poet and his matter. He has the narrator intrude into his story with an apostrophe addressed to the imprisoned Theseus before our heroines even enter the story:

> Me thynketh this, that thow were depe yholde
> To whom that savede thee from cares colde!
> And if now any woman helpe the,
> Wel oughtestow hire servaunt for to be,
> And ben hire trewe lovere yer by yere! (1954–58)

He then has Theseus repeatedly declare that if his lady will save him he will be her lifelong servant. Thus, Theseus's declarations are made to seem fulfillments of the narrator's prescriptions. The narrator's reduction of life's complexities to such romantic simplicities, as though no woman's help were ever self-serving and no means of gratitude possible save endless devotion—not even when one is destined to be helped by more than one fair damsel—is finally mocked by the legend's revelation of just how self-serving and irrelevant such romanticism can be. Theseus will say anything and accept any terms to save his neck; Ariadne will do anything to be queen of Athens. If her moments of seeming innocence make her appear the victim of romancers like Theseus and the narrator, her moments of hardheaded and hardhearted manipulation leave us to ponder whether the narrator is a fool or a knave, an innocent victim himself or a self-serving manipulator.

The narrator's unwarranted treatment of Ariadne as innocent victim culminates in his account of her stellification.

> The goddes han hire holpen for pite,
> And in the signe of Taurus men may se
> The stones of hire corone shyne clere. (2222–24)

Whether one accepts Robinson's explanation of Chaucer's apparent mislocation of the constellation Corona Borealis—" 'in the sign of Taurus' clearly means when the sun is in that sign"[56]—or supposes it an error, deliberate or otherwise, the import of associating Ariadne with Taurus is clear and consistent with Chaucer's characterization of her. In the Prologue Chaucer identified Taurus with the white bull in whose form Jove ravished "Agnores doghtre." This ravishing produced Minos's ancestry. The reference to Taurus also prompts us to recall her mother's passion for a bull and its result, the Minotaur. Though Chaucer omits those occasions in Ovid where Ariadne refers to the Minotaur as her brother, his linking of Ariadne's crown with Taurus expresses her kinship with the bullish, a kinship that has wreaked havoc in the china shop of the narrator's romance. Indeed, the radical and irreducible mixture in Ariadne of "ingenue" and "fortune hunter," to borrow Fyler's terms,[57] gives her a dual nature for which the Minotaur is an appropriate symbol even as it is an appropriate image for the discordant, farcical mixture in this legend of the romantic and the brutal. Apparently, unquestioning obedience to Alceste and the god of Love breeds monsters.

CHAUCER CONFRONTS art's inevitable involvement with evil head on in the "Legend of Philomela." It opens with the narrator questioning the ways of God: he cannot understand why "the yevere of the formes," who eternally contemplates this "fayre world," permitted Tereus to exist, Tereus

> That is in love so fals and so foreswore,
> That fro this world up to the firste hevene
> Corrumpeth, whan that folk his name nevene. (2235–37)

While we may sympathize with the narrator's inability to comprehend why a good God would allow such evil to exist, this opening gives us at least equal cause to question the ways of the narrator and, indeed, of art, for the assertion that the mere mention of Tereus's name corrupts all of the universe that is subject to corruption indicates that to retell his story is to multiply evil and corruption.[58] The narrator himself has become infected just from reading his story:

> And, as for me, so grisely was his dede
> That, whan that I his foule storye rede,
> Myne eyen wexe foule and sore also.
> Yit last the venym of so longe ago,
> That it enfecteth hym that wol beholde
> The storye of Tereus, of which I tolde. (2238–43)

If this makes the poet's task seem almost heroic, as he braves on our behalf the venom of his old books in search of truth in loving, it calls the value of art into question in much the same way as the ap-

parent effects of romance on Ariadne did. For it indicates that
however much the artist may wish to teach virtue, art inevitably
spreads infection as well.

Though the narrator transforms his source, Ovid's *Metamorphoses*,[59] he does not succeed in removing the venom from it. The
original, one of literature's more grotesque tales of rape and vengeance, depicts totally unrestrained passion and cruelty—not only
on the part of Tereus, who first ravishes Philomela and then cuts
out her tongue, but also on the part of Philomela and Procne, who
slaughter Tereus's and Procne's son, stew him up, and feed him to
Tereus, all the while rejoicing in their vengeance.[60] Consistent with
Alceste's charge, the narrator transforms Ovid's savage avengers into
seemingly innocent and pathetic young ladies. Though certain of
the passions have changed, they nonetheless remain unrestrained
and excessive. After five years of marriage, "on a day" Procne begins so to long to see her sister "that for desyr she nyste what to
seye" (2262). She prays "for Godes love" that they may visit one another, "and this was, day by day, al hire prayere, / With humblesse
of wifhod, word and chere" (2268–69).[61] Pandion's tearful grief and
reluctance at Philomela's temporary departure and his prayer that
he may see Procne once more before he dies are also undeniably
extreme, as are Philomela's prayers, her "salte teres," and her repeated embrace of her father as she pleads for permission to go.[62]
That the narrator has been infected by the general excess is evident
from his hyperbolic use of "so" seven times in fifteen lines. In contrast to Alceste, who teaches "al the boundes" to be kept, here no
one respects any limits or shows any restraint.

Tereus's rape of Philomela echoes Tarquin's rape of Lucrece. The
general similarity is reinforced by the comparison of each woman
to a lamb confronted by a wolf. After the rape, Tereus cuts out Philomela's tongue, "lest she shulde his shame crye, / And don hym
openly a vilenye" (2332–33). Tereus fails to silence her, however,
for knowing how to write, she weaves an account of her misfortune
and sends the cloth to her sister. Procne rescues her and the narrator leaves the two dwelling together "in here sorwe." Of their
vengeance he makes no mention, commenting that "the remen-
aunt is no charge for to telle" (2283). Remembering the beneficial
effect of Lucrece's revelation of Tarquin's similar villainy, the ban-
ishment of tyranny from Rome, we may wish to congratulate the

narrator for having braved the story's venom to publish Tereus's villainy. The narrator concludes the legend by warning women not to trust men even though they will not "for shame, / Don as Tereus," lest they lose their "name." Since a fear of shame does no doubt help to restrain base impulses, the narrator would appear to have performed a morally and socially valuable function in making Tereus's shame known.

At the same time, however, the narrator's refusal to recount the vengeance taken threatens to silence his old book even as Tereus sought to prevent vengeance by silencing Philomela. Having asked why God allows such creatures as Tereus to exist, he omits a significant part of the answer: that they may be avenged for all to see and for poets to publish so that man may restrain himself—if not for love or fear of shame, then from fear of the retribution that was believed to await the sinner. If some of the responsiblity for this failure must go to those who gave the narrator his original charge, a charge which requires him to silence much of the truth, some of it apparently derives from his understandable distaste for so grotesque a story. He is "wery" of telling of Tereus after only thirteen lines; his narration is frequently abrupt. Indeed, inasmuch as the venom of the story is still infectious, brevity would seem advisable. Nonetheless, however commendable his desire not to dwell on the particulars, his distaste for the story assists his corruption of its truth. Even the artist's good intentions can contribute to undesirable ends, it would seem.

The narrator's efforts to cut at least a part of the tongue from his tale are finally ineffectual. It will not be silenced any more than Philomela, for it is full of reminders that the original story is one of revenge as well as of ravishment. Thus, the narrator pictures the Furies, those spirits of vengeance, at the wedding of Tereus and Procne. He observes that Procne responded to Philomela's news by being unable to speak "for sorwe and ek for rage." Further, when warning women not to trust men even though they will not do as Tereus did, he adds, "ne serve yow as a morderour"—words lacking any referent in his version of the story. Finally, given the fact that the traditional story has two distinct movements—one concluding in the rape and silencing of Philomela, the other in the sisters' vengeance—he should have ended his narrative after the rape, at the point where he calls on God to avenge Philomela and declares it time to "make an ende sone." For to tell us of Philomela's communication of her fate to her sister and of Procne's response is to begin the revenge movement of the tale and inevitably make us remember what he wishes us to forget: that the vengeance was not left to God. In short, once again the narrator's imperfect suppression of the unacceptable in his old books has undermined his efforts to advance the narrow dogmas of the Prologue. The narrator's lack of control—presumably partly the consequence of the infectious absence of restraint so characteristic of the narrative he is retelling—becomes a means whereby we are reminded of the revenge the supposedly tender creatures take as avenging Furies in their sorrow and rage. Finally, it would seem, the effects of art, only imperfectly in the control of the artist, are governed by the same Providence that allows evil to exist in order to bring forth good from that evil. Even the narrator's silences cry out the truth to those willing to hear. However misnamed or ignored, the truth will out.

TO ARRIVE at the final legends is to confront the possibility that Chaucer left them incomplete because he tired of them. The two passages that best support this common supposition are the narrator's declaration virtually at the beginning of the "Legend of Philomela" that he is weary of Tereus and his assertion in the "Legend of Phillis" that he is "agroted" with telling of those forsworn in love; the latter passage includes a prayer to God to send him grace to perform his legendary. Dismissing the first of these as a "Chaucerian *topos*" and the second as an isolated example of comic relief, Frank declares the supposition itself a legend.[63] While there is no denying the conventional and often comic character of such passages, it should be equally clear that they contribute significantly to the design of the legends, for the narrator's attitude toward his task forms a distinct and easily recognizable pattern. He begins his penance reluctantly, resisting the notion that all men are false: unless books lie, Antony was as worthy as any "wight"; he includes Pyramus because it is "deynte" to men to find a man true in love. While recounting Aeneas's infamous desertion of Dido he warms to his task and soon is roundly and contemptuously denouncing the likes of Jason and Theseus. By now, however, his enthusiasm is waning. He has retold so much male perfidy that he is thoroughly persuaded that Alceste is right: men are false, and he is thoroughly disgusted with his own kind. Demophon and his ilk are not worth the effort it takes to expend "a penne ful of ynke." While it is impossible to know whether or not the narrator's emphatically dramatized weariness expresses Chaucer's own feelings, presumably the pretense that one must spend most of the rest of one's life writing of good women leads to the pretense that one is growing tired because such a repetitive task would be tedious, the resulting repetitive form—however enlivened with ironies and subterranean complications—tiresome.

It is the particular burden of the "Legend of Phillis" to emphasize the universality of human falseness. It begins with the sententious assertion that wicked fruit comes from a wicked tree and proceeds to exemplify this truism by stressing that Demophon followed the "same path" his father trod. His treachery "com hym of nature": as the fox's son is like his father Reynard, as the drake can swim when first placed in water, so Demophon is false in love. Though the narrator makes a narrow application of the general principle—Demophon is like Theseus—the comparisons from nature and the opening *sentenia* imply that the inherited flaw belongs to human nature in general. It is this fact, as much as the preceding legends, that justifies the narrator's concluding advice to women not to trust any man and that supplies much of the irony to his exception of himself from this general condemnation. In arriving at such a conclusion the narrator is reenacting his psychological experience in the *Troilus,* the poem for which he is supposedly doing penance, for it too led him, however reluctantly, to conclude that this world's loves end only in tragedy.

After the narrator's brief account of Demophon's loving and leaving, he covers much the same ground again by translating excerpts from Phillis's letter of complaint.[64] In the process he comes as close as adherence to the Prologue's requirements permits to indicting women for complicity in their tragedies: he allows Phillis to admit she was "to fre" with her love. She also realizes that she trusted too much in Demophon's lineage, a fact intimated the first time around by the emphasis given to his renown as Theseus's son. She hopes that when his ancestors are "peynted" so that men may see their great worthiness, his treachery will also be shown so that people may revile him as a false lover (as the narrator is now doing, of course). She concludes that he is like his father in being an artful and subtle betrayer. That she knew of Theseus's betrayal of Ariadne only underscores her folly in trusting Demophon's lineage. What is evident from Phillis's denunciation of Demophon for being like his father is how like Ariadne she is: as Ariadne was enchanted by the thought of being duchess of Athens, so Phillis is blinded by the glory of its dukes. While she is insisting that Demophon should have remembered what the glory of his lineage required of him, the reader is reminded that she should have remembered what she knew, the shame of that same lineage. Yet again, forgetting—the Prologue's metaphor for human and natural inconstancy—is proved to be as much a female as a male failing.

Though the narrator declares himself an exception to the rule that men are untrustworthy, like Demophon he too is woman's "subtyl fo." By telling the ladies in his audience what they want to hear, that their tragedies are the fault of their lovers, he has employed the false lover's "fayre tonge"; by expending "allases" on the likes of Medea and Ariadne, he has shown that he too can "wepe . . . by craft." In the Prologue's description of how the wayward birds experienced "Daunger" for a period before "Pitee" forgave them and "made Mercy passen Ryght / Through innocence and ruled Curtesye" (162–63), the narrator adds that he does not call innocence "folye" and "fals pitee." Perhaps not, but in the legends he repeatedly calls the ill-considered pity of his heroines innocence. Even now, after clearly showing us Phillis's folly, he is unwilling to repudiate Alceste's formulas by explicitly asserting that truth. No doubt the untenable character of the narrator's labor of love contributes to his weariness.

Weariness, whether the narrator's or Chaucer's, is evident in the opening lines of the final legend, which are so flat and uninspired that one may well feel it was Chaucer who was spent. How else are we to explain the reversal of the fathers' names? (In Ovid, Danaus, not Aegyptus, is the father of Hypermnestra; Aegyptus, not Danaus, is the father of Linus.) There are inappropriate elements in this legend similar to those Chaucer has used throughout to create an ironic perspective and to characterize the narrator. For example, Chaucer's suppression of the fact that Hypermnestra's forty-nine sisters married and obediently slaughtered Linus's forty-nine brothers is less than total: he provides Linus's father with "many a sone" and Hypermnestra's with "many a doghtre" and has Aegyp-

tus observe that he dreamed he would be slain by one of his neph-
ews but did not know which one and that he must be "siker."[65] But
a mere change of names has little or no visibility and thus seems
pointless.

The possibility that the misnaming is a deliberate error cannot
be dismissed out of hand, however, for the opening lines place an
exaggerated emphasis on the names of the characters. Chaucer does
not tell us that there were two brothers, Danaus and Aegyptus, and
that they had, respectively, a son and a daughter, Linus and Hypermnestra. He tells us that there were two brothers, that one "was
called Danao," that he had a favorite son and that he "shop hym a
name, and called hym Lyno," that the other brother "called was Egiste," that he had a legitimate daughter, and that he "dide hire for
to calle / Ypermystra." To labor so redundantly to tell us what each
person "was called" and yet to reverse the fathers' names is so comic
a nod that one may doubt it accidental. Certainly such an error is
consistent with Chaucer's characterization of the narrator as generally careless, as one who translates because "he useth thynges for
to make," and as at present overcome with weariness. The explicit
concern in the legends with proper naming confirms the appropriateness of this blunder. Further, such an error continues the
dramatization in the legends of the impediments to meaningful art
resulting from the Prologue's requirements. When one is required
to narrate story after story, all briefly and all to the same formula,
such errors are virtually inevitable; the demands themselves pro-
hibit the detail and differentiation that distinguish one individual
from another and thus give meaning and memorability to individual names. Paradoxically, such general truths as human frailty are
apparently best taught through singular instances.

On the other hand, given the virtual invisibility of this reversal
to Chaucer's audience, one may doubt the error intentional. That
Chaucer may have blundered in a way similar to that in which he
repeatedly makes his narrator err reminds us that both the external circumstances and the personal limitations with which the narrator is depicted as struggling are akin to those with which Chaucer
himself presumably had to deal. Though the "trial" of the narrator
in the Prologue is ultimately the product of the poet's creative
imagination, it presumably represents realities with which the poet
had to contend; similarly, though the difficulties that the narrator

has in his translations are deliberate creations of the poet, no doubt these difficulties are similar to those Chaucer experienced as poet. Indeed, given the doubt as to authorial intention that must attend our perception of any individual blunder, though not their cumulative weight, one may easily feel—in more cases than the present one—that the narrator's difficulties were the author's. If the legends depict a narrator often stumbling in the dark due to the inadequacy of his guiding lights, his human models, and human understanding of truth in loving; if they depict a narrator frequently incapable of recognizing or accepting the truth and unable to prevent the falsity and viciousness of his old books from corrupting his new book; if they depict an all too human poet who distorts his source materials to please his audience and satisfy his own desires, however unmanly and foolish a procedure that is shown to be, no doubt the reason is that Chaucer found these things to be so. The narrator is a comic figure by which the poet can explore and expose the intellectual experience of Everyman; he is also an image with whom Chaucer chose to identify himself. Though it is necessary to distinguish between poet and narrator in order to recognize the drama explored in this chapter, it is also necessary to realize that the narrator represents the poet in order to appreciate the moral and philosophical seriousness of Chaucer's comedy.

The exaggerated and laborious attention given to naming this legend's dramatis personae contributes to the undeniably parodic character of its opening lines. Chaucer has here reduced the Prologue's stipulations to a completely barren formula and applied that formula so mechanically that the opening can only be read as a *reductio ad absurdum* of what the narrator has had to do all along. Like the salivation of Pavlov's dog at the sound of his bell, the accusation "false" springs forth at the mere mention of a man's name. We are introduced to Danao and told straightway that he has "many a sone / As swich false lovers ofte conne" (2565); we then meet "Egiste, / That was of love as fals as evere hym liste" (2571). Conversely, naming the legend's heroine produces a similarly automatic assertion that she was endowed with "alle thewes goode." Chaucer's momentary descent into parody at the beginning of his final story is an appropriate culmination of the ironic dimension of the legends, for given Alceste's and the god of Love's demands and the character of the narrator, such a moment is inevitable.

The descent into parody suggests that whatever Chaucer's original intention for the legends and whether or not he tired of them, he realized that continuing was pointless. The narrator has demonstrated all of Alceste's program that is demonstrable, all men in some measure being false; Chaucer has demonstrated through his narrator's performance the moral, intellectual, and artistic folly of creating one's art according to the dictates of desire—whether one's own or one's audience's—rather than in the light of a skeptical and reasoned examination of the authority of old books and the "preve" of experience. At the same time, by making the narrator's falsifications visible and by demonstrating that the narrator, in translating, psychologically reenacts his matter, Chaucer has made those falsifications true reflections of the "doctrine" and "soth" of his old books. We see the "folhaste" of Antony and Cleopatra, of Pyramus and Thisbe, in the narrator's haste and folly; hear the fraudulency of the silent Jason in the hollow language that results from the narrator's conformation of his narrative to his audience's desires; recognize Lucrece's misunderstanding of the good in his unqualified approbation of her; discover the perfect image of Ariadne's monstrosity in his mixture of the romantic and grotesque. The narrator encounters himself in his old books, reveals himself in his new translations, and in the process brings his readers face to face with themselves. Indeed, one may even suspect that Chaucer structured his narrator's progress to bring it to this conclusion, for we have reached the point, the same point reached at the end of the *Troilus*, where all that remains is to recognize that legends of feigned loves can never be more than parodies of that love which will "falsen no wight." Further, the ridicule of parody readies the will to accept that which has been intellectually demonstrated.

There is more to be said about the abrupt ending of the legends, but that must wait upon an examination of their tragic order. Whatever Chaucer's original intention, the narrator's translations have reached an appropriate terminus.

The Order of Justice

IV

N ow that we have seen that the legends are not what the god of Love and his queen would have them be—a failure resulting from the contradictory character of their demands, from the narrator's haste, from the complexity and elusiveness of truth, and from psychological reality's irrepressibility, the narrator himself manifesting the very failings he would ignore—a more accurate assessment of the world there depicted and of its relationship to the Prologue's world should be possible. Though the action of the Prologue is set in spring, it presents the order inherent in all creation as a circular movement through contrary states, an order most evident in the natural cycles of the day and year, in the return of the birds to their mates each spring, in the daisy's course as it follows the sun, in Alceste's descent into hell and reascent to bliss.[1] The narrator's similar progress from his wintry books to his spring flower and back to his old books, a progress whose result is the legends, indicates that we will encounter a world in the legends contrary to the Prologue's, a world dominated by the cold sword of winter rather than by "th'atempre sonne." Our expectations are not disappointed. *Legend* after legend depicts deceit and betrayal, recrimination and complaint, separation and death—not truth, reconciliation, and "resureccioun." Tragedy has replaced comedy.

Similarly, as the Prologue provides a vision of unity—presenting the Alceste-daisy as the union of red and white, dramatizing the reconciliation of the narrator and the god of Love, and discovering the same truth in dreams, books, and nature—so the legends depict multiplicity, fragmentation, and division. In the invocation to Cleo in the proem to Book 2 of the *Troilus,* Chaucer stresses the

mutability, multiplicity, and variety that characterize historical reality: customs in love change over time; no three at one time have
ever done and said all alike in love. So here, when we follow the
narrator back to his old histories, we encounter diversity and change:
the "sondry usages" of various lovers "in sondry ages" and "sondry
londes," conflict both between male and female and within the individual, divergent authorities. Discord and disagreement have replaced harmony.

Yet the legends ought not to be simply the Prologue's antithesis,
any more than the Prologue is simply a vision of harmony. When
the Prologue represents cyclical order as universal, it implies the
presence of that order in the legends as well. If the Alceste-daisy is
the flower of flowers, the lady of ladies, summing up all the beauty
and goodness to be found in any creature, then the heroines of the
legends must manifest some of the same beauty and goodness. In
Boethian terms, to descend from the one to the many, from a vision of the transcendent to an encounter with the historical, is to
enter a world of multiplicity and partiality where psychologically
divided men and women pursue partial goods, but one that still
manifests the stability and unity of its source.[2] It is to the question
of whether or not the legends confirm the Prologue's philosophical
vision that we should now turn.

Some definition of the diverse tragedies of the legends is provided by the recurrent references to "Fortune, that hath the world
in governaunce" (1044).[3] The narrator invokes Fortune as well as
Love to explain Antony's desertion of wife and country for Cleopatra and Medea's assistance to Jason: she owed Antony a "shame";
Medea, a "foul myschaunce." Indeed, most of the heroines could
lament with Dido, "I have fulfild of fortune al the cours" (1340).
To love worldly goods is to bind oneself to Fortune's turning wheel,
to submit the self to inexorable change.[4] This fatal necessity finds
its perfect expression in the characterization of Dido's time in the
cave with Aeneas as simultaneously "the first morwe / Of hire glad-
nesse, and gynnyng of hire sorwe" (1230–31). The tragic end of
their love is inherent in its beginning.

Consistent with this philosophical perspective, the legends repeatedly reveal the inadequacy of the partial goods to which the
heroines of the legends give themselves. Though there are moments which reveal that their heroines are driven by the same flesh-

ly appetites as their villains, as when Cleopatra enshrines Antony's "dede cors" or Medea laments her preference for Jason's golden hair to her own "honeste," usually Chaucer depicts them as succumbing to nobler infirmities, to values more easily mistaken for real goods.[5] As Jason sets out heroically to conquer the golden fleece because of its fame, so Hypsipyle responds to the "renome" and "grete los" of its would-be conquerors, Jason and Hercules—a fame whose vanity is revealed when Hypsipyle's nemesis, Medea, wins it for Jason. As Ariadne is enchanted by the prospect of being queen of Athens, so Phillis is so moved by the "gret renoun" of its next lord that she overlooks his similarity to his father. (It is not just Diomede who sees love as conquest.) The partial good that is the particular undoing of the legends' heroines, however, is honor, "name." Both Cleopatra and Thisbe die to show how "trewe in lovynge" a woman can be; both Dido and Phillis, primarily in shame for their loss of honor. The ultimate demonstration in the legends of the destructiveness of pursuing "name" is, of course, "The Legend of Lucrece," where we watch the innocent Lucrece scorn forgiveness and violate her devotion to truth that she may preserve her reputation. If the narrator is the spokesman for this world of appearances— the reverse of Lady Philosophy, as it were—as he blindly affirms his heroines in their blind affirmation of the false and the mutable, the legends in their relentless reiteration of the tragic consequences of such passions demonstrate, as Lady Philosophy does, that the pursuit of the false binds one in separation from the good to the turning wheels by which destiny orders this world.[6]

Chaucer further underscores the tragic character of the legends by associating the circles that result from Fortune's "governaunce" with the cyclical alternation of day and night.[7] In the "Legend of Thisbe," for instance, the narrative's tragic action is joined to the passage of day into night.[8] The lovers meet "whan Phebus gan to cleere," after Aurora "hadde dreyed up the dew"; they agree to rendezvous that very night "in o place at o tyde," the grave of King Ninus, and then await impatiently the sun's setting. Night comes; Thisbe steals away. When Pyramus discovers her torn wimple in the moonlight, he regrets the folly of urging her to such a perilous place at night and laments, as though they were victims of the night, "Allas . . . the day that I was born! / This o nyght wol us lovers bothe sle" (833–34). Linking their fate with the coming of night heightens its tragic inevitability and implicitly associates it with nature's cyclical order.

The identification of the lovers with the natural cyclical order of the day is even more pronounced in the "Legend of Dido." After describing the meeting of Aeneas and Dido, Chaucer turns "to th'effect," "to the fruyt of al." He describes Dido complaining of her love "upon a nyght, / Whan that the mone up reysed hadde his lyght" (1162–63) and declaring her intention to have Aeneas. We move directly to the morning of the hunt: "The dawenyng up-rist out of the se" (1188). Dido is like Aurora that morning; she sits on her horse "as fair as is the bryghte morwe, / That heleth syke folk of nyghtes sorwe" (1202–3). Aeneas sits on his horse "lik Phebus to devise." The comparison of Aeneas to the sun, of Dido to the dawn, recalls the daisy's daily "resureccioun" with the sun from night's hateful darkness. But the reminiscence is profoundly ironic. Though Dido is compared to a light capable of healing the sorrows of night and has been credited with bringing Aeneas "to paradys / Out of the swolow of helle," she is herself the one suffering the sorrows of night. Her effort to heal herself by adhering to Phoebus-Aeneas leads to the darkness of the cave, where she experiences the "firste morwe" of that joy which is the beginning of sorrow. When we return to the narrative after the lengthy denunciation of Aeneas, it is again night. Dido is expressing her fears that he will leave; Aeneas is pleading that it is his destiny to conquer Italy. For all of Dido's apprehension and pleading, he does steal away "on a nyght," so that when she awakes the only cure for her sorrow will be death. Having committed herself to one who will be true to his own transitory nature and destiny, she does indeed bind herself to and define the "cours" of Fortune and nature.

As in the *Troilus,* where he represented Criseyde's affinity with nature, Fortune, and Venus by giving them all two faces, so here Chaucer defines man's divided nature and its similar affinities by associating it with the duality of the day.[9] Man's dark side is evident in his propensity for stealing away under the cover of darkness. As Aeneas deserted Dido, so Theseus abandons Ariadne: "Ryght in the dawenyng awaketh she, / And gropeth in the bed, and fond ryght nought" (2185–86). Awakened that he may flee before morning comes, Linus ends the single day of Hypermnestra's narrative, their wedding day, by abandoning her before daybreak to a vengeance her father will presumably exact in the cruel light of day. This affinity with darkness finds its ultimate expression in the legends in Tarquin. Seeing Lucrece "dischevele" one night, he spends the following day remembering "hire beaute and hyre cheere" and then returns to ravish her:

> Doun was the sonne, and day hath lost his lyght;
> And in he cometh into a prive halke,
> And in the nyght ful thefly gan he stalke. (1779–81)

His stalking in the night culminates when he sits on her bed and she cries out, "What beste is that?" In the morning the only recourse she can imagine to put this darkness from her is to commit suicide.[10]

The behavior of the heroines similarly testifies to their equivalent duality. They too have a penchant for stealing away at night. Witness the parallel between Jason and Hercules as they plot to "bedote" Hypsipyle, and Jason and Medea as they plan in bed the conquest of the golden fleece. The treasure won, Medea departs with Jason "unwist of hire father." As Jason's quest for his false good, the golden fleece, leads him to forsake Hypsipyle and his own truth, so her love of his "yelwe her" prompts her to abandon her father and her "honeste." Similarly, as Theseus steals away from Ariadne at night, so he and Ariadne and Phaedra had all stolen away from Crete at night with a great treasure, presumably at Ariadne's and Phaedra's devising.[11] The ultimate undoing of several of the heroines is their eagerness to love and be loved. Alceste, we remember, unites pity and "daunger"; she wins the narrator forgiveness but does not dispense with the proving penance. In contrast, the heroines of the legends are at first all pity and love, and then, when their too easily won love is betrayed, all remorse and anger. Having squandered their "honeste," they turn the cold and pitiless sword of justice on themselves or, in the case of Medea and Procne, on their children. Their inability to be simultaneously merciful and just perfectly illustrates the Boethian idea that man divides the good into partial goods, those reflections of the good whose partiality ensures their lovers a tragic fall.

If one of the effects of linking the individual tragedies in the legends to the imagery of the turning day is to reinforce our sense of the naturalness and inevitability of such change, another is to en-

sure that we visualize their rising and falling action as circular. The
individual legends are not simply separate circles, however, for a
number of factors give to them a cyclically repetitive character: the
very fact that they are a series, the frequent repetition in action and
imagery, the persistent use of a complaint for the denouement, the
ever present narrator with his unflagging sympathy for his heroines and mounting contempt for false men. As a result the legends
unite to form a spiral, an image simultaneously of recurrence and
progress.

The significance of this order is heightened by the comparison
of Jason's appetite for women to matter's appetite for form:

> As mater apetiteth forme alway
> And from forme into forme it passen may,
> Or as a well that were botomles,
> Ryght so can false Jason have no pes. (1582–85)

The image of a bottomless well suggests appetite's insatiability; the
image of matter's progress from form to form, the cyclical change
that results from pursuing it. The repetitive cyclical character of the
legends represents the inevitable consequence of living according
to the unharmonized promptings of Venus and Mars, even as does
the Wife of Bath's progress from husband to husband in her quest
to satisfy her thirst with water from the Samaritan woman's well.

This image of desire similarly manifests the life of the imagination. In medieval thought the motion or activity proper to the rational soul is from the transcendent to the mutable and back to the
transcendent. The motion proper to the irrational faculties is from
the corruptible to the Creator and back to the corruptible. Only the
rational soul can ascend from the many to the one, there to rest.
The imagination is tied to the sensible particulars from which its
images derive and inevitably contaminated with the passions natural to the sensitive soul, concupiscence and irascibility. Its instability, its thirst for ever new images of its persistent desires—images
that provide only momentary stasis—is reflected in the narrator's
(and the reader's) pell-mell progress from tragedy to tragedy. Its
inability to adhere to the one, to ascend and hold to the form of the
beautiful, is reflected in the legends' recurring cyclical form.[12]

The characterization of cyclical progress as matter's desire for
form invites us to see in the cyclical union and separation of the

lovers the pattern of Nature's perpetuity, her recurrent generation and destruction of all perishable things through the union and dissolution of matter and form. Theseus's great speech in the "Knight's Tale" taught Chaucer's audience to see the order in this progression of the species and to recognize in it proof of the unity and stability of this world's source. The location of the appetite that perpetuates the species in matter recalls the view of medieval philosophy—derived in large part from Aristotle but reflected significantly in both Boethius and Dante—that the created universe is turned in its circling courses by its desire for the perfection of the unmoved mover, by the *reduci igne* manifest in the daisy.[13] Though the image derives from Guido delle Colonne, Chaucer's use of it encourages reflections like those resulting from Bernardus Silvester's picture of Nature's appeal to Nous on behalf of Silva, primordial chaos, that Silva be rendered more beautiful by the gift of form.[14] Similarly, the idea of the instability of appetite recalls Bernardus's characterization of matter as incapable of being permanently harmonized by the form it desires.[15] Nature's order, life by succession, results from the desire and the deficiency of the created. If concupiscence is a source of disorder in the human species, it also guarantees that male and female, matter and form, unite to ensure generation and progression.

Further implications of the cyclical form of the legends are evident in Jason's progress from woman to woman. After Jason departs, Hypsipyle prays

> That she, that hadde his herte yraft hire fro,
> Moste fynden hym untrewe to hir also,
> And that she moste bothe hire chyldren spylle,
> And alle tho that sufferede hym his wille. (1572–75)

The fact that her words predict what is to happen implies that her prayer is answered. The fairness of the prayer that the bereaver be bereft suggests the justness of Medea's fate. The iron law of justice, a law that ravishes all things born to the light of day back into the darkness of night, is just—as Hypsipyle's own death shortly after she utters this prayer confirms, since she is one of those who "sufferede hym his wille." In their tragic form the legends dramatize the justice that binds all those who abandon the good to the mutability of the things they have preferred to the good.

Finally, such things as the repetitive nature of the legends, the comparison of male desire to matter's appetite for form, and the association of various of the tragedies with the cycle of the day give the reiterated drama of loving and leaving an air of inevitability. Even as the narrator's castigation of his villains requires moral judgment from us, we realize the inevitability of these tragedies. As the narrator observed of Dido's passion for Aeneas, "Love wol love, for nothing wol it wonde" (1187). Theologically, man is fallen, like Demophon, vicious fruit of a vicious tree; philosophically, his nature shares in the corruptible. Culpable participation in tragedy is his fate. Like the *Troilus* the legends declare, "swich is the world" that the "yevere of the formes" has wrought.

IN THE language of theology, when men and women turn from reason to the appetites and bind themselves to destiny's wheels of fire, they separate themselves from the order of grace and bind themselves to the order of justice.[16] In medieval tradition the end result of such choices is damnation. To understand Chaucer's dramatization of the order of justice in the legends, we must see that the world the narrator creates from his old pagan books is significantly analogous to the nature and order of hell. Having told us in the opening lines of the poem that one can know of heaven and hell only what one hears told or finds written, Chaucer makes his poem a book full of traces of these moral and metaphysical absolutes. Kiser has already pointed out infernal imagery in three of the legends; she interprets it as a device by which Chaucer transforms his classical heroines into saints, their lives into legends, for the ultimate purpose of parodying exemplary narrative's reductive representation of reality.[17] In order to add to her evidence and propose an alternative reading of the significance of this dimension of the legends, we need to see that the Prologue predicts that the legends will be an infernal descent, that their infernal intimations are much more pervasive and subtle than Kiser argues, and that they are informed in significant ways by Dante's vision.

As we have already observed, fundamental to the order of the *Legend of Good Women* is the opposition of the Prologue and the legends. Since the Prologue presents a paradisiacal world, a garden in which the god of Love and his saints manifest themselves, having come forth from heaven even as Dante's saints came forth from the celestial rose to reveal themselves, this principle of opposition implies that the legends will manifest the infernal. Confirming this implication is the fact that the legends are presented to us as the consequence of the narrator's cyclical progress from his wintry books to his spring flower and back to his books, for this cyclical progress is given definition by the cycles associated with the daisy and Alceste: the daisy's daily descent into darkness and morning "resureccioun," Alceste's descent to hell and reascent to bliss. Further confirmation is provided by the characterization of the Alceste-daisy as the narrator's light in this dark world, his guide in this work as in all his sorrows, and by Chaucer's depiction of the narrator imitating the daisy's imitation of the sun. Not by allusion but by his presentation of the narrator's behavior as lover and poet, Chaucer makes his narrator an Orpheus, a singer seeking to journey to the light through the *infernum* of the legends.

Further support for the view that the legends are an infernal descent is provided by the language of Chaucer's invocation of Virgil at the beginning of the "Legend of Dido":

> Glorye and honour, Virgil Mantoan,
> Be to thy name! and I shal, as I can,
> Folwe thy lantern, as thow gost beforn,
> How Eneas to Dido was forsworn. (924–27)

Chaucer is here echoing Dante. Certainly he had in mind Cato's question at the foot of purgatory: "Chi v'ha guidati, o che vi fu lucerna, / uscendo fuor de la profonda notte / che sempre nera fa la valle inferna?" (Who has guided you, or what was a lamp to you issuing forth from the deep night that ever makes the infernal valley black?; *Purg.* 1, 43–45); and quite possibly, Statius's characterization of Virgil "come quei che va di notte, / che porta il lume dietro e sé non giova, / ma dopo sé fa le persone dotte" (like one who goes by night and carries the light behind him and profits not himself but makes those wise who follow him; *Purg.* 22, 67–69).[18] Chaucer's invocation of Virgil as guide through the *Aeneid* in the language Dante applied to Virgil as his guide through hell implicitly characterizes the narrator's progress through his old books as a journey through hell. Since the fourteenth century, Dante's Virgil has been understood to represent human reason—that capacity natural to all men—and the works of reason, pagan poetry and natural philosophy.[19] Virgil's poetry represents what it is, human wisdom and eloquence. In a sense Virgil is old books. In Dante's drama of the mind, reason and its fruits provide sufficient light to lead humanity through the darkness of sin and most of the way back to prelapsarian perfection: that is, through hell and much of purgatory. Even as we have seen that the interaction of Chaucer's narrator and his legends dramatizes the capacity of books to deceive and even corrupt, so we shall see that old books represent and are for Chaucer much what they were for Dante, potential guidance through a sinful world. A further parallel in support of such a view of the *Legend* is that both Dante's Virgil and the narrator's old books are commissioned by a greater light, Beatrice and the Alceste-daisy.

Chaucer's *Legend* has analogous parallels with a work often considered its twin, Gower's *Confessio Amantis*.[20] Both have prologues that introduce a series of brief, largely classical narratives at least nominally concerned with love; both prologues comment upon the state of the nation, represent themselves as commissioned, and depict their narrators as lovers; both assert the value of old books. The characteristics of the *Legend* that we are considering suggest that their affinity is even greater than has been appreciated. Though Gower's narratives dramatize a confession rather than a penance, they constitute a systematic exploration of Amant's spiritual condition, one in which their primary function is to illustrate the various sins. Amant begins his journey through the sins by declaring himself no Arion, no singer capable of redressing the wrongs in his society through the harmonizing power of song—that is, no Orpheus—even as Dante declares himself no Paul, no Aeneas (*Inf.* 1, 31–33); it ends when Amant, freed from the delusions of love, attains self-knowledge, even as Dante achieves mastery over himself at the top of purgatory. Clearly, the *Legend* merits being read in the light of these analogues.

Kiser characterizes the snakepit Cleopatra constructs as a "miniature" hell and compares her leap into it with the infernal descents of Christ and Alceste. She is careful to note that Cleopatra's fate is willfully self-inflicted and concludes that the purpose of this adaptation of Cleopatra's life to a hagiographic pattern is to show that such "formal correspondences" between the classical and Christian are superficial.[21] Comparing Cleopatra's leap to Dante's entrance into hell will permit us to see further. Looking across the Acheron, Dante asks Virgil what law ("qual costume") makes those on this side so ready ("sì pronte") to cross, for though the damned souls are weeping and gnashing their teeth, cursing God, their parents, the human race, and much else besides, they nonetheless fling themselves into Charon's boat. Virgil explains that those "che muoion ne l'ira di Dio" (who die in the wrath of God) "pronti sono a trapassar lo rio, / ché la divina giustizia li sprona, / sì che la tema si volve in disio" (are eager to cross the stream, for Divine Justice so spurs them that their fear is changed to desire; *Inf.* 3, 124–26). Simultaneously, they flee before the wrath of God and rush to embrace their own fate. Like everything else in the universe, they desire their place, their fulfillment, and this is their proper end.

The same law is evident in Cleopatra's behavior. After the defeat at Actium, unable to have any "grace" of Caesar, who is apparently still "wod" from Antony and Cleopatra's marriage and still accompanied by troops "crewel as lyoun," Cleopatra flees to Egypt "for drede and for destresse."[22] She enshrines Antony's "dede cors," digs her snakepit, and, declaring her truth, leaps naked in among the serpents "with ful good herte."[23] She too is simultaneously driven and drawn. Indeed, one cannot imagine a more powerful image for the terrifying eagerness of the damned to seek their own fulfillment than that of Cleopatra leaping naked in among the serpents to fulfill her truth to Antony.[24]

After crossing the Acheron, Dante enters the circle of the lustful and asks Virgil to identify the people he sees being driven on the dark wind. Virgil responds that the first "fu imperadrice di molte favelle" (was empress of many tongues), she who was so licentious "che libito fé licito in sua legge" (that she made lust licit in her law): namely, Semiramis (*Inf.* 5, 52–57).[25] Next he points out she "che s'ancise amorosa, / e ruppe fede al cener di Sicheo" (who slew herself for love and broke faith with the ashes of Sichaeus)—that is, Dido—and next, "lussuriosa" Cleopatra. Though Virgil goes on to name others who do not appear in the legends, the prominence and conjunction of Cleopatra and Dido there and here is striking, especially because it is unexpected: Chaucer went out of his way to include Cleopatra, for unlike the other heroines of the legends she was not one of courtly literature's traditional "betrayed women."[26]

The opening of the legend linking those of Cleopatra and Dido adds to the affinity to Dante:

> At Babiloyne whylom fil it thus,
> The whyche toun the queen Semyramus
> Let dychen al about . . . (706–8)

While the reference to Semiramis is from Ovid, that to Babylon is Chaucer's addition; he must have assumed his audience would associate it with the city "of many tongues," the most common image of the city of this world and, consequently, of the confusion of Hell.[27]

Confirmation that Chaucer's opening legends dramatize a submission of reason to desire analogous to that found in Dante's second circle is provided by the slight but significant alterations he made in Ovid's account of Pyramus and Thisbe, for these alterations align Thisbe's legend with Dante's account of the fate of Paolo and Francesca. After Virgil names "le donne antiche e' cavalieri," Dante asks to speak with Paolo and Francesca. They leave the whirling troop, and Francesca gives him an account of how, as she says, "amor condusse noi ad una morte" (love brought us to one death; *Inf.* 5, 106):

> Amor, ch'al cor gentil ratto s'apprende,
>   prese costui de la bella persona
>   che mi fu tolta; e 'l modo ancor m'offende.
> Amor, ch'a nullo amato amar perdona,
>   mi prese del costui piacer sí forte,
>   che, come vedi, ancor non m'abbandona. (5, 100–105)

(Love, which is quickly kindled in a gentle heart, seized this one for the fair form that was taken from me—and the way of it afflicts me still. Love, which absolves no one beloved from loving, seized me so strongly with delight in him [or "with his charm"],[28] that, as you see, it does not leave me even now.")

If the reference to her "bella persona" and his "piacer" suggest the passion in which their love is rooted, her justification—that love afflicts the gentle and obligates the beloved—reveals that she is still and, thus, forever a prisoner of the romanticizing ideology of courtly love—an ideology that attributes, Dante implies, a gentility and necessity in fact foreign to such passions.[29] Their punishment is ever to desire, never to find relief. Forever will he hunger for a "fair form" that is no more, and she for a "charm" that his silence throughout the scene proves equally nonexistent. Their love has made them eternally one, but it is the union of the "una morte" to which love has brought them.

Chaucer's accommodation of Ovid's narrative and Dante's sense begins with his original explanation of why Pyramus and Thisbe cannot meet: in Babylon, "Maydenes been ykept, for jelosye, / Ful streyte, lest they diden som folye" (722–23). "For jelosye" appeals to the viewpoint of the lovers and reflects the required courtly perspective, a perspective the lovers echo repeatedly, as when Thisbe prays that their parents will bury them in one grave "withouten more envye." "Lest they diden som folye" requires us to view their intended tryst "in o place at o tyde" (the grave of Ninus) from another point of view, however, one that judges it folly.[30] How thoroughly they are prisoners of the courtly ideology is clear from Thisbe's declaration that she will show by her death "that a woman can / Ben as trewe in lovynge as a man" (910–11), as though life were only a game in some court of love. Like Cleopatra before her, Thisbe goes to her death reaffirming her love:

> And thogh that nothyng, save the deth only,
> Mighte thee fro me departe trewely,
> Thow shal no more departe now fro me
> Than fro the deth, for I wol go with thee. (896–99)

A comparison with Ovid's "quique a me morte revelli / heu sola poteras, poteris nec morte revelli" (you only able to be separated from me by death will not be separated by death) reveals that Chaucer has added to the idea that death cannot part them the fact that they are equally inseparable from death itself.[31] Though each commits suicide, each rightly declares himself "felawe and cause ek" of the other's death. Each slays his other self. Their love, like Antony and Cleopatra's, has found its consummation in "una morte."[32] Viewing Paolo and Francesca, Dante laments, "Alas, how many sweet thoughts, how great desire, brought them to the woeful pass" (*Inf.* 5, 113–14). Thisbe prays that they may lie in "o grave" together "sith love hath brought us to this pitous ende" (904). While "pitous ende" cannot be declared a precise translation of "doloroso passo," Pyramus and Thisbe's piteous end is Paolo and Francesca's woeful pass, a union in the one time, one place, of the eternal grave.

Asked by Dante to explain the occasion of their love, Francesca says its "prima radice" was a book: when they read of Lancelot first kissing Guinevere, then they kissed and read no further; "Galeotteo fu 'l libro e chi lo scrisse" (A Gallehault was the book and he who wrote it; *Inf.* 5, 137). Gallehault was, of course, the go-between in the affair of Lancelot and Guinevere, their pander. Though Ovid explicitly declares that Pyramus and Thisbe "had no go-between," Chaucer tells us that they fell in love "by report," as "the name of everych gan to other sprynge / By women that were neighbores aboute" (719–20).[33] This parallel comments upon those in Chaucer's audience who would have him celebrate such passions as the "Legend of Thisbe" dramatizes and, equally importantly, upon the role of the narrator as poetic spokesman for this viewpoint. When the narrator ends the legend by celebrating Pyramus and Thisbe's truth in loving, we see how near he is to being one with them, much as Dante suggests the affinity of his pilgrim with Paolo and Francesca by having him swoon "di pietade." Confirming the narrator's participation in the moral failing of his hero and heroine is Chaucer's characterization, previously noted, of their actions and his narration as foolishly hasty, even as Gower used their story to illustrate Amant's sinful "folhaste."[34]

Chaucer's dramatization of the circle of the lustful, of those deceived by love, culminates in Dido's measureless passion for Aeneas. With the characterization of Aeneas as an artful seducer and deliberate traitor, we begin a descent to a darker world, where men and women knowingly and willingly sacrifice others to their own desires. Though our knowledge of Virgil's Aeneas inevitably qualifies our acceptance of the narrator's depiction of Aeneas's perfidy, the arrival of Jason on the scene unequivocally places us among a new "sekte," those who are not themselves deceived by love but deliberately deceive to satisfy their "foul delyt," those whose distinguishing trait is their duplicity. His kind, we are told, feign truth and counterfeit pain. Jason is also a prominent figure in the *Inferno*. We meet him in the first ditch of the eighth circle, Malebolge, the eternal home of the fraudulent. There he leads with him "all who practice such deceit" (*Inf.* 18, 97), even as in the *Legend* Jason is the "rote of false lovers" (1368). We have followed Dante down to the realm of fraud.

The first *bolgia* of the fraudulent is inhabited by two classes of sinners circling in opposite directions, the panders and the seducers. Dante first meets Venedico Caccianemico, he who led Ghisolabella to do "la voglia del marchese" (*Inf.* 18, 56), and then Jason, leading the seducers. This union of panders and seducers may well explain the unprecedented role Chaucer assigns Hercules in this story, that of pander.[35] He pictures Hercules extravagantly praising Jason to Hypsipyle, declaring Jason's only fault a reluctance to love, affirming it his own greatest desire to see Jason married. All this has been purposed between them, to "bedote" Hypsipyle.[36] As Dante's Jason is of "aspetto reale" even in hell, manifesting the "courage" and the "craft" with which he secured the golden fleece, so Chaucer's Jason is "of his lok as real as a leoun"—though his emphasis, as we have seen, is on Jason's fraudulent appearance, his Jason being in fact more capon than lion. Similarly, though Chaucer affirms Jason "goodly" in his speech, as Dante had noted his use of "parole ornate" to beguile Hypsipyle, in Chaucer's representation of Hypsipyle's seduction Jason acts "as coy as doth a mayde; / He loketh pitously, but naught he sayde" (1548–49).[37] If it is Chaucer's purpose, as it was Dante's, to use Jason to dramatize the nature of fraud, he also wishes to show how frequently its path is made smooth by the eagerness of the intended victim.

Further evidence that Chaucer's subject in this legend is fraud is provided by his otherwise inexplicably long account (virtually a third of the whole) of how Peleus persuaded Jason to undertake the quest for the golden fleece,[38] ostensibly out of love for him, actually in the hope he would be slain:

> And in his wit, a-nyght, compassed he
> How Jason myghte best distroyed be
> Withoute sclaunder of his compassement. (1414–16)

Similarly manifesting fraud, at least to one familiar with Dante's analysis of that sin, is Medea's winning for Jason the "name" of a "conqueror / Ryght through the sleyghte of hire enchauntement" (1650), for besides the manifest fraudulence of Jason's reputation and the suggestion that Medea is betraying her father in helping him, such diviners and workers of magic as Medea is here suggested to be are consigned by Dante to the fourth circle of Malebolge.[39]

The "Legend of Lucrece" carries us deeper into hell. Like Gower in the *Confessio*, Chaucer characterizes Tarquin's rape as an in-

stance of tyranny.[40] In the Prologue, we recall, Chaucer represented—partly dramatically, partly symbolically—the commonplace
expressed by John of Salisbury that a king is a reflection of God.
Here we have a dramatic and symbolic expression of a corollary of
that idea, one also expressed by John of Salisbury, that a tyrant is
an image of Lucifer.[41] Though the narrative begins with Colatyn
and Tarquin ostensibly celebrating virtue, when we are told that
Lucrece was "dischevele, for no malice she ne thoughte" (1720), we
reassess their motives. Colatyn's folly and pride are obvious, but the
malice referred to is Tarquin's. He seeks wifely chastity, that image
of beauty and virtue in one, not to celebrate it but to destroy it.

In his enumeration both of what Tarquin sees when spying on
Lucrece and of what he turns over in his mind the next day, Chaucer stresses that Tarquin's "blynde lust" derives as much from Lucrece's virtue (her words, her manner, her "cheere") as from her
beauty (her yellow hair, her shape, her hue).[42] If her virtuous beauty sets him on fire, it also forces him to recognize that she is unat-
tainable, so that he despairs, "and ay the more that he was in dis-
payr, / The more he coveyteth" (1770–71). Her memory arouses not
"plesaunce" but "delit, / Or an unrightful talent, with dispit." His
"coveytynge" is grounded in despair and mixed with something close
to its contrary, a contempt bordering on hatred for that which it
desires. In his satanic malice, he would seem as determined to destroy her wifely chastity as to possess her. When he stalks in like a
thief, seizes her like a wolf, and responds to her pleas for "grace"
with the threat that if she does not submit he will destroy her name,
we realize that this is all he has power over: her name. Ultimately,
there is nothing he can do either to possess himself of her beauty
and virtue or to destroy it. All he can do, if he does succeed in gain-
ing her willing submission, is discover that she is not the perfect
union of beauty and virtue he desires, or, if he fails, make a saint,
multiplying that glory which is forever out of his grasp. Malice and
despair are indeed his lot. In his simultaneous desire and contempt
for the good and in his powerlessness to attain it, he perfectly expresses the medieval psychology and metaphysics of evil.[43]

That he fails to make a saint in this case (though Lucrece was
considered one in ancient Rome) is clear from her scorn for forgiveness—"I wol not have noo forgyft for nothing"—and her subsequent suicide. Her behavior is perfectly characterized by Piero

delle Vigne's explanation of his suicide in the *Inferno:* "L'animo mio, per disdegnoso gusto, / credendo col morir fuggir disdegno, / ingiusto fece me contra me giusto." (My mind, in scornful temper, thinking by dying to escape from scorn, made me unjust against my just self; 13, 70–72). Her scornful disdain of forgiveness and her suicide to avoid shame make her equally unjust to herself.[44] In both instances, we see the tragedy that occurs when a noble soul turns that nobility against the self.

The legends of both Ariadne and Philomela continue Chaucer's dramatization of the sin punished in the final circle of Dante's hell: treachery. (Significantly, the two stories are also juxtaposed in Gower's *Confessio,* where the first exemplifies ingratitude—Theseus's desertion—and the second, tyrannical "ravine.")[45] Kiser has noted a number of infernal allusions in the "Legend of Ariadne": the depiction of Minos as "juge infernal" (as in the *Inferno*); the characterization of the Minotaur as "fend"; Ariadne's rescue of Theseus from the prison to which he has been "dampned," even as Alceste saved Admetus.[46] We are indeed among the damned here. The designation of Minos as "juge infernal," deriving no doubt from Dante, signals the role played in this legend by retribution.[47] It opens with a reference to the vengeance the "goddes of heven" have taken, depicts Minos as delighting only in avenging his son, and ends with the narrator calling on the devil to "quyte" Theseus.[48] Treachery is similarly everywhere. We watch Scylla betray her father and country to the enemy, Minos; Ariadne does the same to her father and country by helping Theseus. As Minos's rejection of Scylla immediately avenges her betrayal, so Theseus's abandonment of Ariadne on a deserted island avenges hers. The gods dispose that treachery repays treachery.

Chaucer's dramatization of the nature and function of hell in the legends is no doubt the explanation of one of its puzzling features, the fact that Chaucer characterizes the "derk and wonder lowe" prison to which Theseus has been "dampned" as a "foreyne."[49] His laments apparently ascend to the heroines, listening in the moonlight, through the drain of their privy. Though the stench of hell is one of its most prominent features, and artistic representations of hell amply depict the scatological, once again Dante illuminates Chaucer's purposes. Immediately after meeting Jason in the first *bolgia,* Dante encounters the flatterers in the second. They are "attuffata in uno sterco / che da li uman privadi parea mosso" (plunged in a filth that seemed to have come from human privies; *Inf.* 18, 113–14). Neither the poetic justice of this punishment nor the relevance of Theseus's analogous circumstances to his blandishments needs elaboration.

Equally important to this legend's intimation of the character of divine justice is Ariadne's translation to "the signe of Taurus." Chaucer's association of her with Taurus inevitably recalls her kinship with the Minotaur, whom Dante termed the "infamy of Crete" and made an image of brutishness (see *Inf.* 12, 11–21). Dante's (and Ovid's) designation of Ariadne as the Minotaur's "sister" fits well the Ariadne we witness ensuring that she, rather than her sister Phaedra, will be not only Theseus's love but also his duchess and queen. As we have noted, the Minotaur is an appropriate sign for the mixture of sentimentality and savagery that characterizes both Ariadne and her tale. As Taurus, the image of the ravishing bull, was used in the Prologue and in the *Troilus* to represent the necessity and malignity inherent in the universe, so here Taurus, the Minotaur, Ariadne, and the narrator's tale all intimate the mythic source and end of this necessity and malignity, the monstrous antithesis of the freedom and goodness of God.[50] Chaucer's depiction of human treachery and brutish promotion of self in this legend, where everyone acts with a contempt for others like the "dispit" with which Minos feeds the youth of Athens to the Minotaur, does indeed recall Dante's frozen Cocytus. Both are worlds from which the softening warmth of God's love is totally absent.

Dante's dramatization of the ultimate in treachery and cruelty culminates in images of cannibalism—Count Ugolino gnawing upon Ruggieri; Satan's three mouths devouring Judas, Brutus, Cassius— as again Dante individualizes the conventional. Chaucer concludes his exploration of the depths of man's inhumanity with a third story of brutish treachery, one that ends in a similarly cannibalistic way. Though the narrator omits the revenge, in which Procne and Philomela feed Tereus his own son, we see enough to know where we are. That the "Legend of Philomela" was designed to conclude our descent is suggested by both its rhetorical and its narrative beginnings: the explicit question as to why the maker of this "fayre world" allows infectious evil to corrupt it, and the depiction of Tereus and Procne's marriage as made in hell. Their wedding is attended not by Juno and "Imeneus, that god of wedying is," but by the three Furies, those spirits of vengeance and daughters of the Night from Dante's hell, and the owl "that prophete is of wo and of myschaunce," itself associated with Hades in the Proserpina myth.[51] If Alceste, the model of "wyfhod," teaches "al the boundes" that lovers ought to keep and thus illustrates the harmony that love creates in the cosmos, here we see only the antithesis of love: a passion that knows no bounds; a ravishing that destroys all bonds, betrays all trust, and produces a revenge too cruel to behold.

Chaucer suggests the nature and depth of Tereus's perfidy by associating him with Tarquin. Tarquin stalked "ful thefly; Tereus is "this fals thef." Both are wolves attacking lambs. Just as Lucrece sat by her bed with her hair down "for no malyce she ne thoughte," so when Pandion committed Philomela to Tereus's care, "no malyce he ne thoughte." The change from Ovid, where Pandion is full of foreboding, is especially significant, for it characterizes the intent lying behind Tereus's determination to have her "how so that it go," even as Tarquin had determined to have Lucrece at whatever cost (see 1773–74).[52] In both cases we see passion's sacrifice of all for the moment, joined to the deliberation and determination of the act willed by and for the self in contempt of all else. Further, by stressing Pandion's failure to suspect malice, Chaucer underscores Tereus's betrayal of those who have trusted and fostered him. Again, treachery and ingratitude loom as large as brutality.

Chaucer gives definition to the significance of Tereus's rape of Philomela by stressing the relationships it violates. Although we already know the familial relationships of the characters, when Tereus arrives in Greece, we are told that

> Unto his fadyr-in-lawe gan he preye
> To vouche-sauf that, for a month or tweye,
> That Philomene, his wyves syster, myghte
> On Progne his wyf but ones han a syghte. (2272–75)

Committing Philomela to Tereus's care, Pandion addresses him as "sone," refers to her as "my yonge doughter," and urges him to greet Procne, "my daughter and thy wif," on her father's behalf. Similarly, when Tereus confines Philomela to the cave, she cries out, "Where is my sister, brother Tereus?" While being raped, she calls on her "syster," on her "fader dere," and on "God in hevene."   The designation of Tereus as son and brother extend the special sacredness of family bonds to the more general and legalistic ties that unite humanity, even as the legend's final lines remind us of the universal brotherhood of man. Thus Chaucer stresses the sacredness of the bonds of love and loyalty that ought to bind people together at the same time that he suggests the magnitude of the malice that would destroy all bonds. The relevant gloss is the characterization of hell in the "Parson's Tale" as a place where all love becomes deadly hate:

> "The sones and the doghtren shullen rebellen agayns fader and mooder, and kynrede agayns kynrede, and chiden and despisen everich of hem oother bothe day and nyght," as God seith by the prophete Michias. / And the lovynge children, that whilome loveden so flesshly everich oother, wolden everich of hem eten oother if they myghte.   (*CT* X, 200–201)

Though the narrator refuses to recount the revenge that God takes through the instrumentality of such avenging Furies as Procne and Philomela, we see both the necessity for it and the justice of it, for left to its own devices, such venomous malice would corrupt and destroy all. In the legends of Tarquin, Ariadne, and Tereus we do indeed catch a glimpse of the three faces of Satan.

Having reached the bottom, the last two legends begin an ascent to the light, but one that still takes place within the confines of hell. Chaucer's dramatization of Phillis's "to fre" love of Demophon seems to place us back in the second circle among those mastered by love. Central to this dramatization is the theme of forgetting. When Phillis rebukes Demophon in her letter by observing that if he would "have in memorye" what he did to her, he would see little glory in it, she in effect rebukes herself, for this appeal to remember is located between her lament that she trusted in his "lynage" and her revelation that she knew all along the treachery inherent in that "lynage." Had she kept in mind what she knew, she would have realized that there is also no glory in loving the fruit of such a tree, for all his "renoun" as lord and duke of Athens. To appreciate the import of her forgetfulness, we need to remember Boethius's treatment of the theme, his picture of himself in his grief as one who has forgotten both his own nature as an immortal soul created to participate in divinity and the end toward which all things tend, the good (*Consolation* 1, pr. 2, 6). Boethius depicts forgetfulness as intrinsic to the human condition: first of all, the soul forgets the good it once knew when it descends from its stellar home into this world, this *infernum;* further, this forgetfulness is exacerbated when man abandons his reason to pursue the world's false goods. The value of bad fortune, of course, is that it helps one to remember one's true source and ends by freeing one from attachment to the mutable and the false. Rather than turning from the false to the good, however, Phillis commits suicide, "swych sorwe hath she, for she besette hire so" (2558). Hell is the consequence of abandoning oneself without repentance to such obliterating passions, a condition in which the good is forever forgotten.

Phillis's recognition of her own culpability, her own too great freedom, inevitably calls into question the legend's automatic treatment of Demophon's failure to return as simply another instance of male infidelity. Contending with the characterization of him as another of Jason's sect is the depiction of such love as soul-destroying. Significantly, this is the first desertion that has not involved another woman (the final legend is the second). Apparently, Demophon merely preferred staying in Athens, that home of philosophy. One remembers that the preceding legend ends with the narrator warning women that they will never find a true man "but it so be that he may have non other." Following that assertion with this legend simultaneously indicts the narrator once again for his naiveté about male perfidy and forces us to question Demophon's reasons for not returning. Though the narrative explicitly compares Demophon to his father, it begs comparison with the *Aeneid:* it opens with a navy full of sick and wounded being battered by the hostile seas as it returns from Troy, until the gods have compassion on Demophon and his men and allow them to land in Rhodope, where Phillis plays Dido.[53] This analogy raises the possibility that Demophon also had a higher destiny. It is noteworthy that the clerical interpretation of the *Aeneid* regarded it as an account of the mind's journey through the *infernum* of this world to the good; Aeneas's desertion of Dido signifies his triumph over libidinous passion.[54] But the chief inducement to such reflections is the cumulative weight of the legends. After so many demonstrations of the bitter fruits of passion, the need to seek one's truth elsewhere is inescapable.

The "Legend of Hypermnestra" is our exit out of hell. Indeed, given Hypermnestra's similarity to Alceste—she alone of all the legends' heroines in any way sacrifices herself that another may live—we may well wonder whether we are still in hell. A number of factors distinguish her from Alceste, however. The most important of these is the fact, noted by both Fyler and Kiser, that Chaucer's attribution of her virtue to "the Wirdes, that we clepen Destine," deprives her of any merit for it.[55] Further, it is not entirely clear that she deserves our approbation. Though she is said to be as "pyetous, sad, wis, and trewe as stel," we are also told that she did not "dar" to "handle a knyf / In malice"—a fact explained astrologically as the consequence of Venus's oppression of the "crewel craft" of "rede Mars." If this absence of malice accounts for her inability to kill her husband, as her father demands, the exemplification of this absence by her fear of knives undermines the characterization "trewe as stel." In a poem written as an apology for Criseyde, it is a reminder that she too did not "dar" to "handle" sword or dart (*T&C* 4, 771–72). Even more crucially, it reminds us that Alceste unites Venus with Mars, from whom she derives her red. True virtue is neither male nor female, of course, but an androgynous union of qualities that the legends have been asked to sever: masculine rigor and feminine pity. Only those capable of uniting justice and mercy, as Alceste did, can escape the "prysoun" in which the legend leaves Hypermnestra.

Chaucer's account of her salvation of Linus limits our sympathy with her and demonstrates that she is no Alceste. We may approve her refusal to be her father's preemptive Fury and sympathize with her suffering as she is torn between pity and fear of death, but it is predominantly her fear of knives and her distaste for blood that motivate her awakening of Linus, not her "wifly honeste." When she looks at her hands and imagines them all bloody from the deed, we may be moved, but not so when she imagines herself with her "throte korve a-two" and concludes "thanne shal I blede," for the conclusion is too literal and too anticlimactic. It is of the same order as the assertion that the Prioress would weep for a mouse "if it were deed or bledde." Hers is a sensibility, one the courtly tradition assumes to be particularly feminine, that is overwhelmed by thoughts of blood. Killing her husband is simply temperamentally impossible for her.

Finally, Hypermnestra fails to come to grips with the issues and thus avoids all moral choice. She no more debates Linus's guilt or

innocence than she does the merits or demerits of her father's demand. Her "Be as be may, for earnest or for game, / He shal awake"
(2703–4) constitutes a surrender to the pressure of making such
a choice. Her capitulation to her tenderhearted nature is equally
evident in her illogical conclusion that either she or her husband
must die. Though the narrator blames Linus for not taking her with
him and laments that she was "so weik" and so helpless that her
father caught her before she could escape, the fact that "she sat hire
doun ryght tho" indicates that she is as much a victim of her own
lack of steel. There is a relevant Dantean analogue: those who are
located just outside hell proper with the "angeli che non furon ri-
belli / ne fur fedeli a Dio, ma per sé fuoro" (angels who were neither rebellious nor faithful to God but stood apart; *Inf.* 3, 38–39).
Chief among these is "l'ombra di colui / che fece per viltade il gran
rifiuto" (the shade of him who from cowardice made the great
refusal; *Inf.* 3, 59–60). Though it may seem harsh to characterize
Hypermnestra as "per sé," her fate is determined by her inability
to choose between doing her father's will and leaping from the
loft with her husband. Neither justice nor mercy, much less the
union of the two that constitutes true love, would seem within her
power.[56]

The picture of Linus's departure is hardly sympathetic. In his
haste to save himself he shows no concern for his wife whatsoever;
he is accused of the *Legend*'s archetypal sin—forgetting. He seems
as hard as his wife is soft. Nonetheless, Chaucer's picture of Linus's
departure inevitably raises questions similar to those raised by Demophon's failure to return. When the narrator asks Linus "why ne
haddest thow remembred in thy mynd / To taken hire, and lad hire
forth with the" (2717–18), the specification "lad hire forth" as what
he should have done—when, in fact, Linus escaped by leaping from
a loft—must give us pause. In the context of Chaucer's presentation of the legends as an *infernum*, it calls to mind both Virgil's efforts to lead Dante forth from hell and, perhaps even more important, Orpheus's effort to rescue Eurydice. The relevant version of
the latter story is Boethius's, of course, as Chaucer translated it. "The
lord and juge of soules" was so charmed by Orpheus's music that
he gave him his wife again, only requiring that Orpheus not look
behind him at his following wife until they were out of hell. But the
"moste ardaunt love of his wif brende the entrayles of his breest,"

and love is "a grettere lawe and a strengere" than any man may give,
so that "whanne Orpheus and his wyf were almost at the termes of
the nyght (*That is to seyn, at the laste boundes of helle*), Orpheus lokede
abakward on Erudyce his wif, and lost hire and was deed" (*Consolation* 3, m. 12). Though the narrator faults Linus for not looking
back, Orpheus's fate reminds us that had he done so, he not only
would have failed to save her but would have destroyed himself as
well. Similarly, though Virgil encourages Dante to speak with those
in hell, he is careful to keep him moving and to remind him when
he tarries that his end lies beyond hell. However drawn Dante may
be to those he meets there, they and all they represent must be left
behind.

The moralization with which the Orpheus fable ends, equating
the *infernum* to which Orpheus descends with this world, illuminates Chaucer's intimations of the nature and order of hell in the
legends:

> The fable apertenith to yow alle, whosoevere desireth or seketh to
> lede his thought into the sovereyn day (*that is to seyn, into cleernesse of
> sovereyn good*). For whoso that evere be so overcomen that he ficche his
> eien into the put of helle (*that is to seyn, whoso sette his thoughtes in erthly
> thinges*), al that evere he hath drawen of the noble good celestial he
> lesith it, whanne he looketh the helles (*that is to seyn, into lowe thinges of
> the erthe*). (*Consolation* 3, m. 12)

As Chaucer's legends constitute a revelation of the final consequences of sin, so their demonstration that this world is infected
with hell's venom proves a powerful argument for turning elsewhere. If one is not to be a Cleopatra, so enamored of such "erthly
thinges" as Antony's "dede cors" that she leapt in pursuit "into the
put of helle," then one must learn that to escape "or that it be day"
requires one to remember the good and look to it. Others must follow under their own strength. Thus, though Linus may seem from
one point of view nothing more than another false lover, in the context in which we have been examining the legends in this chapter,
his sudden departure calls to mind the hard fact that truth in loving
requires one to attend to the good and prefer it to all earthly things.
Pity requires that one awaken one's beloved; justice, that one de-
cisively choose the good. Ideal love, that love figured in the Alceste-
daisy, unites Hypermnestra's pity and Linus's steel.

Having seen that the legends are both dramatizations of this world's tragedy and revelations of the moral and metaphysical ultimates which such tragedies entail, we can make at least tentative sense of their abrupt ending, for their sudden conclusion leaves the reader in Hypermnestra's position. If we are capable of recognizing in the final image of the *Legend of Good Women,* that of Hypermnestra fettered in prison, the fate of all those who for whatever reason are unable to escape the dark night of hell—the imprisoning chains by which destiny binds those who abandon the good for earthly loves—we can, if we have the will and the power, turn ourselves to the good. Chaucer's purpose in repeatedly confronting us with the tragedies that result from an adherence to false goods and by revealing the eschatological consequences of such loves, would seem to be to free us with his art from those illusions that prevent our turning to the good. He leaves us, as it were, "at the termes of the night" that we may choose whether to step forth into the light of day or look back and be lost.

In the philosophical tradition in which Chaucer is writing, such infernal descents as those of Orpheus and Aeneas were treated as figures for the mind's journey *per creaturas ad creatorem*.[57] The journey through hell was a revelation of this world and of the essential nature of its goods. It is in such terms that Dante himself explains the literal subject of his poem, "the state of souls after death," in the letter to Can Grande: "Taken allegorically, its subject is: Man, as by good or ill deserts, in the exercise of his free choice, he becomes liable to rewarding or punishing Justice."[58] Chaucer reverses this traditional *descensus ad inferos*. His literal subject is this life, but he makes his narrator's depiction of this life—a depiction deriving from old books and enabled by the Alceste-daisy's guiding light—an intimation of the joys of heaven and the sorrows of hell. However darkly, the legends demonstrate, this world manifests the eternal world; this life, the next. We are told in the Prologue that Alceste shows what she is. So the villains and heroines of the legends, "le donne antiche e' cavalieri," show what they are. In both cases, we see them choose the ends that determine their being. Men's and women's acts and intentions are seen in their essential nature, even as they will be for all eternity. In their "exercise of [their] free choice" we glimpse the fate of their "souls after death."

Besides being a depiction of "the state of souls after death," the

Commedia allegorically represents in the pilgrim's literal journey through hell, purgatory, and heaven the function of reason and its fruit (that wisdom of which old books are the repository) and of love and its fruit (the grace of which the beloved is vessel) in the earthly pilgrims' salvation, in their recognition of the vicious, in their purgation of it, and in their ascent to virtue. Once again, what Dante does allegorically, Chaucer does literally; the *Legend* with its intimations of heaven and hell is the product and expression of his love for the Alceste-daisy on the one hand, of his encounter with old books on the other. Dante represents the pilgrim's journey as his spiritual autobiography: now among those who subjected reason to desire he swoons in an excess of sympathy for Francesca; now among the wrathful he lashes out in apparently righteous anger at Filippo Argenti; now he succumbs to an ignoble fascination with the quarrel of Adam and Sinon. Similarly, Chaucer makes the narrator's encounter with sin in his old books a participation: now to the peril of his soul his judgment is overwhelmed by pity for Dido even as hers was by pity and love for Aeneas; now he raises his voice in anger against the deceiver Jason even as he is himself telling a fraudulent tale; now he would silence his old book by omitting Procne's and Philomela's revenge even as Tereus sought to silence Philomela to prevent revenge. His encounter with the depths of hell in his old books is, as we have seen, a descent into his own spiritual depths, one which also recalls Gower's inquiry into Amant's spiritual state by means of stories illustrating the deadly sins. Indeed, in their dramatization of poet's participation in the moral ambiguities of the world he creates, the legends can be said with justice to be more honest and more subtle than Dante's equivalent representation of his pilgrim's participation in hell.

But we must remember that the narrator's return to his books at Alceste's command, his descent into hell in imitation of her, is undertaken as penance. One recalls Tarquin's suggestion to the men at the siege of Ardea that they "ese" their hearts with speech. To encounter sin and even imaginatively reenact it in literature is, it is implied, a potentially redemptive process, for it can lead to self-knowledge. And indeed, the narrator's journey through his old books is something of a progress. He abandons his tentative efforts to insist on male goodness, confronts in sorrow man's betrayal of woman, and comes to ponder the place of evil in the cosmos. He even permits Phillis to admit openly her own complicity in her un-doing. This process is also purgatorial in that the narrator's imag-inative participation in the tragedy of human loving seems gradu-ally to tear his soul from its attachment to earthly things—necessary preparation for loving the good. At the same time, however, the efficacy of the narrator's penance is fatally limited by his apparent failure to recognize that his legends are a participation in the evils he encounters in his old books, a failure that culminates in his ad-vice to women to trust no man in love except himself. To the end he remains unaware that his legends in their "folhaste" constitute a betrayal of the good manifest in the Alceste-daisy, albeit one forced upon him by her dream counterpart.

In this infernal descent, the narrator is the reader's guide and point of identification; we inevitably participate in his failure. By simultaneously confronting us with the narrator's failure, Chaucer would enable our success. Even as the narrator discovers himself in his old books and creates his moral identify as he translates them, so through reading his translations we can discover and create our-selves. His unwitting descent into folly and viciousness makes it possible for the reader's accompanying descent to be conscious and thus an ascent to self-knowledge and efficacious penance. While it may seem excessively fanciful to judge that Chaucer has sacrificed his narrator for the reader's sake, accompanying Chaucer's confes-sion (through the persona of his narrator) that he enjoyed writing love poetry, and his dramatization that as such it is a spiritually dan-gerous undertaking, is the very real implication that he exposed himself to its dangers at least in part in the service of his audience. Presumably, he hazarded the venom of old books and adopted the stance of lover in the hope that doing so in charity would advance his soul. This charity is nowhere more evident than in his rejection of an art that preaches salvation at a safe distance from art's temp-tations (in the manner of the "Parson's Tale") for the more hazard-ous art that participates in sin in order to enable salvation.

Unlike the intertextual drama of the narrator's translations, in which the reader is directly confronted with his manipulation of his sources, the intertextual relationship of the legends and Dante's *Commedia* is silent. Chaucer makes no explicit references to the *Commedia;* he does not openly reproduce it or take issue with it; he does not advise us to read it. The fact that it must have been virtually unknown in fourteenth-century London may have influenced this decision (as may literary rivalry), though we should note that its obscurity did not prevent his parodying it in the "House of Fame" or repeatedly echoing it in *Troilus and Criseyde*.[59] Many of the shared ideas and the analogous images were common cultural property, of course.[60] (Dante's use of Aristotle's classification of vice to organize the *Inferno* was apparently unprecedented, but Chaucer has not reproduced that: his descent—from those who succumb to passion, to those who deliberately seduce, to those who employ force to betray—does not depend on Dante for intelligibility.) Modern readers may need the *Commedia* to authorize a dimension of the poem so alien to our expectations, but presumably the *Legend*'s original audience—which was drenched in anatomies of sin and the mythology of hell, however unknown Dante may have been—would not. If the imitation suggests Chaucer's admiration for Dante as a poet, the silence also suggests a refusal to endorse Dante's pretense to have seen what lies beyond the veil that separates this world and the next. Chaucer began the *Legend*, we recall, by simultaneously declaring his faith that there is joy in heaven and pain in hell and avowing that there is "noon dwellyng in this contree" who has been in either. What we know of such moral and metaphysical absolutes, he implies, we know provisionally, by such intimations of them as can be garnered from experience and old books. We see them darkly through such natural remembrances as daisies and such literary ones as Ariadne. To claim more, one must transcend the ethical and philosophical limits proper to poetry.

The Conclusion of the Legends

V

For all the aesthetic logic of Pandarus's assertion that "th'ende is every tales strengthe," it often seems as though Pandarus's own creator little regarded it. What could be more anticlimactic and inconclusive then the endings of the *Book of the Duchess* and the *Parliament of Fowls*? When Chaucer does provide an emphatic ending—a concluding moralization, for instance—it is likely as not to seem inadequate and even wrongheaded, akin to the inappropriate sententiousness parodied in the "Nun's Priest's Tale." The conclusions of his two most substantial works, *Troilus and Criseyde* and the *Canterbury Tales,* are well-known conundrums, given their apparent rejection of the very art that produced them. And then there are the numerous works Chaucer left as fragments—whether for biographical reasons, as presumably the "Squire's Tale" and the *House of Fame,* or by artistic design, as the "Tale of Sir Thopas" and the "Monk's Tale," where the incomplete state of the work is as aspect of its finished form. The *Legend of Good Women* is a particularly problematic instance of a work left incomplete. Indeed, the *Legend* has the dubious distinction of seeming—at least to many readers—doubly incomplete: it lacks all the legends apparently promised, and the last legend provided itself seems truncated.

Frequently, recognizing a work abandoned in progress is a simple matter. Such is not so obviously the case with the *Legend* as is sometimes supposed, however. Unlike the *House of Fame* or the "Squire's Tale," it does not break off in midnarrative. Similarly, since on the surface it has an open-ended serial form lacking any conventional means of formal closure (such as a concluding Alexandrine or a final speech in which the old order is buried, the new asserted), it does not announce its lack of completion by the absence of some obligatory or conventional feature. The only reason we suppose it incomplete is its failure to satisfy the expectations it has itself raised. While presumably no one takes as a literal expression of Chaucer's intention, Alceste's insistence that the narrator spend the greater part of the rest of his life writing of good women, virtually all critics have supposed that Chaucer intended more than we have. The hierarchical division in the Prologue between the nineteen ladies "in real habit" who follow the god of Love and the huge "traas" of good women who follow them seems to imply at least nineteen legends, especially if we imagine the nineteen comprising Alceste and the eighteen women with whom she is compared in the *balade* that accompanies the description of this procession.[1] At the very least, the Prologue would seem to require the inclusion of Alceste's story among the legends; the god mandates its inclusion "whan thou hast other smale ymaad before" (F, 550), an order that certainly implies a final position for it. And indeed, telling Alceste's story last would have been one way to provide a sense of closure, for given the Prologue's treatment of her as the ultimate example of womanly truth in loving, her legend would produce a sense of climax and completion—or it would if the legends were the celebrations of female goodness they represent themselves to be.

Significantly, our reason for supposing the final legend itself incomplete is similar: its ending does not fulfill the expectations we have acquired from reading the other legends. Taken in itself, its final line—"This tale is seyd for this conclusioun"—can be supposed to point to what has just transpired, Hypermnestra's imprisonment, or be interpreted as a statement without external reference (beyond that in "this tale"), a way of saying "The End." Skeat's and Robinson's reason for supposing that it must have been intended to point to some unsupplied "application," some generalized remarks about the perfidy of men and/or the goodness of women, is the fact that the other legends end in that fashion.[2] Given the frequency with which Chaucer disappoints our expectations, especially when it comes to endings, and his strategy in the *Legend* of creating expectations he has no intention of fulfilling, perhaps we should not be so quick to prefer our notions of how Hypermnestra's legend ought to conclude to its actual (and adequate) end-

ing. Taking a hint from the scribe's final line in the Bodleian manuscript (Arch. Selden B.24), "and thus ended Chaucere the legendis
of ladyis," we ought first to explore the possibility that the poem's
present ending fulfilled Chaucer's intention not only for the "Legend of Hypermnestra" but also for the *Legend* as a whole.[3]

There is some evidence external to the *Legend* that bears upon
such a probability. I refer, of course, to the Man of Law's discussion
of the supposed contents of Chaucer's "large volume" called "the
Seintes Legende of Cupide" and to Chaucer's reference to the *Legend* in the Retraction as "the book of the xxv. Ladies." We might
suppose such references to the work as a thing accomplished con-
clusive proof that Chaucer regarded it as complete were it not for
his similar references to the manifestly incomplete *House of Fame*.
In fact, what strikes one about these allusions to the *Legend* is that
even as they treat it as a thing achieved, they remind us of its lack
of completion. Though some critics have supposed the Man of Law's
inaccurate list of the poem's contents to be Chaucer's way of keeping track of what he intended to do once he had the time, surely
Sullivan is right to insist that the list is the Man of Law's and that it
functions to characterize him.[4] It confirms the implications from the
General Prologue of the *Canterbury Tales* that the Sergeant of the
Law is not really so learned and wise as he seems. While the list does
include numerous heroines Chaucer might have included and may
even once have intended to include, our appreciation of its characterization of the Man of Law depends on our realization that
Chaucer never wrote legends of, say, Dejanire or Hermione or
Hero—or, for that matter, of Penelope and Alceste. If Chaucer had
completed the *Legend* by narrating the lives of the women mentioned by the Man of Law, he would have destroyed much of the
significance of the Man of Law's prologue. The inescapable implication is that at the time he was writing that prologue, Chaucer did
not intend to include the additional women in the Man of Law's list
in the legends, possibly not even Penelope or Alceste. Either he had
realized that he was not going to complete the originally intended
sequence of legends and took advantage of this fact for some humor—partly at the Man of Law's expense, partly at his own—or he
never intended to include all the women mentioned.[5]

The omission from the *Legend*'s G Prologue of the god's requirement that the dreamer include the women listed in his *balade* can

be interpreted in support of the view that the humor of the Man of Law's prologue reflects a change in plans. Assuming G the revision, one may suppose this modification in our expectations a consequence of Chaucer's realization that he was never going to get all those legends written—but it is by no means certain that G is the revision. And there is another explanation of the god's failure in G to refer the narrator to the ladies in his *balade:* the fact that he no longer sings it. If G is the revision, these lines had to be either dropped or altered. Thus, the difference by no means eliminates the possibility that Chaucer intended an incomplete poem from the beginning. Even if we suppose this a modification reflecting a belated awareness on Chaucer's part that he would never write that many legends, the G Prologue still implies more legends than we have. In either case, that is, whether Chaucer only belatedly realized he would never complete the lengthy sequence implied by Alceste's and the god's demands or never intended to complete it, the Man of Law's prologue suggests that the present incomplete state of the legends had one degree or another of intentionality.

The Retraction's title—"the book of the xxv. Ladies"—similarly underscores the incomplete state of the poem and simultaneously suggests the possibility that what we have is what Chaucer intended. There is some slight question about the reading "xxv."[6] Both Robinson in his first edition (1933) and Skeat chose from among the manuscript variants the number nineteen. Robinson dropped this emendation in his second edition (1957) after Manly and Rickert's collation of all the manuscripts revealed that it occurs in only three manuscripts representing just two minor branches.[7] The fact that each of the other variants from the predominant reading of twenty-five occurs only once—the obvious result of scribal error—might lead one to suppose the double occurrence of the number nineteen, improbable on the basis of chance, due to authorial revision.[8]

What makes this supposition unlikely, besides the overwhelming predominance of the number twenty-five and despite the undeniably slight authority of the manuscripts that give nineteen, is the existence of another reason to account for the latter number's appearance: the reference in the Prologue to the nineteen ladies following the god of Love. Some, at least, of the Retraction's scribes were apparently puzzled by the reading twenty-five, which neither describes what we have nor strikingly confirms any expectations from the Prologue; it thus seems, as far as the reader can tell, totally arbitrary. Like some modern editors and critics, they apparently seized on the passage in the Prologue to solve neatly the question of Chaucer's intentions. But the more difficult reading must be accepted and its implications faced. We can adopt a biographical explanation for the discrepancy between the title and the extant poem: perhaps Chaucer actually wrote twenty-five legends and sixteen have been lost; perhaps Chaucer still intended to write sixteen more, even though in the Retraction he is repenting for having written any; perhaps Chaucer forgot how many he had actually written. But the business of the literary critic is to seek where possible an artistic explanation for textual facts. In the light of such a principle, one must entertain the hypothesis that Chaucer chose a title that does not describe what he wrote over one that does—say, the book of ten ladies, or the perfectly adequate title he had already used in the Man of Law's prologue, "the Seintes Legende of Cupide"—because he wanted the poem's title to indicate its incomplete state, as though that were an essential feature of its literary character.

The possibility that Chaucer regarded the poem as finished raises the question of what we mean by the terms "complete" and "finished" when we apply them to literary texts. When we distinguish between the two terms at all, we ordinarily use "complete" to refer to the wholeness of the work, to express our conviction that we have all that was intended and that what was intended was a whole; we use "finished" to characterize a work that we judge not only complete but also as polished as its author was inclined or able to make it, one that has received its finishing touches. In ordinary usage, the latter term includes the former: finished works are complete; incomplete works are unfinished; but complete works may be unfinished. The anomaly is the deliberate fragment, the finished work that appears incomplete. It is the possibility that the *Legend* is such an anomaly that Chaucer's subsequent references to the *Legend* require us to consider.

Some light can be shed both on this problem and on what these terms entail by comparing the *Legend* with the *Canterbury Tales*, for they are alike not only in that they seem incomplete but also in that they both dramatize their own genesis in their prologues and, in the process, define much of their scope and character. Considering the question of whether or not the *Canterbury Tales* is a whole, Howard has used a different distinction between "incomplete" and "unfinished," one that Northrop Frye applied to the *Faerie Queene*.[9] As I understand Howard's argument, he is persuaded that Chaucer realized the distinctive features of his idea for the *Tales:* the form of the whole is defined and in place; if we cannot quite say that we have every kind of tale we were to have, we can say that diversity and multiplicity are amply achieved. Nothing Chaucer might have added would have altered the essential literary character of the work as we have it. Thus, Howard judges that though the whole poem is unfinished, it is complete in that Chaucer realized its informing and defining idea. Many would no doubt allow the *Legend*'s completeness in Howard's sense of the term: even as we ordinarily assume that Chaucer intended more legends, we normally suppose that the additional legends would have been more of the same, additional realizations of the idea of the legends, whatever our conception of that idea may be. Whether or not one accepts the view that the legends are more or less randomly ordered beads on a string, it is clear that the *Legend* must be complete in Howard's sense of the term for it to be complete in the ordinary sense.

In her recent discussion of the *Tales* in relation to Arabic frame narratives, Katherine Gittes has taken issue with Howard's characterization of that poem as "unfinished but complete" and has proposed viewing it as "finished but incomplete."[10] While I see no way in which the *Canterbury Tales* can be called finished (unless Gittes means by "finished" either what Howard means by "complete" or simply that Chaucer is no longer writing tales), her point is that the work has the open-ended character she finds typical of Arabic frame narratives, which she regards as its ultimate model. Her contention is that the form is always open to addition and hence could never be fully complete.[11]

Whatever one thinks of the assertion that the form of the *Tales* is permanently open, there is certainly a level at which this appears to be true of the *Legend,* much truer of it than of the *Canterbury Tales*. Unlike the drama that accounts for the *Tales,* which provides two possible end points and two controlling plans for the storytelling (the supper at the Tabard Inn after each pilgrim has told four tales, proposed in the General Prologue, and the arrival at the shrine after each has told one tale, seemingly anticipated in the Parson's

Prologue), the drama presented as the genesis of the legends provides no definite stopping point and no control over the number
of legends to be told prior to that point. Alceste's demand that the
poet spend the greater part of the rest of his life writing of good
women creates an indefinitely expandable form and implies that
the poem can only end, even if it ends with her legend as the god
seems to imply that it should, when the poet is near or on his death-
bed. Further, unlike the *Canterbury Tales,* the *Legend* as it exists lacks
any formal ending, any equivalent to the Retraction. What one ex-
pects from a poem that defines itself is congruity between the
foreseen ending and the actual ending. One of the reasons we suppose the *Canterbury Tales* incomplete is that its ending is not con-
gruent with the ending foreseen in the General Prologue; presumably one of Howard's reasons for supposing its idea complete is that
the "Parson's Tale" and the Retraction can be regarded as satisfying
the expectations of the Parson's prologue. In contrast, Chaucer's
dramatization of the genesis of the legends does not permit us to
anticipate anything but an arbitrary ending. Alceste's and the god's
demands require a series of indeterminate length, one without any
inherent stopping point. All the poet can do is stop at some point
or, if you prefer, decide that enough is enough and tell Alceste's
story. In Gittes's terms, at least, that would finish the poem, but it
would not complete it.

But this permanently open-ended quality belongs to Alceste's
conception of the poem. As Howard is right to insist that Harry
Bailey's initial plan for the pilgrimage was not necessarily Chaucer's, so we must insist that Alceste's conception of the legends is
not necessarily his; indeed, as we have seen, the contradictions inherent in her and the god's plan indicate that it is necessarily not
Chaucer's.[12] According to Alceste's conception, we should note, the
legends could end in midsentence in the midst of a narrative—that
is, be without any ending at all—and yet be complete provided it
stops in that way because of the poet's death. Only let him die per-
forming his penance, and her intention for the poem will be fulfilled. Presumably, Chaucer had some other terminus in mind for
the poem (and for his life!). And yet the poem stops precisely as
though it *had* been ended by such an accident.

We should not suppose this congruity—between the ending

provided and the ending inevitably implied by Alceste's demand for a perpetual series—itself an accident, a chance consequence of Chaucer's own biography. It is too neat and too similar to other ironies that result from the relationship of the legends to the Prologue. We have seen evidence that Chaucer intended the general disparity between Alceste's demand for legends of good women and the narrator's inappropriate selections in the congruity between that inappropriateness and Chaucer's characterization of the narrator as heedless. In the same way, we should see a suggestion that Chaucer intended the disparity between our expectations of a substantial series and the number he actually supplied in the congruity of the provided and implied endings. By ending the narrator's series as though by biographical accident, Chaucer puts that accident, whatever its character and however invisible, inside the poem; he makes it a part of the narrator's biography, as it were, and provides the poem with an ending, an intended conclusion that fulfills his purposes. His ending for the poem is a dramatization of Alceste's non-ending, her demand for a poem that merely stops. Thus, the apparent incompleteness of the poem becomes evidence of its completeness.

One retreats from such paradoxical complexity, seeks a simpler idea of the legends. Surely, the god of Love's demand that Chaucer include Alceste's life among the legends is proof that they are incomplete and unfinished. But the insistence on Alceste's inclusion belongs to the same level of the poem as Alceste's demands, the level at which the narrator lives. Once again we are forced to distinguish between the idea of the poem articulated on its surface and the underlying idea that defines its character and form. Though the surface drama requires a legend about Alceste, the underlying order of the poem prohibits her tale from appearing among the legends. As we have seen, contrast between the Prologue and the legends is a fundamental principle of the poem's structure: the springtime garden world of revival and resurrection in the Prologue contrasts with the tragic world of division and death pictured in the legends. The comedy of Alceste's resurrection cannot occur in the legends without violating this order. No doubt that is why Chaucer manages to give us the essentials of her life in the Prologue. Once again the conclusion is inescapable: Chaucer's idea of the legends requires them to be incomplete from the point of view of Alceste and the god of Love.

The notion that the poem should be regarded as finished is not new. It was first proposed (without ever being seconded, as far as I know) by H. C. Goddard.[13] Reading the poem as an almost savagely ironic response by Chaucer to the demands of the ladies in his court audience, Goddard declared its incomplete state the last of its many jokes, Chaucer's final comment on the absurdity of the imposed task and on the unavailability of good women to praise. Goddard's proposal needs to be seconded and then amended; his understanding of the significance of the poem's intentionally fragmentary form was inadequate, but there is ample evidence beyond that already considered to confirm that its present ending is indeed part of the poem's design. Once again, comparison with the *Canterbury Tales* can help us appreciate some of this evidence.

To regard the *Legend's* incomplete state as part of its finished form is to place it in the company of the "Tale of Sir Thopas" and the "Monk's Tale," works whose intentional incompleteness is indicated by their being interrupted by their pilgrim audience. The "Monk's Tale" provides a particularly instructive parallel, for it too has a prologue drama that implies a virtually endless series of tales (the Monk claims to have a hundred in his "celle"), and the tales themselves are similar in form, being briefly narrated tragedies. Given these similarities, a consideration of the reaction of the Monk's audience may give us some insight into how Chaucer must have thought some of his audience would react to the *Legend*. Chaucer dramatizes two related reactions to the Monk's tragedies, associating each with a corresponding idea of comedy. The Knight takes the Monk's tragedies to heart and finds them distressing. It is a "grete disese," he tells us, to hear of so many sudden falls, a "lytel hevynesse" being enough for most people; in contrast it is a "gladsom" thing to hear of people waxing fortunate. His definition of comedy according to plot structure—all's well that ends well—is reflected in his own tale, which follows Arcite's tragic death with the happily-ever-after marriage of Palamon and Emily. The Host, who has been bored, seconds the Knight's interruption but deems the Monk's tragedies profitless because there is no point in bewailing the past, and annoying because they contain "no desport ne game"; he nearly fell asleep. For the Host, comedy is what produces mirth and laughter. Obviously, similar reactions to the tragedies of the *Legend* are possible.

Though the structure of the *Legend* does not permit Chaucer to dramatize audience reaction in the manner of the *Canterbury Tales,* it does provide a means of internalizing possible responses, for Chaucer has his narrator repeatedly react in the manner of an audience to the works he is translating. While the narrator's responses are often unreliable—inappropriate and disproportionate, controlled by a priori considerations, calculated to limit and control our responses—Chaucer has not so distanced us from his narrator that we cannot appreciate and even participate at times in his reactions. Not surprisingly, the narrator's response to the repetitive character of his task is analogous to the responses of the Knight and the Host to the Monk's serial tragedies. Increasingly, he seems bored: he is weary of Tereus even before he begins his story; the "Legend of Phillis" finds him "agroted" with telling of false men. Associated with this weariness, accounting for it in part, is his increasing contempt for and disgust with his own kind. He is depressed as well as weary. While this does not surprise us, we ought to wonder that Chaucer allowed his narrator to voice such sentiments. If he intended, say, sixteen more legends, it is a strangely counterproductive procedure to allow the narrator to prompt the reader to feel weary and "disesed" at this point. Such statements as we find in the antepenultimate and penultimate legends make artistic sense only in those positions. Their presence necessitates ending the legends soon; indeed, they virtually constitute an announcement that the ending is at hand.

The intimation that the end is near only underscores the poem's lack of a forceful ending. Again, comparison with the "Monk's Tale" is instructive (assuming that it was intended to end with the Croesus story).[14] Though the Monk's tragedies are clearly interrupted by the Knight's "Hoo, . . . good sire, namore of this," Chaucer provided them with an apparent ending: the final lines of the last tragedy restate the general definition of tragedy with which the Monk began. Both the general character of these closing remarks, which are more or less applicable to all the preceding narratives, and the sense of return are strong signs of closure.[15] In comparison, the ending of the "Legend of Hypermnestra" does not even persuade us that it is done, much less that the legends as a whole are, even though its final lines could mean "this is the end." If we are struck once again by the way the ending of the *Legend* leaves it incomplete, the narrator's weariness and his prayer for the grace to persevere in his penance raise the possibility that this incompleteness should be regarded as the consequence of his having quit.

The suggestion that the abrupt ending of the legends is meant to represent the narrator's abandonment of his penance gains confirmation from both the Prologue and Chaucer's dramatization of the narrator's efforts as translator in the final legends. Alceste's demand that the narrator spend the greater part of the rest of his life writing of good women and false men leads us to anticipate weariness and boredom. Is there anywhere a translator so avid and compulsive, so accustomed to making and so "nyce," that he will devote a lifetime to writing poetry of such a repetitive character? To imagine a long life for the narrator is to imagine him giving up. Is there anywhere a lover so true that he will perform such an endless penance for his lady? If, as Alceste claims, all lovers are false, then logic requires us to suppose that the narrator will abandon his translations, since he undertook them as a lover. While it is one of the purposes of the legends to imply—in defiance of Alceste—that goodness is not dependent upon sex, it is equally their purpose to demonstrate that humanity is flawed. Finally, of course, the legends are written from the same ultimate perspective as the *Troilus* and prove, among other things, the same final truth: that all human love is "feigned" in comparison to that love which will "falsen no wight." Throughout the legends, Chaucer has been dramatizing his narrator's fallible humanity, his participation in the failings depicted in his old books. Having characterized in the Prologue the inconstant order of the natural world and of human nature as forgetful, Chaucer concludes the legends by having the narrator climactically demonstrate his forgetfulness.

The demands of the poem's logic are confirmed by the ironies of its denouement. As the narrator's weariness and prayer for grace predict his departure, so do his reactions to the antepenultimate and penultimate legends. He ends the first of these by warning women to beware of men, for they will find them true "ful lytel while," and averring that he would say the same of any man, even his own brother.[16] He ends the second by advising women to trust no man in love except himself. The irony of his exclusion of himself from the general condemnation, as though he had no kinship with false men, is only made more emphatic by the principal burden of this legend: its demonstration that all men are brothers in their forgetful frailty; that mankind, wicked fruit of a wicked tree, is false by nature. The narrator's exclusion of himself is the pride that precedes a fall; it demands an immediate demonstration that he is no exception to the rule. His sudden departure in the final legend is the needed proof that he belongs to the brotherhood of man.

What logic predicts and the ironies of the denouement confirm is also revealed by Chaucer's practice in the legends of establishing analogies between the dramas there recounted and the narrator's activities as translator. In the final two legends we return to instances of the classic form of human inconstancy, loving and leaving. To regard the abrupt ending as another case of desertion is to see in it just one more instance of this pattern and yet another proof of the dangers inherent in translating old books, whose viciousness may still be infectious. Indeed, the poem's final line—"The tale is seyd for this conclusioun"—can be viewed as pointing to the narrator's departure, to his dramatic enactment of the "application," the missing but inevitable conclusion: trust no man, for we are *all* false.

According to Alceste's assertion that it is now regarded a game among men to see how many women they may shame, when a man leaves one lady it is for another. The narrator expresses the same sentiment even more directly at the end of the "Legend of Phillis." If we ask who Alceste's rival is, for whom the narrator has deserted her, the poem's answer is the daisy. The validity of the supposition that the narrator has abandoned his translations that he may resume his devotion to the daisy is evident in the *Legend*'s structure. In the Prologue, let us recall once more, Chaucer depicts the natural order as a cyclical progression through contraries, one illustrated by the daisy's imitation of the sun, by Alceste's infernal descent and final stellification, and by the seasonal separation and reconciliation of the birds. In his turn the narrator participates in this order: he follows the daisy as it follows the sun; his translations are in effect an infernal descent; like the birds, he spends winter with one love, his books, but returns to the other in spring. The *Legend* itself is the consequence of the cyclical order of the narrator's life. He abandons his books for the daisy only to be returned to them by his dream. As a reflection and product of this natural cyclical order, the *Legend* must itself be circular; it too ought to end with a return. The abruptness of the poem's ending accords perfectly with the narrator's depiction of the effects of spring upon him: "Farewel my bok, and my devocioun!" In sum, the poem's structure invites the supposition that its "conclusioun" is the narrator's inevitable seasonal return to his other love.

Much besides the drama of the narrator indicates that the *Legend of Good Women* is finished. The conviction that the legends are incomplete is usually accompanied by the unspoken assumption that they have little or no structure, that they are more or less randomly ordered beads on a string. As we saw in the last chapter, however, their sequence is patterned; its underlying structure defines a movement of descent and reascent. Chaucer begins with two tragedies depicting mutually faithful lovers—Antony and Cleopatra, Pyramus and Thisbe—and follows these with two depicting male desertion, those of Aeneas and Jason. This descent into increasing viciousness culminates in the three legends that depict ravishment. The last two legends ascend from these depths by resuming the loving-and-leaving pattern.

The final legend answers the first. As we saw in the last chapter, Cleopatra's grand gesture in affirmation of her truth in loving—her leap into the grave of snakes—is an apt and powerful image for the hellish death that results from "feigned" loves. Linus's leap from the bedroom he shares with Hypermnestra, one made without looking back, constitutes an escape from the grave. If the narrator judges the former to be truth in loving and the latter faithlessness, the poem as a whole intimates a perspective that makes the former look like folly and willfulness, the latter like wisdom and the better part of valor. With Cleopatra we enter hell; with Linus we leave it. This movement defines the legends as a cyclical whole and returns us, along with the narrator, to the daylight world of the daisy.

The perception that the legends dramatize an infernal descent and that they are a structured whole makes it possible to recognize significance in the fact that Chaucer tells nine legends recounting the tragedies of ten heroines. Similarly, in each of Dante's other worlds there are from one point of view nine circles; from another, ten. Nine is a multiple of the trinity; ten is the number of totality, wholeness, completion.[17] It is for similar reasons, of course, that each of Dante's three journeys takes thirty-three cantos, the whole poem, one hundred.

We have seen yet further evidence that Hypermnestra's legend was designed to be a finale. First, there is the parody with which it opens: the absolutely formulaic denunciation of men as bad, caught perfectly in the tone of "That other brother called was Egiste, / That was of love as fals as ever him liste." The pretense that books prove the god's and Alceste's simplified vision can be carried no further. Similarly marking the end is the fact that alone among the heroines, Hypermnestra recalls Alceste; Chaucer uses her dissimilar similitude to Alceste to give a definitive answer to the idea that truth in loving is female and falsity in love is male. I refer, of course, to the reminder the final legend provides that truth in loving unites the white of Venus and the red of Mars, the lily and the rose, pity and "daunger," tenderness and steel; and to its demonstration that Hypermnestra satisfies only half the equation, even as Linus seemingly manifests only the other half. Its demonstration that truth in loving is neither male nor female but the consequence of a balance of qualities conventionally associated with each is of the order of a final statement. It does dramatically what the ending of the "Monk's Tale" does explicitly. It recapitulates and sums up. In the process, it returns the mind to Alceste and thus ends the sequence.

Though the end of the *Legend* requires us to imagine the narrator once again kneeling before the daisy, it also points the reader toward that reality to which the daisy and Alceste and the lady fashioned from the two in the narrator's dream all point, that reality to which nature and books and visions all lead: namely that "oon, and two, and thre, eterne on lyve, / That regnest ay in thre, and two, and oon" (*T&C* 5, 1863–64). As the tragedy of Troilus and Criseyde requires both audience and poet to turn from feigned loves and from poetry about such loves, so finally must the *Legend*'s tragedies. Though we may feel contempt for Linus in his apparent failure to give Hypermnestra even a thought, the dramatic allusion to the Orpheus myth inevitably reminds us that in the last analysis (the analysis that corresponds to final tales) one is responsible for one's own soul. At some point one must stop looking back to earth.

Similarly, at some point the poet must stop writing tragedies that implicitly call his audience to God, and answer that call himself. It is up to the reader to follow.

All these factors argue that the *Legend of Good Women* is complete and finished. That its finished form depicts an incomplete action, that it leaves the narrator's poem apparently incomplete, is its final representation of the order of this life. While we imagine at the poem's end the narrator kneeling before the daisy, the poet in prayer to God, we need to remember that the narrator leads a separate life only within poems and that the narrator of the *Legend* is not a fiction created for this poem only; his fictional biography is continuous with that of the *Troilus*'s narrator and, presumably, with that of the pilgrim-Chaucer. If the *Troilus* compels its poet to abandon love and poetry for God, even in the midst of arriving at that realization Chaucer imagines himself writing another poem, a comedy; he imagines himself realizing himself in his narrator in another poem about worldly loves. Probably it was the comedy of the Prologue to the *Legend,* Alceste's comedy, that he had in mind. If the *Legend* compels us to imagine (and by imagining to participate in) the poet's departure, both its implicitly circular form and its intimation that May constrains an involvement with the world require us to imagine the poet returning from the heights of contemplation to writing poetry once again. It should hardly surprise us that when Chaucer returned to creating his narrator anew in a new poem—the *Canterbury Tales*—it too led inevitably to a retraction. The mind's ascent to God by way of his traces in creation, the journey the *Legend* enacts, must be perpetually renewed. This process is never complete; it is merely terminated. Like the *Legend,* human lives are wholes only retrospectively. The order of the whole poem, including its finished incompletion, mirrors and enacts the human condition.

Given the medieval assumption that this life is only preparation for another life, one spent contemplating God, and the medieval conviction that this world is so ordered as to direct man repeatedly to that end, the reader may well feel that an ending which simultaneously dramatizes renewed engagement with the world and a turning from it, the mind's return to the daisy and the mind's flight to God, is the quintessential ending for a medieval poem. We are called to an end beyond this world, but we can rise to it only by traveling the world's circular courses. It is Fortune's and Nature's wheels of fire that perfect us to that ultimate end. Though the full realization of this ending takes place only in the mind of the reader, the *Legend* provides the evidence and the impetus for this realization. In its demand that the reader bring it to fulfillment and fruition, in the radical way in which it requires us to write its ending, the poem expresses the simultaneous power and powerlessness of poetry—which enables, but can only enable, the reader to create it in the mind.

Poetry as
Secular Sacrament

VI

Lee Patterson has recently argued that the *Legend* documents and participates in man's relentless oppression of woman.[1] Both the conception of feminine goodness here evident and the literary tradition that promotes it are the products and tools of this masculine tyranny. Patterson notes, for instance, that Lucrece, exposed to Tarquin's oppression by her husband's pride in her goodness, commits suicide to preserve her husband from shame.[2] While Lucrece's self-victimization is presumably unwitting, in Patterson's view Chaucer's complicity is fully conscious: it is Chaucer's purpose not only to show that the literary tradition of feminine goodness is a part of this tyranny but also to depict himself, as love poet, as "at once sustained and oppressed" by this tradition. As he is the ultimate inventor of the penance of which he is victim, so if he is to write poetry, to achieve for himself literary authority, he can do it only within and by means of this oppressive tradition: "Writing can be enacted only within a literary tradition so powerful that it coopts all innovation."[3] In this view the poet has no choice—he cannot walk out on history. Chaucer does all he can when he manifests his own inevitable complicity.

One of the compelling scenes in the tradition to which Chaucer was heir in his "literary belatedness," one Chaucer takes up and ultimately invests with his own authority, is Virgil's account of the meeting of Aeneas and Dido in the temple depicting the fall of Troy. The idea of Aeneas's appearance in a temple that recounts his own history obviously had a powerful appeal to Chaucer's imagination. Besides repeating it in the "Legend of Dido," he created variations on it in the *Book of the Duchess,* where the events of the dream begin in a room decorated with the story of Troy and both "text and glose" of the *Romance of the Rose,* and in the *House of Fame,* where the dreamer is transported to a temple of Venus adorned with the story of the *Aeneid.* These decorations present the imagery, mythology, and ideology of courtly romance even as the stained glass and wall paintings in a medieval church surrounded the worshiper with the sacred history defining the life of the Christian. The fact that Aeneas becomes visible to Dido only after he is within the temple emphatically proclaims the role of cultural inheritance in giving definition to humanity and in forming mankind's perceptions. As this recurrent scene suggests that a man is as fixed and determined by his cultural inheritance as by his individual history, so it graphically represents the double bind of the poet as product and maker of these mind-forged manacles.

Chaucer's depiction of this aspect of the scene is more complex than Virgil's. Virgil's Aeneas takes hope from the pictures on the walls, seeing them not only as evidence that his fame is known in Carthage but also as proof that its inhabitants are capable of pity (*Aeneid* 1.459–63). Chaucer's Aeneas reacts with despair to finding the Trojan "shame" so widely known, to see that they who were once "in prosperite" are now so "desclandred, and in swich degre." The reaction of Chaucer's Dido enacts the assessment that Virgil's Aeneas made of its significance, however. Seeing Aeneas, remembering that she "hadde herd ofte" of him, and moved to see "swich a noble . . . disherited in swich degre," Dido pities and loves him, so that "refreshed moste he been of his distresse." The verbal echo of Aeneas's response to this art in Dido's response to Aeneas underscores the crucial role of romance tradition in engendering and validating her passion. He is the very embodiment of the culturally imposed mythos she worships, its word made flesh.[4]

Chaucer's dramatization of the narrator's complicity in Ariadne's passion makes much the same point. When Chaucer denies the normal temporal distance between events and narrative by having the narrator directly admonish Theseus to serve any woman who may help him, and then has Theseus act out and echo the proffered advice, he makes the narrator a shaping force in the events of the narrative as well as in its telling. Given this denial of distance, when the narrator begins this legend with a perversely romantic account of Scylla's betrayal of her country, he not only anticipates Ariadne's similar betrayal but conditions it as well. As an "auctor" embodying the courtly tradition, he is twice the author of her opinion that her behavior is according to the "wone" of gentle women. We do indeed seem to inhabit a prison house of language in which poets are the Daedalean jailors.

But we have also seen that the hell of the legends is not inescapable. Chaucer does not represent literature as monolithically determined and determinative. The art of Dido's temple defines Aeneas as lovable in Dido's eyes, as shamed in his own. This freedom of interpretation limits the capacity of culture to compel and provides the individual with at least some possibility for thought and action. The legends amply demonstrate this freedom as well. The narrator opens Dido's story by announcing that he is going to follow Virgil and take his tenor from Ovid. The qualification he places on his imitation of Virgil—"as I can"—implies the incompatibility of Virgil and Ovid, and announces the plurality and diversity of his poetic inheritance. The narrator attempts this reconciliation, we recall, by taking advantage of a silence, a lacuna, in Virgil's account: seizing upon the fact that Virgil does not narrate the events inside the cave, he gives an account that transforms Virgil's Aeneas into Ovid's. The narrator uses the poetic freedom provided by literature's indeterminacy to eradicate freedom. Out of received diversity he would create a crushing romantic monolith, one that would enforce the god of Love's vision. But Chaucer makes us witness to this would-be act of oppression: the narrator's account is characterized as a mere rumor and shown to be the product of his desires. We further see that much of the power of culture to enslave derives from our having made it in our own image. Ariadne the innocent victim of romance, we remember, is simultaneously Ariadne the brute beast, who uses romance to compel all to submit to her desires. As we are made witness to the narrator's complicity in his own enslavement, so Chaucer's art ensures that the "Legend of Dido" makes us as aware of Virgil's tenor as of Ovid's; thus he restores to us a measure of freedom.

Certainly one of the hallmarks of Chaucer's art is its presentation of diverse viewpoints. One thinks first of the various perspectives inherent in the multiple narrators and various genres of the *Canterbury Tales* and of Chaucer's refusal there to privilege any one point of view.[5] More subtle but equally undeniable are the diverse styles and perspectives associated with Troilus, Pandarus, and Criseyde in the *Troilus*.⁶ The chief burden of this study has been to demonstrate a similar presence of diverse perspectives in the *Legend*. First there are the remembrances of old books that repudiate the courtly dogma imposed in the Prologue, such as Hypsipyle's prayer that her bereaver might slay her own children, or the appearance of Ariadne's crown in the sign of Taurus. More generally, there are the multiple points of view that result from the *Legend*'s participation in diverse literary traditions. Coexisting with the romantic, derived from such sources as the *marguerite* tradition and Guillaume's *Roman,* is the bourgeois realism (if this is an acceptable term) familiar from Jean's continuation.⁷ As the *Legend* draws upon both medieval metamorphoses of Ovid, the courtly and the moralized, so it reflects the classical Ovid, recreating his realistic dramatizations of passion's power, occasional glory, and frequent madness and absurdity.⁸ Equally evident are the echoes of the philosophical and theological traditions of the age, especially as they occur in Boethius, Alain, Jean, and Dante. The poem is a product of a complex network of textual relations, and though Chaucer surely sought a unified vision, he gives authority to no single tradition. Multiple viewpoints coexist and repeatedly correct one another.

The *Legend*'s participation in a variety of traditions is recreated in its own dramatization of its relationship to the rest of Chaucer's literary *corpus*. The passage in which Chaucer passes his own previous poetry in review may be self-advertisement, but its primary purpose is to create yet another context for reading the *Legend*. The review begins with the god of Love's denunciation of the *Romaunce of the Rose* and the *Troilus* as heresies against his law, continues with Alceste's list of those texts that make "lewed folk" delight in serving love, and concludes with an enumeration of those that treat of "other holynesse." However simplistic, Chaucer's catalogue of his own canon in terms of these three points of view brings those perspectives to bear upon the *Legend* and underscores its complex interconnections with his own *oeuvre*. The *Legend* recreates several times over the black knight's experience of loss, and the rose lives again in the daisy. We revisit the realm of fame, see the *Troilus* simultaneously repudiated and reconfirmed, and experience Philosophy's consolation. Aeneas in the temple is a case in point. Indeed, for much of Chaucer's variously educated audience, his own canon may have provided the only literary context capable of actualizing the poem's manifold potential.

The chief consequence of the *Legend*'s intertextuality and the irony it produces is the double take. Constantly we look again, either because what we saw was not what we expected or because a moment's reflection reveals that what we saw was not what it seemed. Reading the *Legend* is a perpetual process of revision, of seeing again. In the very midst of the temple scene that expresses culture's coercive power, its capacity to co-opt our sight, between Aeneas's reaction to its art and Dido's conditioned reaction to seeing him, Chaucer has his narrator ask,

> if that God, that hevene and erthe made,
> Wolde han a love, for beaute and goodnesse,
> And womanhod, and trouthe, and semelynesse,
> Whom shulde he loven but this lady swete?
> Ther nys no woman to hym half so mete. (1039–43)

To a Christian audience the question can only repudiate the narrator's conclusion that none is so suitable for God as Dido. But the question does more than bring the Virgin to mind; in its context it recalls another temple, another history recounted in stained glass and wall paintings with its own "disinherited" and its own man of sorrows, and another set of assumptions and values. These reflections influence in turn our response to what follows. The effect is to locate our reading within both temples.

Throughout the poem Chaucer dramatizes and enacts a complex process of prevision, vision, and revision. In the Prologue the god and Alceste demand that the poet revise the heresies of the *Roman* and the *Troilus* by writing a new series of poems whose form and content they dictate. Their demands not only shape the narrator's translations but also condition our response to them; indeed, historically, their provisions for the legends have often dominated our vision of them. At the same time, however, the Prologue's ironies preview and predict a much more complex, ironic, and intellectually playful drama. The serial form of the legends also makes reading them a complex interaction. No legend outside of the series would have the same impact it has within the series, any more than one of the *Tales* is the same thing read in isolation and in con-

text. We recall, for instance, that the narrator ends the denunciation of Jason with which he opens the "Legend of Hypsipyle and
Medea" by arguing that often the false fox gets to eat the tender
capon rightfully belonging to the "good-man" and by adding that
this example is seen "on Jason" by Hypsipyle and Medea. Given Alceste's and the god's demands, the narrator's picture in the immediately preceding legend of Aeneas slyly stealing Dido from the deserving Iarbas, and his characterization of Jason as false, of
Hypsipyle and Medea as tender, we inevitably assume that the story
to come will show Jason stealing his victims from someone more
deserving. Only when we finish the legend do we realize Jason has
done no such thing, there being no rival lover for him to victimize
in either story; only when we remember Hypsipyle's prayer that she
who "hadde his herte yraft hire fro" might also find him untrue to
her do we see Medea as the fox, Jason as the capon, and Hypsipyle
as the rightful owner. The revision caused by the discrepancy between prediction and fact makes us review, in its turn, the erroneous predictors. For instance, we remember yet again Virgil's account of Aeneas's stay in Carthage, where Dido, consumed with
passion, tries to steal him from his divinely appointed destiny.

In effect, the legends form with themselves a complex intertextuality. As Pyramus and Thisbe's "pitous ende" in "o grave" reenacts Antony's and Cleopatra's sequential suicides, including the determination of the heroine to show her truth; as Jason's perfidy
interacts with Aeneas's, and Hypsipyle's and Medea's eagerness and
folly with Dido's, so Tereus and Tarquin mirror each other. The
"Legend of Phillis" is virtually a pastiche of the previous legends depicting loving and leaving. The narrator all but replaces any account of Demophon and Phillis's relationship with assertions that
he traveled the "same path" his father did, as if prevision could dispense with vision altogether. What narrative we are given—the account of how Demophon was driven ashore in Rhodope by hostile
seas and sought succor at court, where he was honoured for his renown and pitied by Phillis—recreates the arrival of Aeneas in Carthage. Like Jason he is a false fox gifted with a "fayre tonge." If
Phillis plays Dido, she also reenacts Medea: her admission that she
was too free of her love recalls Medea's lament that she preferred
Jasons's yellow hair to her own "honeste." And her accusation that
Demophon is like his father in his treachery only forces us to rec-

ognize how like Ariadne she is in her desire to be wife to this "duk and lord" of Athens. Though the narrator uses these similarities to lighten his narrative and intellectual burden, their actual effect is anything but reductive. Even as they locate tragedy's inevitability in our shared humanity, like all the analogies resulting from the serial form of the legends, they involve the reader in a complex and virtually endless process of revision.

As we have seen, the poem's varied and insistent textual interaction—with itself, with Chaucer's own canon, with the diverse traditions to which he was heir—functions to free the poem, its readers, and even experiential reality from the courtly tradition and the ideology it would enforce. Such diverse literary relations inevitably expose the tentative and hypothetical character of a text, simultaneously diminishing its power to reduce and subdue experience to the cultural codes it embodies and increasing its power to illuminate experience. Indeed, the note of skepticism with which the poem begins and the refusal to privilege any single tradition suggest a deliberate effort to hold in abeyance all dogmas and the literary and cultural traditions by which they would impose themselves. If the poet cannot write without them, he can gain some freedom from their dictatorial power by exploiting their diversity and by establishing the provisional character of the text as a representation and interpretation of reality. But this is a temporary strategy, though one which can never be fully abandoned; its paradoxical purpose is the intellectual freedom that will enable one to discover the truth and permit one, once it is discovered, to submit to it. The goal of the poem's cultural relativity is escape from relativity.

We have seen that the *Legend* presents the truth to which man should submit as a union of justice and mercy, and have characterized this virtue as androgynous in that it unites the "Pitee" conventionally associated with the female and the irascibility typically identified with the male, in that it joins Venus and Mars. But part of what is being repudiated is just such conventional views of men and women. The poem seeks to make us see that neither virtue nor vice is male or female. The means of escape from biological determinism, from one's temperament (whether predominantly irascible or concupiscible), and from cultural definitions of masculinity and feminity is the same. The *Legend* locates this freedom in truly loving the good. Freedom for the poet from his "literary belatedness" has the same source. Though Patterson is right to insist that the *Legend* shows Chaucer's awareness that the traditions to which he was heir are expressions and instruments of men's tyranny over women, this apparently did not invalidate them altogether in Chaucer's mind, if only because, as the *Legend* demonstrates, the truth makes itself known even when poets try to suppress it (as when we glimpse, in spite of the narrator, Procne and Philomela's revenge). The poet can escape from history's tyranny, from the vicious circle of oppressing even while being oppressed, only to the degree that he can discover and adhere to the good. The poem dramatizes the refrain to the *Balade de Bon Conseyl:* "And trouthe thee shal delivere, it is no drede."

Chaucer's term for the product of this intertextuality—both the internal and external relations of the poem—is "remembraunce," that activity to which old books are the "keye." The poem makes the same claim for the natural order—the daisy is also a "remembraunce." The metaphor is crucial—nature and books enable us to remember. Boethius's *Consolation* is the appropriate key for unlocking this metaphor.[9] Boethius associates his epistemology of reminiscence with the myth of the soul's preexistence. Prior to this life and its cultural codes, the soul inhabited a star and occupied itself in contemplating the good. Upon descending into the *inferna* of this world and of the flesh, it forgets its former knowledge of the good and substitutes this world's erroneous opinions for that knowledge. The purpose of its sojourn in this life is the reacquisition of that prior knowledge. The world's dissimilar similitude to the good makes the good knowable, reminding us of both what it is and what it is not; but to perceive it, to actualize our innate but forgotten knowledge, we must subdue the passions aroused in this life and employ the light of reason that we may escape the blinders of common opinion.[10] The *Consolation* not only describes this reascent but enacts it as well: first, Lady Philosophy quiets Boethius's passion, and then she constructs with him an argument that enables him to remember the good.[11]

Boethius employs this myth of the soul's vision, fall, and reascent to vision to account for man's intellectual and moral hunger for the good. Though it implies ultimate escape from this world, reunion with the transcendent good beyond time, Boethius's primary concern in the *Consolation* is to demonstrate that the mind can discover and adhere to the good while in this life, even as it is being hurled round the wheels of Fortune and Nature. Especially crucial to this remembering is the study of the stars, for they demonstrate not only the rationality and stability of this world's source but also the order inherent in man's divided nature. The diurnal movement of the fixed stars and the contrary motion of the planets, evidence of the twofold motion of the World Soul, correspond to the analogous twofold motion of man's soul: the war within him of reason (which moves from the transcendent through the mutable and back to the transcendent, there to rest) and passion (which moves from the mutable to the transcendent and back to rest in the mutable); they also demonstrate that the rationality can order the passion even as the movement of the fixed stars dominates the errant motion of the planets.[12]

We have seen that Chaucer depicts the order of the created in terms of similar circles. The cyclical progress of the daisy and the Alceste in the Prologue demonstrates in particular the power of rational loving to discover and adhere to the good and to attain thereby translation to the celestial realm, where the soul enjoys its true freedom by participating in the good. The cyclical order inherent in the legends, on the other hand, demonstrates in particular the irrational progress of those who bind themselves through passion to the wheels of Fortune and Nature by which destiny orders this world, to attain thereby translation to an infernal world where the soul's freedom is forever lost. Guided by the Alceste-daisy on the one hand and by his old books on the other, the narrator and, with him, the reader participate now in rational, now in irrational motions of the mind.

The order of the *Legend* as a whole is similarly circular. It is itself the consequence of the narrator's cyclical movement between his May flower and his old books, a movement that transports him from a paradisiacal dream to the *infernum* depicted in his old books. The Prologue depicts the narrator's return to his old books as an imitation of the Alceste-daisy. The infernal descent, that traditional image of the terrestial pilgrimage as a quest to rediscover and hold to the good, gives definition to the narrator's experience as lover and would-be poet-philosopher. But the definition provided is profoundly ambiguous, for the narrator's efforts are associated with both successful and unsuccessful exemplars of the infernal descent—with Alceste, Hercules, and Troilus on the one hand; with Proserpina, Criseyde, and Orpheus on the other.[13] The recurrent intimations of the demonic in the legends, intimations often informed by Dante's *Inferno,* confirm this definition of the narrator's efforts as translator; and those efforts themselves confirm the ambiguity of this characterization.

The germ for Chaucer's depiction of the narrator's troubled interaction with his old books—his participation in the failings they depict, enact, and enforce; his hesitant efforts to transcend those failings—may well have been Dante's dramatization of his persona's interaction with those he meets in hell, as when he swoons in sympathy with Francesca or listens fascinated to the quarrel of Master Adam and Sinon or exults in anger at seeing Filippo Argenti's irascibility punished. But in their interiorization of the viciousness encountered, the legends far surpass their model. The legends dramatize—indeed, are—the narrator's intellectual and moral compromise, his attempt to understand and name the true and the false as they are reflected in his imperfectly rational old books on the one hand, as they have been defined for him by the revelations of his dream on the other; they express his love of the good, his pity for the victimized, and his contempt for the vicious—according to his undeniably limited understanding of these things and insofar as that understanding has not been compromised by his desire to please Alceste and appease the god of Love. His poetry shows that he is himself both victim and victimizer, and it variously inspires in us love, pity, and contempt for him.[14]

As a whole the *Legend* seems designed to dramatize history's tragic possibilities. The poem's structure presages Orpheus's tragedy; it moves from the paradisiacal to the infernal and ends there. In contrast, Dante ascends from darkness to light; Gower moves through the seven sins to self-knowledge. Like the maze from which Theseus must escape after he has overcome its "fend," the Minotaur, the narrator's books are "krynkeled to and fro," full of "queynte weyes for to go"; misled by them, the narrator takes many a false turn before he finishes. As his moral and intellectual failures testify both to their power to deceive and to his own human weakness, so the "clewe" that Alceste provides—her insistence that salvation lies in recognizing the perfidy of men, the goodness of women, the sanctity of love—is in its ideological partiality part of the problem and does as much to prevent as to facilitate his reascent to the light. Though the narrator makes some progress—he quickly comes to admit the failings of his own sex and shows in the penultimate legend at least some willingness to recognize and assert feminine complicity—self-knowledge still eludes him, and the poem's abrupt ending must be seen as potentially enacting both his failure to be true as a lover and his inability as poet-philosopher to find a satisfactory resolution for his translations.

But this tragedy is contained within and righted by comedy. The structure of the poem, its movement from light to dark, recreates the understanding of the human condition expressed by the myth of the soul's preexistence, the conviction that man has within him the truth if he can but recover it. However counterproductive the imposed dogma and however powerful culture and biology may be in disenabling knowledge, in obstructing access to the good within, the poem's faith is that the light of the daisy and the example of Alceste can be sufficient, when remembered, to reveal at least something of the truth; and that the narrator's old books, rightly understood, can provide at least some confirmation of it. The legends' heroines are no Alcestes, but their truth in loving is to hers as the world's false goods are to the good; that is, even as they show us what the good is not, they point beyond themselves toward it. Remembering the good embodied in the Alceste-daisy and recognizing the dissimilar similitude of the legends' heroines activates a dialectical process within the poem, one that enables a progressively clearer understanding and firmer love of its manifestation of the good. Consequently, reminders of the Prologue seem especially pronounced in the final legend, where we witness a sacrifice of self reminiscent of Alceste's and remember through its fragmentation of justice and mercy Alceste's unification of them. The narrator's progress as translator provides a far from satisfactory enactment of this process, but his failure, like the failure of the heroines, is designed to enable our success.

As the sudden ending of the legends potentially enacts the narrator's desertion, so it potentially enacts the narrator's return to the daisy, his dramatic realization of the mental movement resulting from the interaction of Prologue and legends. The Prologue becomes the Epilogue; its prevision, remembered and revised, becomes final vision, a return to the stars. Even as the universe turns inside out for Dante when he reaches its outermost point to find himself at its true center, so in a sense the *Legend* turns inside out. Its beginning, its Prologue, becomes its end; the legends, where the poem seems to end, become intermediate—a bridge, however slippery, between its Prologue as beginning and end. Tragedy becomes comedy.

The drama experienced by narrator and reader within the poem's own intertextuality, within the interaction of legends and their Prologue-Epilogue (if we may speak of an imagined return as within the text), enacts in little the drama of the poet and reader within the complex of literary relationships involving Chaucer's poem and its diverse poetic antecedents and the equally rich interchange between its poetic world and the reader's experience. The narrator's descent into his old books—a descent that is simultaneously an encounter with self, however sublimely unaware of this fact he may be—creates a similar descent by the reader into Chaucer's incomparably richer intertextuality, wherein reader and poet can remember the good and discover themselves. The poem's ultimate metaphor for the process it dramatizes and enacts is penance, that process which divine justice and mercy have ordained that the individual may attain to the good he or she is not. The penitential process dramatized, the transformation of tragedy into comedy, expresses a number of medieval paradoxes. One comes to knowledge of the good through knowing what it is not. One becomes the good one is not through recognition that one is not this good; one attains sanctity by recognizing one's sinful nature. The consequences of the fall are the means for triumphing over it; the demands of justice are the instruments of mercy.

Our initial experience of the *Legend* is largely a misreading, a mis-seeing. Blinded by Alceste's and the god's provisions and by the narrator's rhetorical confirmation of that view in the legends, a first reading leaves us only vaguely dissatisfied with the failure of the legends to substantiate the prescribed view, only dimly aware of Chaucer's alternative subterranean provisions. Only retrospectively, only with a second reading, can the subterranean view—the product of the poem's ironies and incongruities—emerge to form a perspective that disposes the poem in its full richness and order. This revisionary reading process is the inevitable consequence of the poem's internal and external intertextuality. Its circular form, its implicit return at the end to the beginning—a return that can be executed only by the reader—is the ultimate expression of this order. The poem represents this revisionary order as providential. The soul's descent into the constraints of history and desire, its fallen condition in a fallen world, is assumed to begin a drama in which man is inevitably misled by these constraints to experience the tragedy which is their inevitable consequence; this experience in its turn enlightens man and frees him to rediscover the good beyond history.

Above all, what we have been seeing throughout this study is that Chaucer constructed the *Legend* not just to represent this vision of life but to enact it, to make the experience of the poem the experience of life. The relationship between the poem and the world it imitates is not that of simile, of likeness, but that of metaphor. The poem seeks to be what it means.

Comparison with the first three tales of Canterbury is enlightening in this respect. As we have seen, in the "Knight's Tale" Chaucer creates an image of the order common to microcosm and macrocosm, one comprising rationality, concupiscence, and irascibility. Though the "Knight's Tale" dramatizes the effects of all three faculties in man and the cosmos, Chaucer endeavors to make it ultimately an expression of rationality. In its philosophical inquiry, its measured pace, its distancing of the emotionally disruptive, its highly stylized and deliberate order, it enacts rationality. In turn, the Miller's and Reeve's tales enact the other two faculties, concupiscence and irascibility. It is not just that the first is narrated by the lustful Miller and depicts in its action the universal male desire for the quintessential object of concupiscence—Alisoun—or that it reduces the ultimate narrative of divine wrath to an instrument of seduction; nor is it simply that the second is narrated by the irascible Reeve and depicts an equally universal thirst for vengeance, or that it perverts the ultimate act of concupiscence into an instrument of that vengeance. Patterson has characterized Alisoun as the "presiding spirit" of the "Miller's Tale" (as origin of "the male desire that motivates the tale" and as the embodiment of its "festivity") and rightly so, for its presiding spirit is desire;[15] to read it is to experience the delight that is the source and end of desire. In contrast, the presiding spirit of the "Reeve's Tale" is negation, even death itself; its action, even when that action is sexual, and its moralizing are both driven by irascibility's vengefulness. However amusing it may be, it is impossible to read without distaste. To read the "Knight's Tale" is to experience rationality attempting to order desire and anger; to read the tales of the Miller and Reeve is to experience something close to pure concupiscence and irascibility.

The chief instrument of enactment in the *Legend* is the narrator. We experience the Prologue both as his account of a particular day and as his response to it (an effect crystallized particularly in F by the apostrophe) and the legends as the narrator's translations, as expressions of his intellectual and emotional life. But the poem enacts more than the narrator's life. The Prologue seeks to discover and realize unity. All of its irony and intertextual complexity; its vision of the unity of the daisy, Alceste, and the lady of the narrator's dream; and its characterization, in turn, of this union—the Alceste-daisy—as the flower of flowers and lady of ladies find ultimate expression in the Prologue's integration of diverse literary relationships into a revelation of the oneness of truth. It demonstrates the harmony in God's order not simply by representing it but by manifesting it in its very being. The dominant note in the legends is division. They are dominated by alternation and conflict—in the actors and actions of the narratives, in the alternating pity and scorn of the narrator's responses to those actions, and in the poet's disjunctive intertextuality. To read the legends is inevitably to experience their incompatibility with their sources. In a sense the spirit of the legends is the Minotaur, that monstrous and infernal union of the incompatible. Its perfect expression is the irreducible mixture of the romantic and pathetic with the grotesque and farcical in the "Legend of Ariadne." The reader must either revise and rewrite it or suffer psychological fragmentation while reading it.[16] One cannot weep for the satanic.

The poem recreates the order inherent in the created not only in the apparent hope that the experience of this order can enable us to discover it beyond the poem, in the world and in the self, but also in the apparent conviction that this experience of the deception that enlightens can enable the reader's reformation. By moving the mind first in irrational circles that frustrate and then in the rational circle that rediscovers the good, the poem seeks to habituate the mind to recognizing and desiring the good, to implant in it the *habitus* of virtue.

The metaphor of penance indicates that such a redirection of the will must accompany revision. The poem's goal is individual and social reformation: as the poem would revise our understanding, so it would transform our emotional life to bring it into harmony with this revised understanding. This need finds its expression in the affective dimension of the poem, in the ways in which it seeks to move us. Once again the poem works on more than one level. Its audience is immediately engaged by its surface rhetoric, the consequence of the narrator's engagement with his narratives. This engagement participates in the emotional intensity of romance, its deliberate cultivation of sentiment and pathos, and is in accord with its lexicon of feeling. Pity for the innocent victims of male treachery and contempt for their victimizers dominate. But the surface emotions thus aroused are redirected by the poet's irony.

The poem's rhetoric dramatizes the narrator's emotional life—in the poem's terms, his love, his concupiscence, his irascibility. He is now pouring forth his love for the daisy in song, now trembling before the god of Love's wrath, now simultaneously relieved by Alceste's rescue and frustrated by its terms. Time and again in the legends he responds to the apparent victimization of his heroines with pity, to their betrayers with anger and scorn—an emotional response resulting from his identification with his heroines, from his adoption of their point of view. For instance, he pities Dido as victim and scorns Aeneas as victimizer. But of course he is the author of Dido as victim, Aeneas as victimizer. The pathos in which he revels is enabled by his misperception and misrepresentation. Indeed, a large part of the impetus for misperception is the desire to indulge pathos; both the narrator and his heroines come close to victimizing themselves that they may feel victimized. This is especially evident in the sense of gesture with which most of the legends end: a suicide to demonstrate one's truth, a letter of complaint or rebuke written with no answer expected or even desired. Here the swans immolate themselves that they may sing. Similarly, time and again the narrator rushes to the "grete effects," to the moments of heightened emotions. The *raison d'être* of the narrator's legendary is the arousal of such emotions, and whatever denial of truth's complexity is necessary to arouse them must be indulged.

Behind the narrator stands the poet, thwarting such emotions and redirecting them. By making visible the distortions that arouse these emotions, Chaucer forces us to recognize their illegitimacy. We are made to feel their hollowness. One thinks first perhaps of the narrator's abuse of Jason: his direct defiance of him, as though he would challenge him in person, is mere gesture, a defiance that cannot be answered. The hollowness of the posture reverberates, and we are distanced from his anger. The reader is similarly distanced from the narrator's pity. Only "the holwe rokkes" echo Ariadne's complaint. Above the narrator's pity and scorn, his concupiscence and irascibility, stands the poet's rationality. With his irony he distances us from the narrator's misdirected passions, frees us from them and from the blindness that both enables and results from them. The vicious cycle is broken.

But the *Legend*'s goal and consequence are not to render the reader *impassibilis*. Though the poem repeatedly frees our minds from entanglement with the passions it dramatizes, by depicting their futility and remembering the good, it also repeatedly draws us back into engagement with itself. When the end of the poem returns us to the beginning, it both moves us from darkness to light—from depictions of the false and vicious to representations of the good and true—and begins the poem again, so that it inevitably returns us to the dark. The *Legend*'s end is not just love of the good but also a love of the world that is consonant with the good, the rectification of our concupiscence and irascibility.[17] Our pity for the heroines is now a response to their frailty, not a participation in their feelings of innocent victimization. At extreme moments the narrator's pity is virtually transformed into its opposite—as when we respond with contempt and scorn to the narrator's pity for Ariadne. Similarly, our participation in the narrator's anger at the legends' villains is often tempered by our perception that they are victimized as well as victimizing. Thus the narrator's pity and scorn are transformed into the poet's sympathy and satire, which are directed not least of all at his own persona. The penance by which the poet seeks to make himself and his art the perfect expression of divine justice and mercy is never ending. If the narrator's enthusiasm is the poet's means for involving us with our fellow men, binding us to them in our common brotherhood, his irony is the tool by which he would rectify that involvement. To the poem's dialectic of seeing is joined a dialectic of feeling that unites pity for disinherited man and an anger which demands he reclaim his inheritance. This inheritance is of course his innate capacity to know and love the good.

The goal of Chaucer's poetry is to undo the fall. It is sacramental poetry first in that it has a sacramental view of reality: it depicts a world in which things reveal their maker even as the daisy manifests the day's eye. It is also sacramental in that it would recreate this order in itself, would make itself a similar realization and revelation of the ultimate ends of life. But sacraments are not just revelations. They effect transformation. According to the sacramental view of history, history effects salvation even as penance forgives sins. So Chaucer's art would enable reformation; it is ordered that its experience may make possible the reinstitution of humanity's alienated but natural justice. The poem's ultimate effort to realize this is its opening ending. Chaucer has ordered the *Legend of Good Women* intellectually, affectively, and aesthetically to place the reader at its end on the threshold of new life. But this is and must be an ending which only the free reader can write and enact.

Excursus:
The Two Prologues—
Lover or Clerk

T hough the question of the priority of the Prologues has not
been reargued in print in over fifty years, several critics have
speculated on the reasons for and consequences of revision—all
apparently on the basis of J. L. Lowes's supposed demonstration of
the priority of F.[1] A reconsideration of Lowes's argument, the first
business of this excursus, shows it to be no such demonstration. Indeed, there would appear to be no way to resolve the question, a
circumstance that requires us to treat each Prologue as a separate
achievement rather than as a tentative draft or a rejected version;
hence the second concern of this discussion, characterizing each.
Dismissing the issue of priority may seem a denial of history and a
repudiation of our concern for authorial intention, since the second must have been an intentional adaptation of the first. It need
not have been designed to replace it, however, and this suggestion
brings us to the final concern of this excursus: the possibility that
the two Prologues were created for different audiences and intended to coexist, their differences being more rhetorical than ideological.

Supposing that a first draft would be closer than a revision to
their mutual sources, Lowes claimed to demonstrate the priority of
F by showing its greater affinity with the *marguerite* poetry that lies
behind both Prologues.[2] One need not imagine the exception to this
general supposition—revision with the sources again in hand—to
doubt the priority of F, however, for its undeniably greater reliance
on *marguerite* poetry is the result of its more extensive treatment of
the narrator's devotion to the daisy. Lowes discusses only one instance in which *shared* material is supposedly verbally closer to the

sources in F.[3] His real argument is that G possesses a superior, "organic" unity; F only a "lower," more "mechanical" one—and that this difference is best explained by supposing that Chaucer was piecing together his varied sources in F, whereas in G he was revising his own text.[4] Lowes cites three passages in particular: the panegyric on the daisy, with its attendant apology to fellow poets; the description of the day spent observing the daisy; and the dramatization of the *balade's* inclusion. True, these parts differ in the two versions, but proximity to the French sources is neither a necessary nor an adequate explanation of the variations they contain.

In G the laudatory description of the daisy, which progresses neatly from morning to evening to morning, the expression of regret for not being able to praise it properly, and the narrator's immediate dissociation of himself from the flower and leaf controversy do proceed more directly than in F. In the latter the praise of the daisy is intermixed with representations of the narrator's passion for it; the apology shifts to the second person to call directly on other "lovers" for help; and instead of proceeding to dissociate himself from the flower and leaf controversy—though he has already mentioned it—the narrator returns to praising the daisy, addressing it first as "she," then as "ye," and brings up the flower and leaf again only some 116 lines later.[5] The shifting perspectives of F are not necessarily the consequence of Chaucer's eye being on his sources, however, or the more straightforward order of G the result of revision. The temporal order of G and the logical progression of its ideas are completely natural and could easily appear in a first draft, just as F's shifting perspectives could be the result of amplification.

What is undeniable is that the two passages differ because they have different purposes. G's narrator enjoys walking in the fields in the springtime to observe the daisies. He notes his inability to praise them properly, other "folk" having used all the good words, and hopes that they will not be offended if he repeats their words, since he intends to honor both those who serve the flower and those devoted to the leaf, not being himself a partisan. His work is from another "tonne," old stories that predate "swich stryf." In F, in contrast, the narrator loves the daisy passionately,[6] a fact that accounts for the interruption of his praise of the flower with representations of his passion for it. It also explains the shift to apostrophe, the sudden appeal to other "lovers" for help. The narrator feels acutely his inability to praise his beloved adequately. Thus, however deferred his dissociation of himself from the flower and leaf controversy, the desire to distance himself is more logical now that he appears to be a partisan. This presentation of the narrator also explains the sudden outburst of praise that displaces the dissociation, the narrator's address of the daisy as first "she," then "ye." The abrupt switch from the third to the second person perfectly captures passion. The narrator is so transported with love that he cannot refrain from appealing directly to his beloved. Obviously, neither this matter nor this rhetoric has any place in G, whose narrator's affection for daisies is analogous to a bird watcher's pleasure in the first robins of spring.

That F's abruptness is deliberate is clear from Chaucer's treatment of the issue coming next in both Prologues: the question of why he had earlier spoken of giving credence to old books. In G he explains that we should believe authorities where we may not "assay by preve" and declares his intention to tell many an old story, inviting us to believe them if we like. In F the question is another disruption: the narrator promises to explain when he has time—he cannot "al at-ones speke in ryme"—and returns to describing his passion for the daisy. Raising the question only to dismiss it underscores its intrusive character. It is simultaneously an explanation of narrative disorder and an instance of it. Such a discontinuous manner fits the matter and the narrator's passion; it evidence of art, not of proximity to sources.

The differences in the introduction of the *balade* in the two versions are consistent with the variations we have been observing. In G the *balade* is sung by the ladies accompanying the god and Alceste; it would hardly be appropriate, after all, for its narrator, who is no lover, to sing "My lady cometh, that al this may dysdeyne." In F the *balade* is sung by the narrator. It is not a part of the dream, however, but belongs to the time and action of the writing.[7] About to describe Alceste as she appeared in his dream, the narrator declares her so beautiful that one could sing of her the song he then recites. In F (but not in G, of course), the god will rebuke the narrator for "necligence" in omitting Alceste from his *balade* "Hyd, Absolon, thy tresses." Having the narrator incorporate the song into the Prologue at the time of writing performs a number of functions. It allows the narrator to respond to the god of Love's com-

plaint, appropriate behavior for a lover. Simultaneously, it undermines the god's criticism, since it suggests that the "my lady" of the
balade may have referred to Alceste all along. Most important, it reminds us that the Prologue is not just a description of a dream but
a reaction to it as well, itself the beginning of the penance demanded in the dream.

In this regard, the treatment of the *balade* gives it important affinities with the apostrophes present in F. As Jonathan Culler observes, apostrophes belong to the time of the discourse—not to the
time of the action described—and transform narrative into lyric.[8]
Such devices foreground the narrator as narrator and make the F
Prologue not an account of the narrator's passion in the past tense
but a present expression of it. The lyric mode's implicit invitation
to identify with the lyric voice is undermined, however, because the
depiction of the object of the narrator's passion is so literal, the daisy so insistently a daisy, that the comedy distances us. We find ourselves watching the narrator not only as actor in the past action but
also as author of the present discourse.

The passage describing the day of observing the daisy is the third
whose G version Lowes regards as structurally superior, that in
which the birds defy the fowler. First, the two versions differ fundamentally in content. Neither the initial picture of the narrator
driven by an inner fire to kneel all day by the daisy nor the final
one of him leaning over it on his elbow is in G. Similarly absent are
the account of the birds' infidelity and subsequent reconciliation,
the explanation of this in courtly personifications as the triumph of
"Pitee" and "Mercy" over "Daunger" and "Ryght," and the etymological explanation of "daisy." Second, the place of the two passages
differs in the two Prologues. G's brief version occurs within the
dream, so that (in Lowes's analysis) G has only two parts, the panegyric and the dream, whereas F has three, the panegyric, the elaborate account of the day in the field, and the dream.[9] Simpler may
be better, but once again the differences in content and structure
are interrelated and integral to each Prologue. The function of the
brief passage in G—in which the dreamer experiences spring's flo-
rescence and hears the birds defy the fowler and welcome St. Val-
entine—is both conventional and necessary.[10] Dream visions regularly locate the dream's action in a springtime world redolent with
flowers and resonant with birds. The more substantial passage in F

recounts a day the narrator spends worshiping his flower and thus provides a specific instance of behavior previously characterized as habitual and described only in generalized terms. Rather than setting a scene, it dramatizes the narrator's passion.

Besides being consistent with F's characterization of the narrator, the matter unique to F here has both a high degree of coherence in itself and integral connections with other elements found only in F. In both Prologues the daisy is pictured imitating the sun, the narrator the daisy—evidence in both instances of the bond uniting lover and beloved.[11] This scene's elaboration of these analogous relationships brings out implications in this double imitation that remain largely latent in G. Similarly, explaining that the daisy is rightly called the "ye of day" makes its likeness to the sun explicit and justifies F's characterization of it as the "lyght" guiding the narrator in "this derke world." The description of the narrator as constrained with "gledy desir" to follow the daisy indicates that he too is an analogous sun, he too an eye of day. Though this three-fold analogy of sun, daisy, and lover exists in G and implicitly defines a similar idea of the natural order, the much greater amplification of it in F—a highly integrated and imaginatively unified one that can scarcely be called "mechanical"—insistently imposes the pattern and its implications on our consciousness.

The integration found in F's existential world is also evident in the continuity it establishes between the empirical and the visionary. While the daisy reappears as Alceste in both Prologues, only in F is the god of Love depicted as a similar metamorphosis of the sun. Both Prologues begin by questioning the reliability of human knowledge, whether its source is experience, dreams, or books, and subsequently seem to find validation of that knowledge in the narrator's vision of the oneness of the existential daisy, the historical Alceste, and the daisy queen of his dream. But only F's presentation of the natural world is sufficiently elaborated to dramatize this symbolic assertion that truth in loving can be existentially experienced as well as dreamed of and read about. At the same time, however, by making the dream in F so obviously a transformation of the narrator's experience, Chaucer calls the authority of this vision of unity into question, for the reappearance of sun and daisy in the vision suggests that dreams may be only manifestations of memory and desire.[12] Thus F both more insistently dramatizes the oneness underlying diversity and more profoundly expresses the fear that this unity may be only an invention of the imagination.

The G Prologue also has its own integrity and coherence. Fundamental to it is Chaucer's characterization of its narrator as an aging "clerk." Some, Lowes included, have regarded its references to the narrator's age as biographical evidence that G is the revision, as though it were somehow fundamentally less suitable to depict oneself as a lover in one's (supposed) early fifties than in one's (supposed) middle forties.[13] In fact, Chaucer's characterization of his narrator as an outsider in love is one with his treatment of himself in the *Parlement,* where he has lost his taste for love, and in the *Troilus,* where he declares himself too unlikely for love; thus G's use of this accustomed stance can serve equally as well as an argument for G's priority.[14] What we have here is not biography but the use of a familiar and thoroughly conventional comic role.

The characterization of the narrator as clerk is voiced by the god of Love: Chaucer has grown old and cold and, consequently, thinks it folly to love "paramours to harde and hote." In the god's judgment the narrator is doting, as do these "olde foles, whan here spiryt fayleth; / Thanne blame they folk" (that is, lovers). Though more decorous, this is of a kind with the Wife of Bath's characterization of clerks as inherently hostile to women, since they are born under Mercury rather than Venus, and given to defaming them once they can no longer do "Venus werkes worth" an "olde sho." While we are distanced from the god's analogous characterization, given his intemperate behavior, the absence of any expression or dramatization of passionate love[15] and Alceste's blunt declaration that the narrator "lesteth nat a lovere be" confirm him an outsider in matters of love.[16] This narrator's fondness for the daisy in spring is only a temperate response "lastynge that sesoun" (G, 39).

Consistent with Chaucer's different characterization of his own persona is the more ample part he assigns the god of Love. In the one extended passage unique to G, that in which the god depicts the narrator as a hostile clerk, the god represents himself as the champion of chastity. His appearance in G crowned with lilies and roses anticipates this rather unlikely stance, for though the god of Love is conventionally adorned with flowers and this particular crown matches the red and white of Alceste's daisy-crown, we are rightly taken aback to see Cupid wearing a crown that the "Knight's

Tale" taught us to regard as Diana's.[17] Ordinarily, we associate Cupid with only one of the two contraries represented by these flowers—concupiscence, and that hardly in a chastened state. Behind such symbolism, both enabling it and informing it with considerable irony, lies a pair of traditional medieval distinctions: that of the two Venuses, one representing fleshly concupiscence, the other the "faire cheyne of love" which produces harmony in the cosmos; and that between Venus as the amorous appetite and Cupid as the courtly refinement of that appetite, the *fin amour* to be found in the gentle heart.[18] In effect, courtly ideology maintained that its "ruled Curtesye" partook not of concupiscence but of the love that orders nature and "moves the sun and the other stars." It was the false lover, the member of Jason's sect, who was moved only by lust. To crown the god with Diana's headdress is to claim for love such a chastening power and to imply that this chastening involves a balance, a virtuous mean, between pity and "daunger" (see F 160–66); at the same time, of course, Chaucer's depiction of the god as intemperate calls this claim into question, making it in effect the god's claim.

In this passage the god vows vengeance on the dreamer for his having translated the heretical *Roman* and having told of false Criseyde when he has, "God wot, sixty bokes olde and newe" full of stories of women, "and evere an hundred goode ageyn oon badde."

> This knoweth God, and alle clerkes eke,
> That usen swiche materes for to seke.
> What seith Valerye, Titus, Claudyan?
> What seith Jerome agayns Jovynyan? (G, 278–81)

The passage simultaneously furthers Chaucer's demonstration of the high and difficult art of truth in loving and mocks the god of Love's pretension that he is its sufficient source.[19] Having attacked the narrator rather unfairly as a hostile clerk, now the god sends him to some genuinely hostile clerks for amendment; indeed, it is just such clerks who are the sources of the antifeminism for which the god apparently condemns Chaucer's translation of the *Roman*. The choicest irony is his extended reference to the most celebrated antifeminist tract of the age, for while it is true that Jerome does provide a substantial catalogue of chaste women—"clene maydens," "stedefaste widewes," and "trewe wyves," to quote the god—it is equally true that his recipe for achieving chastity is to flee love and, most particularly, for men to flee women. When the god goes on to ask "what seyth also the epistel of Ovyde," that source of so many of the legends, he only undoes himself all the more, for there were two Ovids in the Middle Ages: the romantic Ovid of the courtly poets and the moralized Ovid of the clerks. To refer to the *Heroides* in this context is to invoke the moralized reading of them as either affirmations of chaste love or denigrations of foolish or illicit love, with the vast majority being in the latter categories (though not quite a hundred bad against one good).[20] Clearly, the god of Love is his own worst enemy.

There is one additional substantial difference, in the summary instructions at the end of the two Prologues. In F the god directs the narrator's attention to the other ladies sitting about them, notes that they are all in his *balade* and his books, and admonishes him to tell their stories—that is, those he knows; though he commands only Cleopatra's legend by name, he implicitly calls for most of the legends we actually have by his reference to the *balade*. In G the god merely orders the narrator to begin with Cleopatra and to include, besides Alceste, "othere smale." He can no longer refer the narrator to the ladies in his *balade,* of course, because it is no longer his. Indeed, in G it is by no means clear that the ladies mentioned in the balade are even among the god's "traas." When the company of ladies assert that their queen can disdain the likes of Penelope, Lavinia, Dido, we do not imagine (not if we can get F out of our minds, anyway) the singing ladies to be naming and denigrating themselves. Alceste and her company are one thing; "al that" quite another.[21] Instead of being prepared by the *balade* for the "stock *exempla*" of courtly love we actually get in the legends, in G the anticipatory literary context for the legends is provided by the god's references to the classics as they were read by moralizing clerics, where Livy and Jerome, Ovid and Vincent of Beauvais, are ethically harmonized or their incompatibilities made explicit. Since what texts mean is determined in part by the expectations with which they are read, by the kind of text they are assumed to be, this insistence that we read the legends as clerical moralizations—or, perhaps more accurately, that we read them from a clerical as well as a courtly perspective—only guarantees all the more that we will find them wanting as instances of truth in loving.

Once again we can see that all the differences in G are of a kind.

The depiction of G's narrator as a "clerk" rather than as a lover, the god's derision of him as an old fool, the sustained irony of the god's defense of the goodness of his female servants, and the direct confrontation of the courtly and the clerical traditions—a directness prepared for by G's open warning to the reader about the unreliability of books: "leveth hem if yow leste"—all heighten the satiric element in this Prologue. The delicate balance in F between the lyricism of love and its comedy has been replaced by the more insistent irony of the rationalist. F's ironies qualify its celebration of the spring of love; G's thrust upon the reader the realist's perception of love's perennial delusions.[22] Ultimately, of course, G is no more a simple repudiation of love than F is a simple endorsement of it; the ideality of the daisy and of the classical heroine it commemorates remains to leaven G. For all their difference in tone, both Prologues intimate love's potential virtues and its inherent limitations.

The consistency in message that underlies the marked disparity in emphasis suggests that the explanation for the differences between the two Prologues may be more rhetorical than ideological. To examine the rhetorical character of the poem is to ask to whom it was addressed, upon what occasion, with what intention. Such questions in turn require distinguishing between the poem's actual audience and occasion and its implied audience and occasion, for though Chaucer may have performed the *Legend,* as a text ultimately written to be read, it is not so much a rhetorical event as an imitation of one.[23] Like the *Troilus,* it creates a fictional narrator, audience, and occasion—or rather, each Prologue creates its own fictional narrator and implies in turn its own audience and occasion. For though the fictional narrator cannot be reduced to a rhetorical device, one of his functions is to establish the desired relationship between poem and audience. Since the narrator is in significant measure an ironic device in both Prologues, a means of projecting two attitudes toward the poem's matter, the implied audience is similarly doubled. In these terms, the poem's rhetorical intent is to move the actual audience from the initial, naive point of view assigned it by the narrator to the more inclusive view gradually intimated.

Since the *Legend* continues the *Troilus,* as it were, we should begin with the audience addressed there. Though the *Troilus* narrator is an outsider in matters of love, love apparently being too high for him to attain (he is sympathetic and at times even a trifle envious), he addresses a gathering of young lovers of diverse experience, to whom he grants a superiority over himself and his narrative even as he proposes to move and instruct them by means of it.[24] The projection of the implied audience, the audience to which we all belong while reading the poem, is not just a product of these moments of direct address, however. Given the fiction that the poem is a performance, we assume the style of that performance to be an accommodation to the audience being addressed: the poem's sophistication, elegance, and refinement express the sophistication, elegance, and refinement of its assumed audience. It is "our" courtliness that accounts for its courtliness. The famous frontispiece of the Corpus Christi Cambridge MS may not record an actual performance, but it is an accurate reflection of the poem's implied audience and occasion, though we are free to imagine ourselves listening to it in "paved parlour" rather than in a garden if we prefer.[25] The poem idealizes its implied audience. It is aristocratic, cultured, sensitive. Its female members are assumed to take pains—rather more appropriately than the Prioress—to be "estatlich of manere" and "digne of reverence," and they, too, are innately "charitable" and "pitous." Its young males are in poised possession of the Squire's accomplishments; all are moved by the Knight's ideals—"chivalrie, / Trouthe and honour, fredom and curtesie." Above all, readers of the poem are temporarily incorporated into the class of those who idealize love. Though the ironies of the *Troilus* define a second audience possessing a more complex point of view, its explicit narrative stance as written for young lovers requires that its moral and philosophical concerns be presented in a form and manner accommodated to that immediate audience: that is, in a way consistent with the poem's courtly surface.

The F Prologue implies a similar audience and adopts a similarly complex relationship with it. Its secular and aristocratic point of view, its refined and witty sophistication, its courtly manner all appeal to and project the same immediate audience. Consistent with this is its use of the religion of love, that parody of Christianity so much less prominent in G, with its simultaneous elevation of love and its playful irreverence (if that is not too strong a term). Its accommodation to such an audience is evident even in the smallest details: in G nothing can lure the poet from his books except a "halyday" or "the joly time of May"; in F he cannot be drawn from his books except "seldom on the holyday" and "certeynly" in May. Though the portrait of the narrator as lover is comic, that too is designed to amuse refined lovers. We do not laugh at the narrator for loving but for loving flowers and literary heroines. Indeed, F's projection of an audience of young lovers is even more insistent than that of the *Troilus,* for there the narrator makes much of his difference from his auditors, whereas here, however ineptly, he is one of them. Again, in the F Prologue as in the *Troilus,* criticism of the adopted perspective is neither hostile nor explicit. The identification of an alternative point of view and identification with it are left to the audience. Membership in the poem's second projected audience—hearers in possession of a more complex appreciation of the nature of love—is by choice.

The differences we have been observing in G all imply a different audience, though one less precisely defined. Gone are the extended depiction of love, the characterization of the narrator as lover, the direct address to other lovers ("Ye lovers that kan make of sentement") and to the narrator's beloved as though they were the poem's audience. G's only direct address to its auditors ("leveth hem [the old stories the narrator will recount] if yow leste!") and its characterization of its narrator as a "clerk" both cast its actual audience in the role of readers, not lovers. What brings us and the narrator together is not our commitment to love but our mutual appreciation of old books. This supposition is supported by the immediate surface appeal of G to what we have been calling the clerical point of view. The audience is now assumed to know who the likes of Jerome and Valerye are, to be familiar with what the "epistles of Ovide" and Vincent of Beauvais's "Estoryal Myrour" say, to get the joke in Cupid's reference to *Jerome against Jovinian.* The one addition to Alceste's catalogue of the poet's works also enlarges the clerical presence in the poem, Pope Innocent's *contemptus mundi* "Of the Wreched Engendrynge of Mankynde." Even the humor of the characterization of clerks as old fools in the person of the narrator appeals to this point of view and evokes sympathy: the narrator is being misunderstood and maligned by the god in just the way "we clerks" are always caricatured by lovers, who assume that "our" realism as to the rarity of true love is envy.[26]

Indeed, all the comedy in presenting the god of Love as believing that his nature and effects are Diana's appeals much more directly than F's similar ironies to those who regard love and chastity as antithetical, not those who consider *fin amour* a fourth degree of chastity. Both Prologues use irony to intimate the conflict between reality as it is defined by lovers and reality as defined by old books. But whereas the superiority granted F's implied audience as experienced lovers places them in the god's corner, members of G's audience are essentially outsiders in the quarrel, distanced though not quite disinterested observers (since they are invited to condescend sympathetically to the feckless narrator, unsympathetically to the blustering god). In short, G's audience is assumed to be at the very least neutral in the quarrel occasioning the poem, perhaps even a trifle partial to the anti-courtly position under attack.

Such a difference in implied audience inevitably raises the question of who constituted Chaucer's actual audience. Pearsall, Strohm, and Scattergood have all challenged the assumption that Chaucer wrote for the court, if one means by the court the immediate circle of the king and queen and the higher nobility.[27] Given what can be discovered of the reading habits of the upper nobility and of Chaucer's actual associations in his literary activity, they think it more likely that he found his actual audience among "the multitude of household knights and officials, foreign office diplomats and civil servants who constitute 'the court' in its wider sense":[28] that is, among those with backgrounds, circumstances, and interests generally similar to his own. If by "Chaucer's audience" we mean "sympathetic readers"—those of like mind and sufficient literary sophistication to appreciate the poet's variety and innovation—such a conclusion seems reasonable with respect to the poetry of the 1380's and 1390's. But Alceste's instruction to the poet in the F Prologue to give the finished *Legend* to the Queen "at Eltham or at Sheene" is also incontrovertible evidence that Anne was an interested member of the audience of the *Troilus* and the *Legend*. The F Prologue may not allegorize her displeasure with the *Troilus,* any more than it celebrates her as Chaucer's patron, but one can hardly imagine Chaucer having Alceste give his persona such orders unless he knew of the queen's interest in the present poem, an interest that presupposes her familiarity with the *Troilus.* And we need only remember the fate of Sheen to suppose that Richard shared this interest. Such considerations strongly suggest that wherever Chaucer may have looked for sympathetic readers, the *Troilus* and the F Prologue were written immediately for the royal circle. Indeed, as both G's different implied audience and the underlying preoccupation of the *Troilus* with the ethical and philosophical remind us, addressing the *Troilus* and the F Prologue to an audience of young lovers was not a necessary consequence of their courtly surface but a choice, one quite possibly determined by the immediate audience to which they were to be presented. This is not, of course, to assign to Anne and Richard the status of patrons in a vital, symbiotic relationship with the poet.[29] On the evidence, it would seem as likely that they were only an occasional audience, but one of sufficient moment to ensure that the poems were accommodated to their point of view.

The simplest explanation, then, for two Prologues that differ in the interrelated roles assigned narrator and implied audience is to assume two different actual audiences. Given the apparent continuity between the *Troilus* and the F Prologue in both implied and actual audience, such an assumption can be taken to support the traditional view that G is the revision, presumably one written after the death of Anne. It is equally possible, however, that Chaucer wrote the initial version of the *Legend* for those in the court circle who more closely shared his point of view rather than for the royal circle, and that the Prologue addressed to Anne was the revision, a response to a request or an occasion that demanded a version of the poem suited to young aristocrats who viewed themselves as lovers. It is noteworthy that though neither Prologue can be read simply as a direct recreation of the court's hostile reaction to the *Troilus,* the implied audience in F is undeniably projected, at least initially, as ideologically closer and more sympathetic to the views expressed by the god and Alceste than that in G, where, if anything, the audience is assumed to be in sympathy with the poet.[30] The only potentially discordant note in the assumption that the two versions of the Prologue reflect a division in Chaucer's actual audience is that it assigns the thinner of the two Prologues to the more sympathetic and familiar audience. This poses no difficulty if we imagine F the revision, an amplified reconception of the poem; but to suppose it the original (as a consequence, say, of weighing more heavily its continuity with the *Troilus* with respect to audience than G's continuity with respect to the narrator's role as an outsider in love) and G a revision freely undertaken for a more sympathetic audience (rather than, say, in response to the demands of an occasion) is to imagine Chaucer diminishing his own work.

The supposition that G was written to appeal to an audience that prefers the "realistic" to the "romantic," one more in tune with the ironic dimension of the poet's intention, does not permit identifying Chaucer's point of view in G with the stance assigned its narrator and audience. For all the greater immediacy of G's irony, its total point of view is no more anti-courtly than F's is courtly. Both preserve a rich and complex view of love. The celebration of the daisy may be less elaborated and Alceste's virtue may seem all the more isolated and singular in G, but both the daisy and Alceste remain to assert not only the ordering role of love in the cosmos but also its potentially redemptive effect upon humanity. Furthermore, when Chaucer tells us in G that he intends to rehearse old stories after their authors and then warns us to believe them at our own discretion, he is not indicting courtly romances and confirming the "sentence" of clerical antifeminism. The god's rhetorical questions finally constitute a genuine question—what do these old books say?—and the poet's skepticism about the reliability of such histories a genuine doubt. We do not need the "Merchant's Tale" to recognize that ironies can be as false and self-deceiving as enthusiasm or to realize that the unspoken text is not necessarily profounder than the uttered. Both Prologues engage their immediate audience, F's lovers, G's readers, in a text that requires them to substitute complexity for piety, whether romantic or clerical.[31]

Finally, of course, the similarities of the two Prologues far outweigh their differences. Both narrate the same fundamental drama in the same basic terms. Both present a narrator who loves daisies part of the year, books the rest; establish the same analogy between the daisy's devotion to the sun and narrator's devotion to the daisy; depict a dream in which the dreamer is attacked by the god of Love and defended by a queen who unites the daisy and Alceste, humanizing in the process their ideal representation of truth in loving; and assign as penance the writing of a legendary of good women. The two Prologues emphasize different aspects of the drama, but each can be said to elaborate a significance that is also present though less prominent in the other—to actualize, as it were, dimensions of the other's potentiality. While the implications of the variations are often considerable and the experience of reading the two Prologues and the attendant legends significantly different, these differences must finally be characterized—at least from a medieval point of view, I suspect—as essentially rhetorical. There is no evidence here that Chaucer had two fundamentally different messages, only that he had two audiences to which to accommodate his vision.

Those of us accustomed to thinking of poems as organic unities, in which no detail can be changed without the whole being transformed, may be uncomfortable with such a view. From the standpoint of medieval rhetoric, however, a poet is someone who has an inherited truth to express. The poet's task is to fashion a rhetorical presentation of that truth, the same truth being capable of many different rhetorical presentations. While it is clear that Chaucer did not view his art this simply—if only because he repeatedly dramatized the making and mismaking of meaning, repeatedly employed his rhetoric to question received truths and inherited rhetorical poses—he apparently did not regard singularity and universality as incompatible in life or in art. In the Prologue to the "Tale of Melibee" the pilgrim Chaucer observes that the gospels differ "in hir telling," some saying more and some less, but affirms that nonetheless their "sentence" is not only "al sooth" but also "al oon." The meaning and the message are not assumed to be an inseparable, organic whole, a nominalist singularity. He goes on to observe that though he may "varie" his speech, he does so not to alter its significance but to "enforce" the "effect" of his "matteere," an observation which, appropriately qualified, we might extend to all the god's plenty—its diverse individuals, its many poetic kinds—of the *Canterbury Tales* or to his two realizations of the Prologue. In the latter (to stick to the matter in hand), Chaucer has varied his treatment of his sources and given us two different realizations of the same fundamental matter not, apparently, because of a change in his concept of the significance of that matter, but in order to better ensure a hearing with his different audiences. That irony and enthusiasm coexist in the rhetoric of both Prologues suggests that Chaucer's intention was not so much to persuade his audiences of the truth of his vision—though he does indeed present them with a persuasive vision—as to free them from prefabricated ideologies and rhetorics, whether romantic or realistic, that they might see and feel this vision for themselves.

Notes

E xcept where otherwise indicated, I have used the following editions. All Chaucer citations are from F. N. Robinson, ed., *The Works of Geoffrey Chaucer,* 2d. ed. (Boston: Houghton Mifflin).

For the *Consolation* I have generally cited Chaucer's *Boece* or (where a Latin text has seemed advisable) Boethius, *Consolatio Philosophiae,* ed. Ludwig Bieler (Turnhout: Brepols, 1957); for the *Roman,* Guillaume de Lorris and Jean de Meun, *Le Roman de la rose,* ed. Felix Lecoy, 3 vols. (Paris: Champion, 1965–70), and *The Romance of the Rose,* trans. Charles Dahlberg (Princeton, N.J.: Princeton Univ. Press, 1971); for the *Complaint,* Alain de Lille, *De planctu Naturae,* ed. N. M. Häring, *Studi medievali,* ser. 3, 19 (1978), and *The Plaint of Nature,* trans. James J. Sheridan (Toronto: Pontifical Institute of Mediaeval Studies, 1980); for the *Somnium,* Macrobius, *Commentarii in Somnium Scipionis,* ed. Jacobus Willis (Leipzig: Teubner, 1963), and *The Commentary on the Dream of Scipio,* trans. William H. Stahl (New York: Columbia Univ. Press, 1952); for the *Confessio Amantis, The Complete Works of John Gower,* ed. G. C. Macauley, vols. 2–3 (Oxford: Clarendon, 1901).

Italian and English citations from the *Commedia* are both from Dante Alighieri, *The Divine Comedy,* ed. and trans. Charles S. Singleton, 3 vols. (Princeton, N.J.: Princeton Univ. Press, 1970–75).

In comparing Chaucer's legends with their antecedents, I have used the following volumes of the Loeb Classical Library (currently published by Harvard Univ. Press): Ovid, *Heroides and Amores,* trans. Grant Showerman, 2d. ed., rev. G. P. Gould (Cambridge, Mass.: Harvard Univ. Press, 1977); Ovid, *Metamorphoses,* 2 vols., trans. Frank Justus Miller (New York: Putnam, 1916); Ovid, *Fasti,* trans. James George Frazer (New York, Putnam, 1931); Livy, *Works,* vol. 1, trans. B. O. Foster (New York:

Putnam, 1919); Virgil, *Aeneid,* 2 vols., trans. H. Rushton Fairclough, rev. ed. (New York: Putnam, 1934).

Translations, other than those listed above or cited in the notes, are mine.

I have also used the following abbreviations:

AHDLMA	*Archives d'histoire doctrinale et littéraire du moyen âge*
BL	British Library
CT	*Canterbury Tales*
EETS	Early English Text Society
ELH	*English Literary History*
Inf.	Dante's *Inferno*
JEGP	*Journal of English and Germanic Philology*
MLN	*Modern Language Notes*
MLQ	*Modern Language Quarterly*
MLR	*Modern Language Review*
MP	*Modern Philology*
MS	*Mediaeval Studies*
Par.	Dante's *Paradiso*
PL	*Patrologia Latina*
PMASAL	*Papers of the Michigan Academy of Science, Arts, and Letters*
PMLA	*Publications of the Modern Language Association of America*
Purg.	Dante's *Purgatorio*
RES	*Review of English Studies*
SP	*Studies in Philology*
T&C	*Troilus and Criseyde*
YES	*Yearbook of English Studies*

I. BACKGROUNDS

1. Between the publication of Robert Worth Frank's *Chaucer and the Legend of Good Women* (Cambridge, Mass.: Harvard Univ. Press, 1972) and Lisa J. Kiser's *Telling Classical Tales: Chaucer and the Legend of Good Women* (Ithaca, N.Y.: Cornell Univ. Press, 1983) the MLA bibliography lists only seven articles and four notes. There have been a number of dissertations, which may bode well for the future; and several discussions of the poem have appeared in more general studies, perhaps most noteworthy being the chapters in Alfred David, *The*

Strumpet Muse: Art and Morals in Chaucer's Poetry (Bloomington: Indiana Univ. Press, 1976); Robert B. Burlin, *Chaucerian Fiction* (Princeton, N.J.: Princeton Univ. Press, 1977); and John M. Fyler, *Chaucer and Ovid* (New Haven, Conn.: Yale Univ. Press, 1979).

2. Victor Langhans, "Der Prolog zu Chaucers Legende von guten Frauen," *Anglia* 41 (1917):162. In "Hugo Lange und die Lösung der Legenden prologfrage bei Chaucer," *Anglia* 50 (1926): 71, Langhans provides a convenient tabulation of sides taken: initially, J. F. Furnivall, M. Bech, and Emil Koeppel assigned priority to G, but Bernhard ten Brink argued for F's originality, and Koeppel—switching sides—joined him. W. W. Skeat came out for G, Max Kaluza for F. But then Emil Legouis, John Koch, and J. B. Bilderbeck all argued for G's priority. Lowes and John Tatlock came to the defense of F, but were answered in turn by John C. French. Finally, Carleton Brown and Lange entered the lists in F's cause. Langhans himself took a new tack, arguing repeatedly that only G was genuinely Chaucer's, but no one has seconded this desperate way out of the mire. (Robinson's designations for the two Prologues stand for their manuscript sources: G for Cambridge University Library MS. Gg.16.4, the sole source for this version; F for Bodleian Fairfax 16, one of several MSS in which this version is preserved.)

3. For J. L. Lowes's view, see "The Prologue to the *Legend of Good Women* as Related to the French *Marguerite* Poems, and the *Filostrato*," *PMLA* 19 (1904): 593–683, and "The Prologue to the *Legend of Good Women* Considered in Its Chronological Relations," *PMLA* 20 (1905): 749–864. Robinson's acceptance of Lowes's point of view (*Works*, 839) has been generally imitated by more recent editors: E. Talbot Donaldson declares it "generally agreed" that G is the revision and prints it (*Chaucer's Poetry* [New York: Ronald, 1958], 958); Albert C. Baugh declares present scholars unanimous in regarding F as the earlier but prints it (*Chaucer's Major Poetry* [New York: Appleton-Century-Crofts, 1963], 213); John H. Fisher also judges G the revision but prints F, though he does put G's variants in the notes (*The Complete Poetry and Prose of Geoffrey Chaucer* [New York: Holt, Rinehart, & Winston, 1977], 620). See also Fisher's argument that G is a revision occasioned by Richard's marriage to Isabella: "The Revision of the Prologue to the *Legend of Good Women:* An Occasional Explanation," *South Atlantic Bulletin* 43 (Nov. 1978): 75–84. While there has been no extended reconsideration of the question since the 1920s, there

have been discussions of the significance of Chaucer's revision, all of which assume with Lowes that F was the earlier: Donald C. Baker, "Dreamer and Critic," *University of Colorado Studies in Language and Literature* 9 (1963): 4–18; John Gardner, "The Two Prologues to the *Legend of Good Women*," *JEGP* 67 (1968): 594–611; and Judson B. Allen, *The Ethical Poetic of the Later Middle Ages* (Toronto: Univ. of Toronto Press, 1982), 271–75. Frank regards G as the revision (*Chaucer and the Legend,* 11–12) but bases his discussion on F; Kiser does not choose between the two, regarding them as essentially similar with respect to her concern, "the problems of poetry" (*Telling Classical Tales,* 22 n.7), though the most important detail for her argument, the characterization of the daisy as a sun through the etymology "eye of day," occurs only in F.

4. Against Chaucer's use of the *Paradys d'amours,* see Robert M. Estrich, "Chaucer's Prologue to the *Legend of Good Women* and Machaut's *Le Jugement dou Roy de Navarre,*" *SP* 36 (1939): 26–29; against the use of Deschamps's *Lay,* see Marian Lossing, "The Prologue to the *Legend of Good Women* and the *Lai de Franchise,*" *SP* 39 (1942): 15–35. Essentially, they demonstrate that every supposed borrowing is of a conventional character and thus uncertain.

5. Lowes's most explicit formulation of his thesis—that G is the revision because it is further from the original sources—occurs in a lengthy footnote to his second article ("Chronological Relations," 749–51). In fact, virtually every instance where he finds F closer to the French and Italian is from a passage not found in G; thus his evidence supports equally well the view that Chaucer revised G by adding passages of borrowed poetry. What Lowes actually argues is that F has a looser structure resulting from Chaucer's compilation of it from a variety of sources, and that G, as the revision, has a tighter, more "organic" structure; in short, he essentially establishes priority on the basis of a critical judgment, one which we shall see to be entirely debatable. For the one instance in which he discusses a detail found in both versions, see Excursus, n. 3.

6. Lowes, "Chronological Relations," 800–801.

7. For instance, reading the two versions to establish priority invites one to interpret autobiographically Chaucer's depiction of himself as a lover in F but as too old to love in G. Thus, a crucial critical decision, how to understand the relation of Chaucer's first-person narrator to the poet, is constrained by an extraneous consideration, the desire to

establish priority. My point is not that the reference to age in G is not autobiographical; it may be, and that is an important possibility critics must consider, but they cannot let the need to establish a text turn that possibility into an a priori supposition that limits interpretation. (Cf. Chaucer's presentation of himself as an unlikely lover in the *Troilus*: that is, before either Prologue was written. Given the fact that Chaucer was presumably even then in his forties, "unlikely" may have meant "too old.")

8. The common assumption that the absence from G of the command to give the *Legend* to the queen shows it to be a revision written after her death in 1394 simultaneously reinforces (and is reinforced by) the additional assumption that the long passage only in G, in which the god refers tht poet to Jerome and Valerius, belongs in content and spirit to the period in which Chaucer was writing the marriage group. Neither assumption has any necessity whatsoever: the reference to the queen can as easily be an addition; the citation of Jerome and Valerius (if the reference is to Valerius Maximus) could even be second-hand: see the repeated linking of the two by Vincent of Beauvais (whose "Estoryal Mirour" is mentioned in the passage and is possibly the source of the "Legend of Cleopatra") in his *Speculum doctrinale, Speculum quadruplex* (1624; rpr., Gratz: Academic Press, 1965), 2.4.98 – 100. The effect of such suppositions, the way in which they become certainties that determine our view of Chaucer's genius and poetic development, is well illustrated by Baugh's introduction to the *Legend* (*Chaucer's Major Poetry,* 213 – 15).

9. A recent, highly novel topical reading is Judson B. Allen's interpretation of it (*The Ethical Poetic,* 264 – 69) as a consolation for Queen Anne on the occasion of her unsuccessful suit for Simon Burley's life before Arundel at the time of the Merciless Parliament. Allen first argues an allegorical interpretation of Alceste, adopted from the Third Vatican Mythographer—that Alcste represents the presumption that mind (Admetus) needs to define the soul—and then associates this allegorical reading of the poem with Anne's literal courage in facing Arundel. At the very least one must protest that Allen provides no evidence that Chaucer knew the Third Vatican Mythographer, that he adduces nothing in the poem to justify reading it as allegorical in this manner, and that nothing in the Prologue's literal drama recalls the occasion. One can arrive at such an identification only by beginning with the occasion, not with the poem. Since poetry does not signify in

this way, its meaning not being arbitrary and unrelated to its particulars, such a reading must be imposed upon the poem. The result is a fundamental distortion.

10. J. B. Bilderbeck was perhaps the first to see the sun as representing Richard (*Chaucer's Legend of Good Women* [London, 1902], 85–87). For the haloed god as the Black Prince, see Margaret Galway, "Chaucer's Sovereign Lady: A Study of the Prologue to the *Legend* and Related Poems," *MLR* 33 (1938): 147–49. In a critique of "Chaucer's Sovereign Lady," Bernard F. Huppé sensibly protests against taking passages out of context in order to read them topically; see "Chaucer: A Criticism and a Reply," *MLR* 43 (1948): 395. In G the god is crowned not with a sun but with lilies and roses; though this crown is also perfectly justified by the aesthetic logic of the poem, by the rapport thus established between the god and Alceste and her red and white daisy-crown, it too has been taken as a topical allusion to Richard and Isabella: first by Hugo Lange, "Zur Datierung des Gg.

10. Prolog zu Chaucers Legende von der guten Frauen: Eine heraldische Studie," *Anglia* 39 (1915): 347–55, and again in "Neue Beitrage zu einem endgültigen Läsung der Legendenprologfrage bei Chaucer," *Anglia* 49 (1925): 173–80; subsequently and apparently independently by Margaret Galway in "Chaucer, Granson, and Isabel of France," *RES* 24 (1948): 279; and most recently by John H. Fisher in "The Revision of the Prologue," 75–84. Fisher's occasional explanation creates as many difficulties as it resolves (see Excursus, n. 17).

11. This supposition is as old as Lydgate's Prologue to the *Fall of the Princes* and was endorsed by Thomas Speght in his 1598 edition; see Eleanor P. Hammond, *Chaucer: A Bibliographical Manual* (New York: Macmillan, 1908), 380. There is no evidence that either had any information beyond the poem itself. The most determined recent effort to identify Alceste with Anne is John Norton-Smith, *Geoffrey Chaucer* (London: Routledge & Kegan Paul, 1974), 63–66: interpreting the F Prologue as partially "a transfiguration" of Anne's "intercessorial role of *advocatus clementiae* in the dispute between the king and the city of London," and judging the celebration of the daisy as poetic inspiration to be an acknowledgment of Anne's patronage, Norton-Smith proceeds to argue that the absence of any of Anne's public symbols from the celebration of the daisy is evidence of the private character of Chaucer's "genuine dependence on Anne as

more than a mere patroness." Thus, the absence of any demonstrable connection between poetic sign and signified reality is assumed to prove one, though only a private one. Derek Pearsall points out Norton-Smith's lack of extratextual evidence for patronage and the fact that where such relationships did exist (as in England during the Anglo-Norman period and in fifteenth-century France), they seem to have been "fully documented"; see "The *Troilus* Frontispiece and Chaucer's Audience," *YES* 7 (1977): 72.

12. Richard Firth Green, "The *Familia Regis* and the *Familia Cupidinis*," in *English Court Culture in the Later Middle Ages,* ed. V. J. Scattergood and J. W. Sherborne (London: Duckworth, 1983), 105−6.

13. For efforts to identify Chaucer's beloved with historical figures other than Richard's two queens, besides Galway's "Chaucer's Sovereign Lady," see Frederick Tupper, "Chaucer's Lady of the Daisies," *JEGP* 21 (1922): 293−317. J. M. Manly demolished Tupper's identification by showing that Alice Chester was an elderly lady of the laundry ("Chaucer's Lady of the Daisies?" *MP* 24 [1927]: 257−59).

14. Lowes, *"Marguerite* Poems," 611−34.

15. For a telling argument that those who denounce any concern with authorial intent as the "intentional fallacy" are themselves indulging an organic fallacy, see Paul de Man, *Blindness and Insight: Essays in the Rhetoric of Contemporary Criticism,* 2d ed. (Minneapolis: Univ. of Minnesota Press, 1983), 22−28. This is not to say that the imposed design is independent of inherited forms or the product solely of the conscious mind, but it is to insist that though the various semiological systems of literary tradition may enable and propose, the author actualizes and disposes. The model of literary creation derived from oral tradition, in which the poet is the medium through which the tradition sings, cannot be imposed on the lettered maker precisely because a writer premediates, a fact doubly true in a tradition of twice-told tales such as Chaucer's. One of the more desperate ways poets declare their freedom from the constraints of traditional forms is by deliberately violating them—as when Shakespeare introduced the matter of tragedy into comic structures to create his problem plays. The *Legend* is just such a violation of conventional norms, just such a union of incompatible traditions. Needless to say, any aesthetic construct can be deconstructed, given the impossibility that any literary design will perfectly control all its constituent elements, and no doubt

deconstructing is a salutary activity. The intent of this study, however, is to construct a reading that will account for the recurrent features of the text and so define the poet's design.

16. Harold C. Goddard, "Chaucer's *Legend of Good Women*," *JEGP* 7
(1908): 87–129, and 8 (1909): 47–112. The other important early
ironic reading is Robert M. Garrett, "'Cleopatra the Martyr' and her
Sisters," *JEGP* 22 (1923): 64–74. For two recent examination of the
legends' ironies as Chaucer's demonstration of the deleterious effects
on art of a predetermined, imposed point of view, see Fyler, *Chaucer
and Ovid*, 98–115; and Kiser, *Telling Classical Tales*, 71–94.

17. J. L. Lowes, "Is Chaucer's *Legend of Good Women* a Travesty?" *JEGP* 8
(1909): 513–69. Robinson provided an influential second (*Works*,
482). Two recent straight readings are John P. McCall's insistence
that Chaucer is celebrating the natural goodness of his heroines,
though aware of their limitations, and reserving the satire for the
men (*Chaucer among the Gods: The Poetics of Classical Myth* [University
Park: Pennsylvania State Univ. Press, 1975], 113–22); and Henry A.
Kelly's contention that legends are Chaucer's effort to reconcile an
Ovidian conception of goodness—suffering in love—with the
Hieronymian insistence that love be chaste and honorable (*Love and
Marriage in the Age of Chaucer* [Ithaca, N.Y.: Cornell Univ. Press,
1975], 101–20). Kelly differs from Lowes in seeing the poem as
attempting to reconcile divergent traditions rather than remaining
rigorously confined to the courtly. His thesis has a priori appeal; un-
fortunately, he devotes little time to demonstrating how the participation of the legends in the two traditions produces reconciliation
rather than the irony we anticipate from their incompatibility.

18. Frank, we should note, escapes the celebration-or-satire dilemma by
reading the Prologue as Chaucer's effort to augment his poetic subject matter by giving an appearance of "courtly orthodoxy" to materials otherwise unacceptable to his audience (*Chaucer and the Legend*,
14–15). While his approach provides a fresh perspective on aspects
of the legends that are decidedly uncourtly (viewing such moments as
realism, not irony), it must ignore the rhetoric of the legends, which
repeatedly forces a romantic interpretation on such unromantic
events. A middle ground would also seem the objective of Raymond
Preston, who argues that Chaucer produced the desired legends in
good faith but with an "ironist's consciousness of what he was doing";

Chaucer takes what the form allows but makes us aware of its limitations (*Chaucer* [London: Sheed & Ward, 1952], 129–45).

19. Jonathan Culler, *The Pursuit of Signs: Semiotics, Literature, Deconstruction* (Ithaca, N.Y.: Cornell Univ. Press, 1981), 58–59.

20. Ovid's *Art of Love* is included in Jankyn's book of wicked wives; the antifeminist Merchant cites the story of Pyramus and Thisbe, the subject of the second legend, as evidence that lovers who have a will to deceive inevitably find a way. As the Prologues introducing Ovid's *Heroides* in medieval MSS illustrate, the clerical tradition moralized Ovid, turning the *Heroides* into *exempla* by treating some as instance of chaste love, others as denigrations of foolish or illicit love. Instances of such material are printed in R. B. C. Huygens, *Accessus ad auctores* (Brussels: Latomus, 1954), 24–28.

21. Fyler, *Chaucer and Ovid*, 98–115 (the passage quoted is on p. 99); Kiser, *Telling Classical Tales*, esp. 101–3.

22. Though virtually all modern criticism of the *Legend* nominally distinguishes between poet and narrator, as when Fyler and Kiser attribute the ineptitude of the legends to the narrator's obedience to Cupid, no one has examined the legends as individualized expressions of the narrator.

23. John H. Fisher, *John Gower: Moral Philosopher and Friend of Chaucer* (New York: New York Univ. Press, 1964), 285.

24. For an extreme example, see John V. Fleming's assignment to the writings of Augustine the status of what he calls a "supertext" vis à vis Jean de Meun's continuation, a supertext being an antecedent text that has authority over, or "commands," the subsequent text (*Reason and the Lover* [Princeton, N.J.: Princeton Univ. Press, 1984], 69–70); thus one can determine what Jean means by reading Augustine. More subtle is Winthrop Wetherbee's treatment of Dante's *Commedia* as the norm to which the *Troilus* is a "parodic contrast" (*Chaucer and the Poets: An Essay on Troilus and Criseyde* [Ithaca, N.Y.: Cornell Univ. Press, 1984], esp. 164–67).

II. LOVING THE ALCESTE-DAISY

1. Nevill Coghill terms the opening lines "a masterpiece of agnostic irony" (*The Poet Chaucer* [London: Oxford Univ. Press, 1949], 95); Preston characterizes their attitude as "the skepticism that is neces-

sary to a philosopher whatever he believes or does not believe"
(*Chaucer*, 115).

2. *Inferno* 3.56–57: "I would not have thought death had undone so
many." The reference is to those in Hell's antechamber, those whom
both God's mercy and his justice disdain, since in life they refused
choice. Robinson (*Works*, 843, n. to line 285) notes the allusion and
cites M. Praz, *Monthly Criterion* 6:21.

3. Frank, *Chaucer and the Legend*, 19–21, 28–36. Kiser similarly emphasizes the seriousness of these lines (*Telling Classical Tales*, 30–35).

4. On the paradisiacal character of the Prologue's garden world, see
esp. David, *The Strumpet Muse*, 39–46. Kiser points out infernal associations to some of the imagery in the legends (*Telling Classical Tales*,
95–131).

5. Robinson (*Works*, 842, n. to line 166) suggests that the reference is to
Horace and the source John of Salisbury's *Policraticus;* Howard
Schless nominates Aristotle and Dante's *Convivio* ("Chaucer and
Dante," *Critical Approaches to Medieval Literature*, ed. Dorothy Bethur-
um [New York: Columbia Univ. Press, 1960], 145–56); Norton-
Smith says "a medieval reader would have thought of Aristotle"
(*Geoffrey Chaucer*, 65 n.13).

6. On the cosmos as a harmony of contraries, see Leo Spitzer, "Classical
and Christian Concepts of World Harmony," *Traditio* 2 (1944): 409–
64, and 3 (1945): 305–65; on the concept in Chaucer's *Troilus*, see
Donald W. Rowe, *"O Love, O Charite!" Contraries Harmonized in Chaucer's Troilus* (Carbondale: Southern Illinois Univ. Press, 1976).

7. On the fowler as Satan, see John Speirs, *Chaucer the Maker* (London:
Faber & Faber, 1951), 98; B. G. Koonce, "Satan the Fowler," *MS* 21
(1959): 174–86.

8. Kiser's valuable discussion of Alceste and the daisy as metaphoric
things, as objects that reveal ultimate truth and, consequently, as suitable poetic symbols (*Telling Classical Tales*, 50–60), oversimplifies by
neglecting the problematic character of human understanding as it is
represented by the poem's ironies and ambiguities.

9. Kiser speaks for most recent criticism when she declares that "The
Legend's ostensible subject, love, is not its real subject at all" (*Telling
Classical Tales*, 9); virtually every important discussion of the poem
since Robert O. Payne's *The Key of Remembrance: A Study of Chaucer's
Poetics* (New Haven, Conn.: Yale Univ. Press, 1963), 91–111, has
treated it as primarily a poem about poetry. The one significant ex-

ception to this preoccupation with poetry, Frank's *Chaucer and the Legend,* also regards the poem's interest in love as merely nominal; it is an enabling vehicle for a collection of realistic narratives.

10. On the *marguerite* tradition and Chaucer's indebtedness to it, see J. L. Lowes, "*Marguerite* Poems." To the *marguerite* poetry cited by Lowes should be added Machaut's "Dit de la fleur de lis et de la marguerite" (James I. Wimsatt, "The *Marguerite* Poetry of Guillaume de Machaut," *University of North Carolina Studies in Romance Languages and Literature* 87 [1970]).

11. For a variety of identifications, see John Tatlock, *The Development and Chronology of Chaucer's Works,* Chaucer Soc., 2d. ser. 37 (London: K. Paul, Trench, Trübner, 1907), 102–20; Tupper, "Chaucer's Lady of the Daisies"; and Galway, "Chaucer's Sovereign Lady."

12. Gardner, "The Two Prologues," 606–7; Frank, *Chaucer and the Legend,* 21–25.

13. Lowes, "*Marguerite* Poems," 627–30. Deschamps does observe that its odor is neither fierce nor proud ("Lay de Franchise" 4, *Oeuvres complètes de Eustache Deschamps,* vol. 2, ed. Marquis de Queux de Saint-Hilaire [Paris: Firmin-Didot, 1880], 205).

14. Payne, *The Key of Remembrance,* 93–96.

15. This statement reflects the traditional view that the courtly surface of Guillaume's poem conceals little irony but that Jean's continuation abounds in ironies due to his addition of uncourtly elements, whether naturalistic, satiric, or philosophic.

16. The term "nonrepresentational" characterizes the style's relative neglect of "realistic imitation" and is borrowed from Charles Muscatine's discussion of courtly romance (*Chaucer and the French Tradition* [Berkeley: Univ. of California Press, 1957], 12–57).

17. "Dit de la marguerite," *Oeuvres de Guillaume de Machault,* ed. Prosper Tarbe (Paris: Techener, 1849), 125–26, st. 6; Jean Froissart, "Dittié de la flour de la margherite," *Oeuvres de Froissart,* vol. 2, ed. Auguste Scheler (Brussels: V. Devaux, 1871), 211–13, vv. 65–120; Eustache Deschamps, "Lay de Franchise," 204–5, vv. 27–65; Froissart's *balade,* "Sus toutes flours j'aime la margherite," in the *Paradys d'amours, Oeuvres,* vol. 1 (Brussels: V. Devaux, 1870), 49–50, vv. 1627–53.

18. "Dit de la marguerite," 124, st. 3; 125, st. 4.

19. Deschamps, "Lay de Franchise," 204, vv. 31–32. See also Froissart's praise of the daisy as the flower "Qui de bonte et de beaute est ditte /

La souveraine" (who in goodness and in beauty is called the sovereign; "Dittié," 210, vv. 29–30).

20. Equally indicative of the moral and courtly idealism of the *marguerite* poems is the significance assigned to the colors of the flowers. See both the lily and the daisy in Machaut, "Dit de la fleur de lis et de le marguerite" (in Wimsatt, "The *Marguerite* Poetry of Machaut," 19, vv. 131–48, and 21, vv. 205–30); Deschamps, "Lay de Franchise," 204–5, vv. 33–39; Deschamps's *balade* 539, "Eloge d'une dame du nom de Marguerite," *Oeuvres*, vol. 3, ed. Marquis de Queux de Saint-Hilaire (Paris: Firmin-Didot, 1882), 380, vv. 4–15. On the relevance of Machaut's description of the lily to subsequent descriptions of the daisy, see Wimsatt, "The *Marguerite* Poetry of Machaut," 32.

21. See, e.g., Machaut's assertion that all he possesses in this world "de gloire / De bien, de pais, d'onneur, et de victorie" comes from it ("Dit de la marguerite," 129, st. 13); and Froissart's that it makes him feel "en souffissance grant / Tous biens (all goods in full sufficiency; "Dittié," 215, vv. 183–84). For the idea that its worth and the good it confers obligate the poet to love it, see Machaut, "Dit de la marguerite," 123–24, st. 2; Froissart, "Dittié," 209, vv. 1–3. See further the assertion in Deschamps's "Lay" that there is no prowess "sanz amour" and the lament "Convoitise les terres perdu a / Qu'avoit conquis Emprise, Amour, Largesce" (Covetousness has lost the lands that Prowess, Love, Generosity had conquered; 210, vv. 211 and 220–21).

22. Moshé Lazar, *Amour courtois et "fin'amors" dans la littérature du XIIe siècle* (Paris: Klincksieck, 1964), 23–26. For a demonstration that the literary idealization of love was imitated in real life in the later Middle Ages, see Larry D. Benson, *Malory's Morte Darthur* (Cambridge, Mass.: Harvard Univ. Press, 1976), 153–62. I have myself used the expression *fin amour* to designate the ideology of love in the literature contemporaneous with Chaucer's work, for it is the characterizing expression used by this literature (cf. Machaut's "Dit de la marguerite," 124, st. 2) and by Chaucer when he tells us that Alceste "taught al the craft of fyn lovynge."

23. *Livre des faits du bon messire Jean le Maingre, dit Bouciquaut,* in *Les Chroniques de sire Jean Froissart,* ed. J. A. C. Bouchon, vol. 3 (Paris: F. Wattelier, 1867), 1.7–8. 573a–574b.

24. Witness Froissart's account of how the queen's tears of pity "amollia le coeur" in Edward when he was determined to execute the six Calais bourgeois in retaliation for the damage the city had done him in re-

sisting the siege (*Les Chroniques de sire Jean Froissart* 1.1.321, 272). Marriage does not, of course, solve the problem of the moral and psychological value of passion, a fact that may explain the depiction of married *fin amour* without reference to the institutional ties, as in Machaut's *Dit de la fonteinne amoureuse* (*Oeuvres de Guillaume de Machaut,* ed. Ernest Hoepffner, vol. 3 [Paris: Edward Champion, 1921]) and Chaucer's *Book of the Duchess.* Alceste is the model for both "fyn lovyng" and "wyfhod."

25. Kiser, *Telling Classical Tales,* 44–45, 56.

26. Compare Froissart's account of the origin of the *marguerite* from the tears of Heres nourished by the sun ("Dittié," 211, vv. 75–80).

27. Note, e.g., Hugh of St. Victor's definition of Nature as an "artificer fire coming forth to beget sensible objects," a definition he supports with an appeal to the claim of the physicists "that all things are procreated from heat and moisture" (*The Didascalicon of Hugh of St. Victor,* trans. Jerome Taylor [New York: Columbia Univ. Press, 1961] 1.10, p. 57), and his identification in *In ecclesiastem homiliae* of this *ignis artifex* with the sun, the source of vegetable and sensible life (*PL* 175.136C–37C; cited in Taylor, *Didascalicon,* 193 n.71), or Bernardus Silvester's account of how "the fiery element of the celestial sphere" causes with its circular turning each thing to assume "the mode of being proper to its kind" and so effects "the generation of things" (*Cosmographia,* ed. Peter Dronke [Leiden: E. J. Brill, 1978], 1.4.1–2; Winthrop Wetherbee, trans., *The Cosmographia of Bernardus Silvester* [New York: Columbia Univ. Pres, 1973], 86–87). Behind such claims lies the medieval platonic tradition's association of the animating principle of the universe, its mind or soul, with the ethereal fire of the heavens. Two texts repeatedly cited by this tradition and presumably known to Chaucer deserve singling out: Virgil's characterization of the "spiritus intus," the "mens," that animates the created as an *igneus vigor* (*Aeneid* 4.724–51), and Macrobius's insistence that "ethereal fire" is necessary to sustain "vitam et animam" in creatures formed from sublunar elements (*Somnium* 1.21.35; *Dream of Scipio,* 181). Also noteworthy is the speculation in the commentary tradition of the *Consolation,* 3, m. 9, as to whether or not Boethius's reference to the soul as "mediam" derives from Plato's associating the World Soul and the sun (see Tullio Gregory, *Anima Mundi: La filosofia di Guglielmo di Conches e la scuola di Chartres* [Florence: G. C. Sansoni, 1955], 143 n.2). For a survey of medieval texts associating the World

Soul with ethereal fire, see Taylor, *Didascalicon*, 193 n.71; for a discussion of the tradition with particular reference to twelfth-century thought, see Gregory, *Anima Mundi*, 175–85; on ethereal fire in Bernardus Silvester, see Wetherbee, *Cosmographia*, 41–45.

28. Though Boethius places his primary emphasis on the harmonious motion of the heavens in their reconciliation of the antithetical elements, he also attributes their life-nourishing "temperies" to their moderate heat. The account of creation in Jean's continuation of the *Roman*—which derives partly from 3, m. 9, and 4, m. 6, of the *Consolation*—similarly credits the harmony of the turning heavens and the temperate heat of the sun, which as the middle planet is neither too warm nor too cold, with harmonizing the warring elements and nourishing life (vv. 16895–974). Jean's account of solar influence also seems indebted to Macrobius's discussion of this *fons ignis aetherii* as the "mens," "cor," and "temperatio mundi"; Ernest Langlois (*Roman de la rose* 4 [Paris: Firmin-Didot, 1922], 306, n. to vv. 16911–15) refers to *Somnium* 1.10, 17; even more apposite is 1.20.7–8.

29. The texts that established this physics of secondary causes in the twelfth century presented celestial fire as the animating force in the cosmos: see Hermann of Carinthia, *De essentiis*, ed. and trans. Charles Burnett (Leiden: E. J. Brill, 1982), e.g., 65rG—65vG, pp. 130–33; Thierry of Chartres, *De sex dierum operibus*, e.g., 17, in N. M. Häring, "The Creation and Creator of the World according to Thierry of Chartres and Clarenbaldus of Arras," *AHDLMA* 30 (1955): 189–90; William of Conches, *De philosophia mundi*, e.g., 1.21, *PL* 171.54–55. Though there is no evidence that Chaucer knew these primary texts, his debt to the literary tradition of philosophical poetry directly influenced by such speculations—the *Cosmographia*, the *De planctu*, the *Roman*, the *Commedia*—is well recognized.

30. Again Froissart anticipates something of Chaucer's implication when he characterizes the sun as refining the flower's beauty ("Dittié," 52).

31. On the general question of astrological influence, in addition to the materials surveyed in Chauncey Wood, "Chaucer and Astrology," *Companion to Chaucer Studies*, ed. Beryl Roland (Toronto: Oxford Univ. Press, 1968), 176–91, see Wood's own study, *Chaucer and the Country of the Stars* (Princeton, N.J.: Princeton Univ. Press, 1970); and the magisterial history of the association of planetary influence with human temperament and medical distemper in Raymond Klibansky,

Erwin Parnofsky, and Fritz Saxl, *Saturn and Melancholy* (London: Nelson, 1964).

32. The genius figure in medieval literature has been the object of considerable recent scrutiny. See Jane Chance Nitzsche, *The Genius Figure in Antiquity and the Middle Ages* (New York: Columbia Univ. Press, 1975), esp. for classical and early medieval influences on late medieval personification; Denise N. Baker, "The Priesthood of Genius: A Study of the Medieval Tradition," *Speculum* 51 (1976): 277−91; and Winthrop Wetherbee, *Platonism and Poetry in the Twelfth Century* (Princeton, N.J.: Princeton Univ. Press, 1972), and "The Theme of Imagination in Medieval Poetry and the Allegorical Figure 'Genius,'" *Medievalia et Humanistica*, 7 (1976): 45−64, esp. for appreciation of the complexity of the late medieval personifications. The association of the genius figure as creative agency (as transmitter of specific and individual natures) with the stars is most evident in Bernardus Silvester's characterization of the intelligences of the celestial spheres as genii in the *Cosmographia*.

33. See Alain de Lille's description of *Natura*: "Que, Noys puras recolens ideas, / Singulas rerum species monetas, / Rem togans forma clamidemque forme / Police formans" (who working on the pure idea of Noys, mould the species of all created things, clothing matter with form and fashioning a mantle of form with your thumb; *De planctu* 7.831; *The Plaint,* 128); Bernardus Silvester's depiction of the "infantia mundi" crying out within the womb of Silva "ad speciem vestiri cultius" (to be clothed with a finer appearance; *Cosmographia* 1.1.39−40; Wetherbee, 68); and Jean de Meun's account of the alchemical transmutation, possible because metals "sont trestuit d'une matire, / Coment que Nature l'atire" (are all of one matter, however Nature may attire them; Langlois, *Roman* [Lecoy's text reads "la tire"], vv. 16119−20; *The Romance,* 273).

34. Alain de Lille's description of the revival of the earth upon the appearance of the personification *Natura* in *De planctu* informs the *Roman* and the Prologue in this respect: "Terra uero, iampridem hiemis latrocinio suis ornamentis denudata, a ueris prodigalitate purpurantem florum tunicam usurpabat, ne uestibus pannosis ingloria adolescentule indecenter compareret aspectui. Ver etiam, quasi artifex peritus in arte textoria, ut uirgineis beatius applauderet incessibus, uestimenta texebat arboribus." (Earth, for long stripped

of its ornaments by plundering Winter, acquired a purple garment of flowers from the bounteous spirit of Spring, lest, dishonoured in ragged attire, she might present an improper appearance to the eyes of the tender maid. Spring, too, skilled craftsman in the weaver's art, wishing to show greater happiness in applauding the maiden's approach, wove garments for trees; *De planctu* 4, pr. 2.45–59; *The Plaint,* 111). So also does his description of spring's revival in the following meter: "Ver, quasi fullo nouus, reparando pallis pratis, / Horum succendit muricis igne togas. / Reddidit arboribus crines quos bruma totondit, / Vestitum reparans quem tulit illa prius" (Spring, like a fuller with renewed strength, mending the meadow's cloak, set the mantles of flowers afire with the glow of purple. He restored to the trees the foliage-tresses that Winter had shorn, restoring the raiment the latter previously took away; *De planctu* 5, m. 3.5–8; *The Plaint,* 113. The *Complaint,* we might note, has been cited as the source for the image of the fowler's "sophistrye": E.S.A., *Notes and Queries,* ser. 8, 3:249–50; cited in Robinson, *Works,* 842, n. to line 137). That the revival of nature upon the appearance of Natura is a reenactment of creation is intimated by the fact that Natura is clothed in the images of things; by the characterization of reviving nature as reclothed upon her revival, clothing being one of Alain's recurrent metaphors for the informing of matter; and by the general similarity of the catalogue of creatures on Natura's garments to Bernardus's description of the universe, which unfolded through the imposition of exemplary forms on matter (*Cosmographia* 1.3, pp. 104–16; Wetherbee, 75–86).

35. On the harmonizing love that Boethius celebrates in *Consolation* 2, m. 8, as both a force emanating from God and the desire of the created for the perfection of the Creator, see two articles immediately addressed to the final lines of Dante's *Commedia:* Howard R. Patch, "The Last Line of the *Commedia,*" *Speculum* 14 (1939): 56–65; Peter Dronke, "L'amor che move il sole e l'altre stelle," *Studi medievali* 6 (1965): 389–422.

36. For Boethius's explanation of how this love orders the cosmos, see *Consolation* 3, m. 2 and pr. 3, where Philosophia characterizes the innate desire of all things for self-realization as a desire for the good; and 4, pr. 6 and m. 6, where she explains how Fate orders the cosmos in obedience to Providence by this same principle. In commenting on 3, m. 9, William of Conches indentifies this infused fire as the same

"divinus amor," the same "benigna concordia," that vivifies all creation, the "Spiritus Sanctus." That he recognized in this "reduci igne"
the principle by which Fate orders all things in obedience to Providence is clear from his association of its *benigna lex* with predestina-
tion; see Charles Jourdain, "Des commentaires inédits de Guillaume
de Conches et de Nicolas Triveth sur la *Consolation de la Philosophie* de
Boèce," in *Excursions historique et philosophique à travers le moyen âge*
(Paris 1888), 61–62, 64 (originally published in *Notices et extraits des
mss. de la Bibl. Imp.* 20 [1862]: 40–82).

37. On Dante's universe as a structure of emanated lights, see Joseph
Mazzeo, *Medieval Cultural Tradition in Dante's Comedy* (Ithaca, N.Y.:
Cornell Univ. Press, 1960), 56–132. For additional discussion of the
role of light imagery in the Prologue, esp. concerning its noetic function, see Kiser, *Telling Classical Tales*, 35–42.

38. Boethius, *Consolation* 4, m. 6. The accounts of Nature's creative activity in Alain's *Complaint* and Jean's *Roman* include in their debt to this
meter its insistence that the same power which fashions creatures also
destroys them (*De planctu* 6.41–42; *The Plaint*, 118; the *Roman*,
vv. 16945–60).

39. E.g., John Gower explains that man "mot be verray kynde dye" because he is compounded of "divisioun": i.e., of the four antithetical
elements, rather than of "o matiere" (*Confessio*, Prologus, 971–90);
Jean de Meun attributes the imperfections of Nature's creations to
the "defaut de leur matires" (*Roman*, v. 16944); Bernardus depicts
Noys as limited in her creative activity by the necessity and malignity
of primal matter (*Cosmographia* 1.2.1–2, 6; Wetherbee, 69–71);
Boethius explains that human souls are free as long as they contem-
plate the divine mind, but "lasse fre whan thei slyden into the bodyes,
and yit lasse fre whan thei ben gadred togidre and comprehended in
erthli membres" (*Consolation* 5. pr. 2).

40. On astrological influence in general, see n. 31, above. It is worth
observing that Chaucer's one apparent echo of the *Cosmographia*, in
the "Man of Law's Tale" (*CT* II, 197–203), imitates Bernardus's catalogue of the future events depicted in the stars (see *Cosmographia*
1.3.31–60; Wetherbee, 76–77).

41. When the daisy appears as Alceste in the dream, Chaucer does give a
fuller account of her gold "fret," white crown, and "real habit grene"
(F, 214–15).

42. G, 160–61. In F, the god wears garments embroidered with "grene

greves, / Inwith a fret of rede rose-leves" (227–28); given the emphasis placed at times on the whiteness of Alceste's crown, this detail suggests that we should see them as jointly red and white, as well as indi-
vidually so.

43. On Emelye as red and white, see the description of her in the garden,
    fairer than a lily and vying with the rose, as she gathers flowers "party
    white and red" (daisies?) to make a garland (*CT* I, 1035–55); Diana's
    "oratorie" is "of alabstre whit and red coral" (line 1910). On Mars and
    Arcite as red, see, e.g., the "rede statue of Mars" in Theseus's banner
    (line 975), Theseus's oath "by myghty Mars the rede," and Arcite's
    entrance with his host through the west gate of the "lists" "under
    Mars" with "baner reed" (lines 2581–83). The association of Venus
    and Palamon with white is less pronounced. If her statue has its
    doves, one imagines its garland of roses as red (lines 1961–63), but
    Palamon enters the amphitheater "under Venus" with "baner white"
    (lines 2584–86).

44. Boccaccio, *Choise al Teseide,* glosses to Book 7, st. 30, 50 (*Opere minori in
    vulgare,* ed. Mario Marti, vol. 2 [Milan: Rizzoli, 1970], 708, 713).

45. The "triplicis naturae" of Plato's World Soul—its composition from
    the individual, the dividual, and a compound of the analogous prin-
    ciples, the same and the different—was customarily referred to the
    three kinds of animation it effected in the cosmos. In his commentary
    on *Consolation* 3, m. 9, William of Conches refers its triple nature to
    the vegetable, sensible, and rational souls (Jourdain, "Des commen-
    taires inédits," 61). Referring soul (in 3, m. 9) to man the "minor
    mundus," Remigius explains its triplicity as man's irascible, concup-
    iscible, and rational faculties, as did the anonymous commentary that
    Silvestre attributes to John the Scot; for both texts, see Hubert Silves-
    tre, "Le Commentaire inédit de Jean Scot Erigène au mètre ix du
    livre III du 'De consolatione Philosophiae' de Boèce," *Revue d'histori-
    que ecclesiastique* 47 (1952): 61. The anonymous commentator printed
    by Silk refers "triplicis naturae" to both threesomes; see *Saeculi noni
    auctoris in Boetii Consolationem Philosophiae commentarius,* ed. Edmund
    T. Silk (Rome: American Academy, 1935), 180. (This commentary
    belongs to the twelfth century; see Pierre Courçelle, "Etudes critique
    sur les commentaires de la Consolation de Boèce (IXe–XVe s.),"
    AHDLMA 12 [1939]: 24–25, 80–81).

46. On the World Soul in twelfth-century philosophical speculations, see
    Gregory, *Anima Mundi,* 123–74. A compact documentation of the

idea's vicissitudes in the face of Christian opposition, including the remedial application of Boethius's reference of it to the human soul, is provided by Taylor, *Didascalicon,* 179–80, n. 10. A concise medieval summary of twelfth-century viewpoints is provided by a fragment deriving from William of Conches, *Philosophia mundi: Un brano inedito della "Philosophia" de Guglielmo de Conches,* ed. Carmelo Ottaviano (Naples: Alberto Morano, 1935), 48–51; on the question of the authorship of this fragment, see Tullio Gregory, "Sull'attribuzione a Guglielmo de Conches de un remaneggiamento della *Philosophia mundi,*" *Giornale critico della filosofia italiana* 30 (1951): 119–25.

47. See, e.g., Hugh of St. Victor's repudiation of Virgil's error in assigning the world a soul of ethereal fire by asserting that sounder understanding refers the words "spiritium pergentem in omnia et in circulos suos revertentem" to a power that nourishes all things (spirit moving outward upon all things and returning upon itself in circles; *In Ecclesiastem homiliae,* hom. 2, *PL* 175.136; quoted in M.-D. Chenu, *Nature, Man, and Society in the Twelfth Century,* trans. Jerome Taylor and L. K. Little [Chicago: Univ. of Chicago Press, 1968], 22 n.46); or Hermann of Carinthia's assertion that what Plato called the World Soul we would call Nature (*De essentiis,* 69rB, p. 154). The most important literary expression of this transfer of the World Soul's powers and functions to Nature occurs in Alain de Lille's *Complaint,* where Natura clothed in the images of things revives the created even as Bernardus's Endelechia has vivified it (see *De planctu* 4, 5, pr. 2, m. 3; *Cosmographia* 1.2.13–16; Wetherbee, 74–75), where she contemplates the ideas in Noys that she may clothe matter with form (*De planctu* 7, m. 4.11–16), where she creates in the soul of man-the-microcosm two contrary motions: rational and irrational thought, which correspond to the motions Plato attributed to the World Soul, motions visible in the westward movement of the fixed stars, the contrary motion of the planets (*De planctu* 6, pr. 3.51–65; see also Rowe, *O Love, O Charite,* 25–27). On the debt of the idea of Nature to that of the World Soul, see Gregory, *Anima Mundi,* 175–245; for a more wide-ranging discussion of the development of the personification, see George D. Economou, *The Goddess Natura in Medieval Literature* (Cambridge, Mass.: Harvard Univ. Press, 1972).

48. Given the association of the vital powers of the cosmos with ethereal fire, as in Virgil, Cicero, and Macrobius, (see n. 27, above; and Taylor, *Didiscalicon,* 193 n.71), and Plato's location of the World Soul

in the middle of the cosmos (Boethius's term in *Consolation* 3, m. 9, is "media"), a close association of the World Soul and the sun was inevitable. See *Timaeus a Calcidio translatus Commentarioque instructus,* ed. J. H. Waszink (Leiden: E. J. Brill, 1975), 99, p. 204. Commenting on 3, m. 9, Remigius explains the indentification of the World Soul as the sun as follows: "Philosophi animam mundi solem dixerunt esse, quia sicut calificat corpus anima, ita solis calore vivificantur omnia, euisque calor diffusus per creaturas facit eas gignere, et re vera ut physici dicunt calore illius omnia et gignunt and gignuntur pariter cum humore, Deo ita disponente" (Philosophers call the sun the world's soul, for just as the soul gives warmth to the body, so all things are given life by the heat of the sun, and its heat, diffused through creatures, makes them generate, and in fact, as natural philosophers say, by the heat of the sun, along with moisture, all things beget and are begotten, God so disposing; Silvestre, "Le Commentaire inédit," 58. William of Conches, we should note, denies the idea that Plato located the World Soul in the sun (Gregory, *Anima Mundi,* 143–44).

49. Lotario dei Sequi, *De miseria condicionis humane,* ed. Robert E. Lewis, *The Chaucer Library* (Athens, Ga.: Univ. of Georgia Press, 1978), 1.3.24–27, p. 99: "Habet enim anima tres naturales potencias sive tres naturales vires: racionalem ut discernat inter bonum et malum, irascibilem ut respuat malum, concupiscibilem ut appetat bonum" (For the soul has three natural powers or forces: reason that distinguishes between good and evil, irascibility that repels evil, concupiscence that seeks good). Similar evaluations of these appetites often accompany the explanation of the "triplicis naturae" of the soul in the commentaries on 3, m. 9. Both Remigius (Silvestre, "Le Commentaire inédit," 61) and the anonymous commentary printed by Silk (*Saeculi noni auctoris,* 180) go on to insist that, properly trained and controlled, these three faculties can reunite creature and Creator. For a list of additional sources providing a similar definition of the irascible and the concupisible, see Silvestre, "Le commentaire inédit," 61 n.1.

50. See Jourdain, "Des commentaires inédits," 64. William clearly regards this fire as God's love of man and man's infused love of God. He observes that this "reduci igne" is the splendor and fervor of love and explains that "ubi . . . est ignis, ibi sunt ista duo, calor et splendor. Similiter in divino amore est splendor quo illuminatur mens, ad cognitionem celestium, et est calor ad comprehendendum et imitan-

dum" (wherever there is fire, there are these two, heat and brightness. Likewise, in divine love there is brightness by which the mind is
illuminated for knowing heavenly things and heat for grasping and
imitating them). William goes on to observe that love works in anyone
who loves God to make him desire heavenly things; he illustrates the
association of this desire with fire by observing that because divine
love filled the apostles with a fervor for heavenly things, the Holy
Spirit is said to have been infused in them "in igneis linguis" (in fiery
tongues). For a discussion of the similar way in which love is depicted
as moving the whole cosmos in William's commentary on the *Timaeus,*
see Dronke, "L'amor che move il sole," 412–13.

51. On the expression "flower of flowers," see Peter Dronke, *Medieval
Latin and the Rise of European Love-Lyric,* 2d ed., vol 1 (Oxford:
Clarendon, 1968), 181–92.

52. On the *forma formarum,* see J. M. Parent, *La Doctrine de la création dans
l'école de Chartres* (Paris: J. Vrin, 1938), 54–58, and the anonymous
commentary on Boethius's *De trinitate,* Paris, Bibliothèque Nationale
MS. Latin 14489, fols. 27v–30r (Parent, *La Doctrine,* 200–205).

53. On Alceste's likeness to the Virgin, see Payne, *The Key of Remembrance,*
107–8; and Kiser, *Telling Classical Tales,* 47–48. Alceste's association
with the rose, the Virgin's "flower of flowers," strengthens this association, as does the sun imagery. Given that the daisy is both a flower
and a sun, reference should perhaps be made to the celebration of
Mary as bearer of the flower of light in the sequence printed by
Dronke, *Medieval Latin and European Love-Lyric,* 186.

54. *Paradiso* 33.21.

55. On the sacred associations of lilies and roses, see the "Second Nun's
Tale," *CT* VIII, 220–80, and Robinson, *Works,* 758, n. to line 220. On
the literary and legendary rose more generally, see Charles Joret, *La
Rose dans l'antiquité et au moyen âge* (Paris: Emile Bouillon, 1892); Bar-
bara Seward, *The Symbolic Rose* (New York: Columbia Univ. Press,
1960).

56. Louis Réau says the use of the *marguerite*-daisy as an emblem for St.
Margaret of Antioch is rare (*Iconographie de l'art chrétien,* vol. 3, *Iconographie de saints,* pt. 2 [Paris: Presses universitaires de France, 1958],
880). For its association with St. Margaret of Cortona, see Richard C.
Prior, *On the Popular Names of British Plants* (London: Williams & Mar-
gate, 1863), 143–44, 147; and Richard Folkard, *Plant Lore, Legends,
and Myths* (London: Low, Marston, Searle, & Rivington, 1884), 174,

424, 431 (neither Prior nor Folkard documents his claims in accurate detail). Caxton associates the daisy with a third St. Margaret: "This Virgin Margaret had twin names; she was called Margaret and Pelagian. Insomuch as she was named Margaret, she is always linked to a flower, for she had in her, flower of her virginity" (*The Golden Legend*, ed. F. S. Ellis, vol. 5 [London: J. M. Dent, 1911], 238).

57. "The Legend of Seynt Margarete," in *The Minor Poems of John Lydgate*, ed. Henry Noble McCracken, vol. 1, EETS, Ext. Ser. 107 (London: K. Paul, Trench, Trübner, 1911), 174, lines 22–28. On the basis of the fact that the daisy blooms year round, Lydgate also associates it with the Virgin Mary, calling her "Duryng dayse, with no weder steyned" ("Balade at the Reverence of our Lady, Qwene of Mercy," *Minor Poems*, vol. 1, 259, line 131. Chaucer alludes to the fact that the daisy blooms all year in F, 55, and mentions it explicitly in G, 57–58.

58. Kiser, *Telling Classical Tales*, 50–61.

59. On Hercules as a type of Christ, see Marcel Simon, *Hercule et le christianisme* (Paris: Université de Strasbourg, 1955), 169–91. On Hercules and Orpheus, another type of Christ, see n. 79, below. Fyler notes Alceste's "imitatio Christi," terms it "shocking," and stresses the disparity between the two, as though Chaucer's purpose were the disparagement rather than the glorification of Alceste (*Chaucer and Ovid*, 118–19).

60. While Kiser is certainly right to stress the affinity of Alceste's meaning as historical *res* (as both flower and heroine) and as poetic metaphor, her attempt to distinguish between Alceste as proper metaphor and the god of Love as improper metaphor—the latter having no reality as *res*—seems misguided. Ironies similar to those she sees undermining the god's integrity as revelatory *signum* (see *Telling Classical Tales* 62–66) are also present in Chaucer's characterization of Alceste (see pp. 40–41). That Alceste and the god mean in different ways is true, but this seems part of the *Legend*'s effort to represent and critique both analytical and intuitive modes of knowing. Here one recognizes the influence of Jean's portion of the *Roman*, where personifications (representation of abstract ideas produced by analysis) and "real," if typical, characters (signifying things) alternate in a dramatization of the uncertainties both of analytical thought and of sacramental allegories. On the two modes of thought and their impact on medieval poetry in general, see Wetherbee, *Platonism and Poetry*, 11–19 and passim.

61. Kiser, *Telling Classical Tales*, 57 n.21. I have been unable to confirm

the alleged definition of "corona" as *margaritum-ae* in the *Thesaurus Linguae Latinae* published by Teubner in 1906–9.

62. French *marguerite* names both pearl and daisy; Latin *margaritum*, pearl, did not apparently mean daisy as well. The French pun is not verbally in the text, of course. The image of a crown made of pearl in the shape of a daisy unites, we might note, two ever fashionable forms of the "corona," the floral wreath and the crown fashioned from precious gems and metals. Besides being a garland and a crown, daisies and pearls, it is a sun with a "corona."

63. The pearl of Alceste's crown has associations that confirm and extend many implications in Chaucer's image of the daisy. The pearl suggests the heavenly reward, the "pearl of great price" that the merchant in Christ's parable sold all to acquire (Matthew 13:45–46, just two verses after Christ's characterization of the righteous as shining like suns in the kingdom of heaven), the reward that awaits those who are themselves priceless pearls, those saved either by innocence or by purification. On the symbolism of the pearl, esp. as relevant to the Middle English elegy, see Marie P. Hamilton, "The Meaning of the Middle English 'Pearl'," *PMLA* 70 (1955): 805–24. This union of flower and pearl, like the *Pearl*'s pearl-rose-pearl transformation (lines 253–72), expresses the transformation of the temporal to the eternal, a metamorphosis simultaneously represented in Alceste's stellification in the immutable heavens. The daisy itself is not only "evere ilyke faire" (F, 55) and "evere ylike fayr and fressh of hewe, / As wel in wynter as in somer newe" (G, 57–58); it is also the daisy as perpetual species or genus, made in everlasting commemoration of Alceste.

64. The association of crown in general and pearl crowns in particular with the saved in general and martyrs in particular is well known. It is perhaps worth recalling that the tonsure was termed a "corona" and understood as a likeness of Christ's crown of thorns; the hope was that the assumption of such a crown of suffering would secure one an eternal crown (see Du Cange, *Glossarium mediae et infinae Latinitatis*, vol. 2 [Paris: Librairie des sciences et des arts, 1937], 572; or *Lexicon Latinitatis Nederlandicae medii aevi*, ed. J. W. Fuchs, Olga Weijers, and Marijke Gumbert, vol. 2 [Leiden: E. J. Brill, 1981], IA3a and IB).

65. The commonplace of *Legend* criticism that the god's sun-crown is a halo was first suggested by William Allan Neilson, *The Origin and Sources of the Court of Love* (Boston: Ginn, 1899), 145.

66. To Chaucer's assertion that men may see Ariadne's crown in the sign

of Taurus, Robinson comments: " 'In the signe of Taurus' clearly means when the sun is in that sign; for the constellation Corona Borealis is almost opposite Taurus and comes to the meridian with Scorpio" (*Works*, 852, n. to lines 2223–24). The only thing that seems indisputable is that Chaucer wished to associate Ariadne and Taurus, which is hardly surprising, given her descent through her father from Jove's ravishing of Europa, her kinship through her mother with the Minotaur, and her own spiritual similitude to such a brute beast.

67. For the idea of being transhumanized, see *Par.* 1.70, and Chaucer's *Troilus,* where Pandarus explains the "newe qualitee" that Troilus feels after the consummation as the effect of having experienced "hevene blisse" (3.1653–59); on becoming a god by participation, see *Consolation* 3, pr. 10.

68. The possibility that Machaut's *Jugement dou Roy de Navarre* was a source for the Prologue was first suggested by G. L. Kittredge, "Chauceriana," *MP* 7 (1910): 472; it was argued at length by Estrich, "Chaucer's and Machaut's *Jugement,*" 20–39. Besides similarities in plot, Estrich saw a shared antifeminist spirit in the two poems. A connection between the *Trésor amoureux* and the Prologue was again first suggested by Kittredge with reference to "Make the metres of hem as the lest" ("Chauceriana," 473–74); for the contention that it influenced the trial scene, see W. O. Sypherd, *Studies in the Hous of Fame,* Chaucer Soc., 2d ser. 39 (London: K. Paul, Trench, Trübner, 1907), 33. With its angry god of Love, its offending poet, and its feminine defenders of the poet, the *Trésor* provides the closest analogue to the situation in the Prologue, though it is hardly a necessary source (for the *Trésor Amoureux,* see Froissart, *Oeuvres,* vol. 3; the relevant action begins at v. 2582).

69. On the debate of the four daughters of God, see Arthur Langfors, *Notices des manuscrits 535 et 10047* in *Notices et extraits des manuscrits de la bibliothèque nationale* 42 (1932): 139–291; and Jean Riviere, *Le Dogme de la rédemption au début du moyen âge* (Paris: J. Vrin, 1934), 309–62.

70. See Richard of Maidstone, "The Reconciliation of Richard II with the City of London," in *Political Poems and Songs,* ed. Thomas Wright, Rolls Ser. (1859; rpr., Wiesbaden: Kraus, 1965), vol. 1, 297–99. Norton-Smith contends the Prologue commemorates Anne's role in this reconciliation (*Geoffrey Chaucer,* 63).

71. Beyond the poets and the king of Navarre, the main characters in

Machaut's *Jugement* and Froissart's *Trésor* are personifications.

72. For relatively recent arguments for and against identifying the god and Alceste with Richard and Anne, see Donaldson, *Chaucer's Poetry*, 956–58; and Bertrand H. Bronson, *In Search of Chaucer* (Toronto: Univ. of Toronto Press, 1960), 54–58. It is no more necessary than it is permissible to reduce the fictive characters to mere signs for historical personages; the god and Alceste may remind us of Richard and Anne without representing them.

73. If Machaut's *Jugement dou Roy de Navarre* is a source, the irony is underscored in the defense that the poet may have written his poems with little attention to what he was about, for in the *Jugement* the poet's accuser insists that he must have known he was defaming women since he writes his poetry with great effort, not when he is drunk (see *Oeuvres de Guillaume de Machaut*, ed. Ernest Hoepffner, vol. 1 [Paris: Firmin-Didot, 1908], 166–67, vv. 865–76).

74. The difficulty with Kiser's attempt to see Alceste here as speaking for the poet (see *Telling Classical Tales*, 84–94) is that it ignores the comedy inherent in her actions, the absurdity of her defense, and the contradictory character of the penance she assigns.

75. For a discussion of the political philosophy inherent in Alceste's remarks on the proper exercise of authority, see Margaret Schlauch, "Chaucer's Doctrine of Kings and Tyrants," *Speculum* 20, (1945): 133–56. The political philosophy inherent in her remarks is, in Walter Ullmann's terms, radically "theocratic": Alceste's appeal is made not on the basis of the accused's rights but on the king's obligation to exercise properly the authority conferred upon him by God. On the theocratic king as intermediary, see Ullmann, *Principles of Government and Politics in the Middle Ages* (London: Methuen, 1961), 130–32.

76. On the need for kings to be simultaneously just and merciful, see, e.g., John of Salisbury, *Policraticus*, ed. Clemens Webb, vol. 1 (Oxford: Clarendon, 1909), 4.8.529; *The Statesman's Book of John of Salisbury*, trans. John Dickinson (New York: Knopf, 1927), 37–40. Worth noting in relation to the Prologue's imagery is the coronation oath cited by Ullman (*Principles of Government*, 130), in which the king is crowned with the "corona justiciae et pietatis."

77. Rowe, *O Love, O Charite*, 131–32, 148.

78. See *Consolation* 3, m. 12; for this intepretation of Orpheus's descent, see the excerpt from William of Conches's commentary on the *Consolation* printed in Edouard Jeauneau, "L'usage de la notion d'*inte-*

gumentum à travers les gloses de Guillaume de Conches," *AHDLMA* 24 (1957): 45–46. Bernardus Silvester provides a similar explanation of the myth in his *Commentum super sex libros Eneidos Virgilii*, ed. J. W. Jones and E. F. Jones (Lincoln: Univ. of Nebraska Press, 1977), 53–55. On the Orpheus myth, see John Block Friedman, *Orpheus in the Middle Ages* (Cambridge, Mass.: Harvard Univ. Press, 1972).

79. On Hercules as a philosopher safely journeying through this infernal world, a successful Orpheus, see Jeauneau, "La notion d'*integumentum*," 40–41, esp. his citation from Guillaume's commentary, p. 52. See also Bernardus Silvester's *Commentum super sex libros*, 30.

80. Gower, *Confessio*, Prologus 1054–88, and 1.1–7; on Arion in the poem, see Russell A. Peck, ed., *Confessio Amantis* (New York: Holt, Rinehart & Winston, 1968), xviii–xix. That Gower saw Arion as another Orpheus is evident from his apparent use of Boethius's characterization of the effects of Orpheus's musical powers (*Consolation* 3, m. 12, 10–13) in describing the effects of Arion's.

81. See *Inf.* 2.32–33. Chaucer's dramatization of the genesis of the present poem in his narrator's obedience to the Alceste-daisy similarly reminds one of his dissociation of himself from Enoch, Elijah, Romulus, and Ganymede in the *House of Fame* 2.588–89, itself a passage echoing Dante.

82. St. Bernard, *Sermon on the Canticles*, in *The Life and Works of St. Bernard*, ed. Dom John Mabillon, trans. Samuel J. Eales, vol. 4 (London: J. Hodges, 1896), 20.6.113. See the equally relevant argument by John of Salisbury that we should reverence persons elevated by such things as office, character, or rank, for while God ought to be the ultimate object of our spiritual affection, he has given us a way to approach him carnally through such bodily manifestations of his wisdom, majesty, and goodness as kings and wise men are. They are to be honored as images of God (*Policraticus* 5.3–4.541b–47b; *The Statesman's Book*, 67–79).

III. THE NARRATOR AS TRANSLATOR

1. Lowes, "Is Chaucer's *Legend* a Travesty?" 546; Robinson, *Works*, 482. See also chap. 1, n. 17.

2. Goddard, "Chaucer's *Legend*" (1908), 101; Garrett, "Cleopatra the Martyr," 67. See also chap. 1, n. 16.

3. Kelly implies that Chaucer left the *Legend* incomplete in part because

he discovered in the course of writing it the inappropriateness of the heroines listed in the Prologue's *balade* and presumably intended for inclusion (*Love and Marriage*, 113–20), but Chaucer's prior familiarity with the unsuitability of many of these women is clear from earlier references to them (see, e.g., the *Book of the Duchess*, 725–34).

4. The classic work on the narrator in the dream visions remains Dorothy Bethurum, "Chaucer's Point of View as Narrator in the Love Poems," *PMLA* 74 (1959): 511–20. On the similarity of the persona to the poet, see Donald R. Howard, "Chaucer the Man," *PMLA* 80 (1965): 337–43.

5. Frank, *Chaucer and the Legend*, 35.

6. Ibid., 14–15. Frank also denies the poem any "moral or theological purpose" (p. 15). He does recognize incidental comedy and irony.

7. The present study lends support to Fyler's view that one of the purposes of the legends is to show the deleterius effect on art and morality of an a priori point of view (*Chaucer and Ovid*, 98–115).

8. For the history of scholarship on the possible sources for this legend, see Frank, *Chaucer and the Legend*, 38 n.2. All of the possible sources for the narrative proper tell Cleopatra's story in sufficient detail to ensure that Chaucer must have known that she fit less than perfectly the prescribed pattern. For instance, Florus in his *Epitome of Roman History* 2.21, Vincent of Beauvais in his *Speculum historiale* 6.53, and Boccaccio in both his *De claris mulieribus* 86 and his *De casibus virorum illustrium* 6.15 all relate that Cleopatra killed herself only after she tried and failed to win Caesar's grace, without including Plutarch's intimation that this was a ruse to enable her to commit suicide (see the *Parallel Lives* 9.82–83). Even in Vincent of Beauvais's account—the briefest and least negative in its depiction of Antony and Cleopatra, and just possibly Chaucer's sole source—Cleopatra kills herself not for love of Antony but to avoid the shame of being paraded as Caesar's captive (the relevant passage is conveniently printed in Pauline Aiken, "Chaucer's *Legend of Cleopatra and the Speculum historiale*," *Speculum* 13 [1938]: 232–33). Chaucer's heroine seems equally committed to her good name, as her final words imply.

9. Though Goddard's satiric reading of this line ("Chaucer's *Legend*" [1908], 62) genuinely offended Lowes ("Is Chaucer's *Legend* a Travesty?" 544 n.106), it is difficult to imagine any other reason for its inclusion, since it is otherwise so totally unnecessary.

10. Ovid makes their *vicinia* the initial cause, not neighboring women.

He represents the parents as opposed but provides no explanation for their opposition: see *Metamorphoses* 4.59–62. Gower, we should note, tells the story of Pyramus and Thisbe as an instance of "fol-haste" (*Confessio* 3.762–66).

11. Fyler points out that traditional representations of the "wantonness" of the wedding lend a certain irony to his insistence on the advisability of being brief (*Chaucer and Ovid,* 101).

12. The *Oxford English Dictionary* defines "due" (def. 3) in this line as "belonging or incumbent as a duty," no doubt as a consequence of what it is assumed the line should say; in fact, the well-attested definition (5b) "merited, appropriate: proper, right" makes perfectly good sense and is consistent with the ironic undercurrent of the lines.

13. While Frank is correct in asserting that Antony "is not the ideal courtly lover" (*Chaucer and the Legend,* 41), it is clear that the narrator seeks to understand him in terms of the ideology of *fin amour.*

14. Kiser's analogous observation—"Cleopatra's pathetic attempt to canonize Antony resembles Chaucer's own efforts to adorn his tales with the superficial glitter of holy rhetoric or to make them conform to sacred plots (*Telling Classical Tales,* 109)—misstates the case by emphasizing the form of the legends rather than the intent of the narrator, for in fact the legends are not particularly similar to the traditional saint's life either in plot or in rhetoric.

15. Garrett, "Cleopatra the Martyr," 68.

16. Fyler sees the story of Dido and Aeneas as the *locus classicus* for medieval treatments of the problem of fame's unreliability and history's uncertainty; see esp. his discussion of Virgil's and Ovid's accounts in relation to Chaucer's in the *House of Fame* (*Chaucer and Ovid,* 30–41).

17. According to Edgar F. Shannon, removing the gods is consistent with Chaucer's usual practice when he retells classical tales (*Chaucer and the Roman Poets* [Cambridge, Mass.: Harvard Univ. Press, 1929], 203).

18. Lee Patterson characterizes the scene in the *Confessions* in which Augustine pictures himself as weeping for Dido but remaining unmoved by the death of his own soul as the *locus classicus* for medieval depictions of texts seducing their readers (" 'For the Wyves Love of Bathe': Feminine Rhetoric and Poetic Resolution in the *Roman de la Rose* and the *Canterbury Tales," Speculum* 58 [1983]: 660).

19. *Aeneid* 4.172.

20. Even if we accept Kelly's contention that Chaucer's audience would

have recognized in the events in the cave a clandestine marriage—betrothal plus consummation constituting marriage—as Dante apparently did (*Love and Marriage*, 210–11; *De monarchia* 2.3.15), Dido's words still reveal how shameful she regards such a marriage to be. In this context, her insistence that she is a "gentil woman and a quene" only remind us that contracting marriage in such a fashion is behaving commonly.

21. Chaucer used mainly Guido's *Historia* (see n.27, below) and Ovid's *Heroides* 6 (Hypsipyle's epistle) and 12 (Medea's). Though Chaucer refers the reader to the *Argonautica* of Valerius Flaccus, he made virtually no use of it (see Shannon, *Chaucer and the Roman Poets*, 211–14, 344–48). To take Chaucer's advice to read the *Argonautica* is to recognize once again how selectively the Prologue requires him to translate.

22. Chaucer's source for this is *Heroides* 6.151–64, except that he substitutes a concrete reference to Medea's murder for a general imprecation that she may lose her children, a change that emphasizes the inappropriateness of the narrator's stance.

23. Frank, *Chaucer and the Legend*, 87. Frank discusses several characteristics that deprive Jason of any stature.

24. On the *Aeneid* as a possible source, see Shannon, *Chaucer and the Roman Poets*, 213–14.

25. On the reduction of Hercules, see Frank, *Chaucer and the Legend*, 89. Shannon observes that in the *Argonautica* Hercules does not come ashore and suggests as a model "the part Achates plays to Aeneas on the occasion of their reception by Dido" (*Chaucer and the Roman Poets*, 213). Closer to home is Pandarus's selling of the "speechless" Troilus, to which this is an abbreviated and cynical analogue.

26. Chaucer's primary source, Guido's *Historia*, is strongly antifeminist in its treatment of Medea; indeed, Frank's characterization of Guido's Medea as "not so much martyr as monster in love" is apt (*Chaucer and the Legend*, 84). Guido's sorceress descends, of course, from the Medea of Ovid's *Metamorphoses* 7.

27. Guido de Columnis, *Historia destructionis Troiae*, ed. Nathaniel E. Griffin (Cambridge, Mass.: Mediaeval Academy of America, 1936), 2.17.

28. See Paull F. Baum's accurate observation that "Jason, bad as he was, was in these two affairs more pursued than sinning" ("Chaucer's 'Glorious Legende,' " *MLN* 60 [1945]: 379).

29. In condensing Guido's depiction of Jason and Medea coming to terms, Chaucer has fundamentally altered it. Guido has Medea advise Jason to give up the quest because it will prove fatal, Jason insist that he intends to try anyway, and Medea then promise to save him in return for a promise of marriage (*Historia* 2.19–22). Chaucer has Medea warn Jason that the quest is impossible without her assistance but immediately assert her willingness to help. Jason thanks her, promises to be her "man," beseeches her aid, and only then declares, "But, certes, for my deth shal I nat spare" (1628). Kelly is certainly right that Chaucer pictures Jason and Medea as marrying (*Love and Marriage*, 203–6). But it seems equally clear that Chaucer's handling of the betrothal and marriage shows its extreme "folhaste": he tells us they agreed to marry and set the time for that same night. So much for the banns.

30. The exaggerated rhetoric of the opening has often been noted. Baum calls it "pompous" ("Chaucer's 'Glorious Legende,' " 378); Preston says Chaucer here is "dramatizing his own antics" (*Chaucer*, 138); Frank stresses the way such exaggeration diminishes Jason (*Chaucer and the Legend*, 85–86).

31. See Kiser's observation (*Telling Classical Tales*, 114) that "it would not be far from the truth to say that Chaucer's role as 'misrepresenter' in the legendary is much like that of the deceitful Jason," an observation whose truth I have sought to substantiate by demonstrating how systematically Chaucer draws the parallel.

32. Medea's lament over her lack of "honeste" appears to derive from Filippo's translation of the *Heroides* rather than from the Latin; see Sanford Brown Meech, "Chaucer and an Italian Translation of the *Heroides*," *PMLA* 45 (1930): 115.

33. *Roman de la rose*, vv. 7097–7100. Raison distinguishes her naming of things properly, which is simultaneously according to her desires and according to their natures, from the practice of French ladies who, when they name things according to their desires, name them metaphorically. An important source of her discussion is Isidore of Seville's distinction between names given "secundum placitum," by convention, according to the pleasure of the namer, and those assigned "secundum naturam," according to the essential quality of the thing named (see *Etymologiae* 1.29.2, in *PL* 82.105). For Isidore, a name was imposed according to the nature of a thing when its supposed etymological meaning characterized the thing named (see

1.29.3; on Isidore's concept of etymologies, see J. Engels, "La portée de l'étymologie isidorienne," *Studi medievali* 3 [1962]: 99–128). Behind Isidore's discussion lies a long classical debate as to whether names in particular and language in general are conventional or natural. In having Raison in effect lay claim to assigning names in two ways normally regarded as antithetical, Jean is characterizing Raison, whose pleasure it is to assign names according to a rational consideration of the nature of the object named.

34. On the possibility of knowing and naming God, see, e.g., the question "utrum aliquod nomen dicatur de Deo proprie" (St. Thomas Aquinas, *Summa theologiae* 1a, q. 13, a. 3; names of perfections are used properly only of God, who is alone perfect, but not in their mode of signifying: that is, not in signifying through man's imperfect ideas of these perfections).

35. Though Chaucer attributes the idea to Plato (*Timaeus* 29B), his immediate source was no doubt Boethius's *Consolation* 3, pr. 12. The expression was a commonplace; see, e.g., the *Roman de la Rose,* vv. 15158–62; and Alain de Lille's *De planctu* 8, pr. 4 (*The Plaint of Nature,* 144). On its implications for the medieval conception of rhetoric and poetry, see Jeffrey A. Hirshberg, " 'Cosyn to the Dede': *The Canterbury Tales* and the Platonic Tradition in Medieval Rhetoric" (Ph.D. diss., Univ. of Wisconsin, 1977), 20–33.

36. Chaucer's treatment of this theme—in the "Wife of Bath's Tale" and in "Gentilesse"—draws upon both the *Roman de la rose* (vv. 6549–62, 18577–866) and Dante's *Convivio* 4. On this commonplace, see Robinson, *Works,* 704, n. to line 1109; and Ernest Robert Curtius, *European Literature and the Latin Middle Ages,* trans. Willard R. Trask (London: Routledge & Kegan Paul, 1953), 179–80.

37. John of Salisbury, *Policraticus* 8.17.788; see Isidore, *Etymologiae* 9.3.4, in *PL* 82.342.

38. For John's definition of a tyrant as "one who oppresses the people," see *Policraticus* 8.17.777d; for private as well as public tyrants, see 8.17.778b.

39. Gower, *Confessio* 7.4899, 5118.

40. Kiser, *Telling Classical Tales,* 107.

41. Both the fainting and the narrator's literal explanation of its consequences—"She feleth no thyng, neyther foul ne fayr" (1818)—are additions by Chaucer. Gower represents her as swooning (*Confessio* 7.4986–87) but makes no mention of Tarquin's use of threats of dis-

grace to force her submission. Both Chaucer's cited sources, Ovid (*Fasti* 2.810) and Livy (*Historia* 1.58), do attribute her submission to her fear of shame. For the possibility that Chaucer used only Ovid, see Shannon, *Chaucer and the Roman Poets,* 221–23.

42. Ovid's Lucretia denies herself the pardon her father and husband grant her as one forced (*Fasti* 2.830); Livy's Lucretia absolves herself of the sin but not of the punishment, declaring that no unchaste woman shall live hereafter by her example (*Historia* 1.58). In neither does she show the scorn for forgiveness evident in Chaucer.

43. Gower, *Confessio* 7, 5060–64.

44. St. Augustine, *The City of God* 1.19. Chaucer's association of Lucrece's great love of her good name with her Romanness (in his explanation of her fainting) seems to derive in general from Augustine's treatment of her and particularly from his explanation of her suicide: "Et Romana mulier, laudis avida nimium, verita est ne putaretur, quod violenter est passa cum viveret, libenter passa si viveret" (And the Roman wife, too eager for praise, feared that she might be thought, if she lived, to have suffered willingly what she forcedly endured while she lived).

45. See *The City of God* 1.18–19. Arguing that Chaucer was aware of the moral problem Augustine discusses—namely, that extenuating Lucretia's self-murder strengthens the charge of adultery; acquitting her of adultery confirms the homicide—Preston concludes that Chaucer "therefore looks for something small to admire" (*Chaucer,* 139–40). Ultimately, Augustine is ready to concede her purity that he may indict her for pride in her suicide. Chaucer's insistence on her innocence by having her faint and his association of both the fainting and the suicide with Lucrece's preoccupation with her good name seem calculated to force one to look not for something small to admire but to Augustine's conclusion, a conclusion confirmed by the pride evident in her scorn for forgiveness.

46. Ovid's term is *honestas,* which intimates something of the complexity of her motivation (*Fasti* 2.833–34).

47. Though the idea that Lucrece was a saint whose day was hallowed may have been suggested by the fact that Ovid tells her story in association with the particular day commemorated as "Fuga Tarquinii Superbi" (see Walter W. Skeat, ed., *The Complete Works of Geoffrey Chaucer,* vol. 3 [Oxford: Clarendon, 1894], 33, n. to line 1871), Chaucer's emphasis on her sanctity according to "hir law" may well be

indebted to Augustine's contrast of Lucrece's love of her good name and the true saint's love of virtue.

48. On the term "foreyne," see Frank, *Chaucer and the Legend,* 115–17.

49. Garrett, "Cleopatra the Martyr," 70; Preston, *Chaucer,* 141.

50. In addition to using as sources Ovid's *Metamorphoses* 8.6–182 and *Heroides* 10, Chaucer appears to have drawn from the *Ovide moralisé.* Its mention of Phaedra along with Ariadne at roughly this point in the narrative may well have inspired her inclusion in Chaucer's narrative; certain details in her speech seemingly derive from the *Ovide,* though there they are assigned to Ariadne. See Sanford Brown Meech, "Chaucer and the *Ovide moralisé*—A Further Story," *PMLA* 46 (1931): 196; and the *Ovide moralisé,* ed. C. DeBoer, in *Verhandelingen der Koninklijke Akademie van Wetenschappen* 30 (1931): 8, vv. 1144–1249, 1310–20. Providing Theseus with two "saviors" is yet another way of showing the absurdity of the credo that any lady's help merits a response of undying passion; to do so, Chaucer had to modify his source, silently making it *less* compatible with the Prologue's demands.

51. Shannon (*Chaucer and the Roman Poets,* 250) thinks the idea of marrying Phaedra to Hippolytus comes from Boccaccio, *De geneologia deorum* 9.29. Meech attributes it to Filippo's translation of the *Heroides* ("Chaucer and an Italian Translation of the *Heroides,*" 117). Whatever its source—perhaps Chaucer's knowledge of Phaedra's own story—the comic improbabilities of the suggestion seem unlikely to have escaped Chaucer; the *Ovide moralisé* (8, vv. 1131–34) indicates that Phaedra is the older of the two sisters.

52. Skeat, *Complete Works of Chaucer,* vol. 3, 338, n. to line 2099.

53. Ariadne's suggestion that Theseus should marry her is from the *Ovide moralisé* 8, vv. 1298–1303.

54. Ariadne's assertion that gentle women always help gentle men seemingly derives from Medea's justification of her aid to Jason in Guido's *Historia* 2.19: "Dignum est equidem ut extraneo nobili et negotioso salutis consilium tribuatur a nobili. Nam prodesse nobilis nobili et quadam mutua urbanitate tenetur" (It is proper that a noble give counsel of safety to a busy foreigner of noble blood, for nobles are bound to help nobles out of a mutual urbanity).

55. See *Metamorphoses* 8.95–103; *Ovide moralisé* 8, vv. 232–37. It is perhaps noteworthy that Guido da Pisa, a fourteenth-century commentator on Dante's *Inferno,* justifies Dante's use of Minos as judge in

Hell on the basis of his justice in dealing with Scylla (*Espositiones et glosae super Comediam Dantis,* ed. Vincenzo Cioffari [Albany, N.Y.: State Univ. of New York Press, 1974], 100).

56. Robinson, *Works,* 852, n. to lines 2223–24.

57. Fyler, *Chaucer and Ovid,* 103; see also Frank's characterization of her as "naive" yet "calculating" (*Chaucer and the Legend,* 128).

58. Fisher supposes "the first hevene" to be a reference to the "outermost sphere," that of Saturn (*Poetry and Prose of Chaucer,* 657, n. to line 2236; 539, n. to *Troilus* 5.1809), thus making there the eighth sphere the innermost. But the reference here must be to the sphere of the moon, since all above the moon was regarded as incorruptible (further evidence that the eighth sphere in the *Troilus* is that of the fixed stars).

59. Though Chaucer's primary source was Ovid's *Metamorphoses* 6.424–674, he apparently also used Chrétien's *Philomela,* a work incorporated into the *Ovide moralisé.* See J. L. Lowes, "Chaucer and the *Ovide moralisé,*" *PMLA* 33 (1918): 303–19.

60. By having Tereus twice ask for his son and Procne twice answer ironically that he will soon be there, Chrétien heightens the sense of "pleasure" taken in the vengeance. See *Philomela: Conte reconte d'apres Ovide,* ed. C. De Boer (Paris, 1909), vv. 1304–1409.

61. Ovid characterizes Procne's request as "blandita" (*Metamorphoses* 6.440).

62. In Chaucer, Pandion's emotions lack the justifying motive they have in Ovid, a premonition of disaster. In asserting "no malice he ne thoughte" (2307), Chaucer is perhaps following Chrétien rather than Ovid, as Lowes contends ("Chaucer and the *Ovide moralisé,*" 310–11; Chrétien, *Philomela,* vv. 725–27). But since the same line occurs in the "Legend of Lucrece," perhaps his purpose is to draw an additional parallel between Tereus and Tarquin.

63. See Frank, *Chaucer and the Legend,* 189–210.

64. Eleanor Winsor Leach notes that Chaucer tells the story twice: see "A Study in the Sources and Rhetoric of Chaucer's Legend of Good Women" (Ph.D. diss., Yale University, 1963), 200, cited in Fyler, *Chaucer and Ovid,* 110.

65. Fyler (*Chaucer and Ovid,* 102) notes that this partial suppression of the other murders deprives Hypermnestra of her singularity and thus her virtue of much of its impact.

IV. THE ORDER OF JUSTICE

1. On the order of the cosmos as contraries harmonized, see Spitzer, "Classical and Christian Concepts of World Harmony"; and Donald W. Rowe, *O Love, O Charite,* 7–39. The emphasis in the *Legend* on the order of Nature as cyclical alternation of contraries derives particularly from the *Consolation* (see esp. 3, m. 2, and 4, pr. 6 and m. 6) and more generally from its twelfth- and thirteenth-century descendants, such as the *Cosmographia,* the *De planctu,* the *Roman.*

2. On man's division of the good, see the *Consolation* 3, pr. 9; on the universal desire for the unity inherent in the good, see 3, pr. 11. Mention should be made of Chaucer's depiction of the relationship of the many to the one in Theseus's speech on the "Firste Moevere" in the "Knight's Tale" (*CTI,* 2987–3040).

3. As tragedies attributed to Fortune's turning wheel, the legends recall Boccaccio's *De casibus virorum illustrium* and his *De claris mulieribus.* Either of these or both may have been sources for the "Legend of Cleopatra" (Shannon, *Chaucer and the Roman Poets,* 181–90). Both undoubtedly did contribute to Chaucer's other work in the *de casibus* tradition, the "Monk's Tale"; see Robert K. Root's discussion in *Sources and Analogues of Chaucer's Canterbury Tales,* ed. W. F. Bryan and Germaine Dempster (London: Routledge & Kegan Paul, 1941), 615–44.

4. See the image Boethius constructs of the good as the providential center of creation, Fate as the agency which orders all that moves about this center. The further the mind moves from the center, the more it submits to Fate. Loving the partial goods is a movement away from the center. See the *Consolation* 4, pr. 6, and the analogous idea in the *Commedia,* where Dante's movement through ever widening and more rapidly circling spheres is simultaneously a movement toward the still center, revealing that Satan, frozen in the ice in the center of Hell, is that point in the cosmos furthest from the love and freedom that constitute its true center.

5. Boethius enumerates possessions (by which one seeks sufficiency), pleasure, power, fame, and honors (high office and reverence) as the false goods. On the inclusion of love as one of Fortune's gifts, see H. R. Patch, *The Goddess Fortuna in Mediaeval Literature* (Cambridge, Mass.: Harvard Univ. Press, 1927), 90–98.

6. Compare Chaucer's depiction of Pandarus in the *Troilus* as a perverse

Lady Philosophy (see Alan T. Gaylord, "Uncle Pandarus as Lady Philosophy," *PMASAL* 46 [1961]: 571–95; and John P. McCall, "Five-Book Structure in Chaucer's *Troilus*," *MLQ* 23 [1962]: 297–302) and the analogy created there between Pandarus and the narrator (Rowe, *O Love, O Charite*, 153).

7. Compare Chaucer's similar association of the circular course of Troilus's tragic love of Criseyde with the turning day and year (Henry W. Sams, "The Dual Time-Scheme in Chaucer's *Troilus*," *MLN* 61 [1941]: 94–100).

8. This association is reproduced from Ovid's *Metamorphoses*.

9. See Rowe, *O Love, O Charite*, 93–95.

10. Chaucer has only increased the prominence of the similar references to day and night in Ovid's *Fasti* 2.721ff.

11. The narrator's description of the event gives Theseus the active role (see 2150–56), but Phaedra's original plan was for him to flee, accompanied by his jailor; Ariadne determined that she and Phaedra should join them.

12. On the two motions of the soul, see Rowe, *O Love, O Charite*, 25–28. For a discussion of the imagination in literary contexts relevant to Chaucer, see Wetherbee's observations on *ingenium* in *Platonism and Poetry*, 94–98, and his "Theme of Imagination in Medieval Poetry."

13. See Aristotle, *Metaphysics* 1072b; with reference to Dante (in addition to Patch, "The Last Line of the *Commedia*," and Dronke, "L'amor che move il sole"), see Francis Fergusson, *Dante* (London: Weidenfeld & Nicolson, 1966), 102, 104–7, 166–70, 193–95.

14. See the *Cosmographia* 1.1; Wetherbee, 67–69. Also noteworthy is Alain de Lille's use of Nature to initiate the creation of a new man in *Anticlaudianus*, ed. Robert Bossaut (Paris: J. Vrin, 1955), 1.1.

15. Wetherbee, trans., *Cosmographia*, 38.

16. In his commentary on the *Consolation*, Nicholas Trivet explains that while the man pursuing false goods "recedes, with reference to the end, from the order of the divine will in one way, he nevertheless falls into the order of the divine will in another; for in leaving the order of mercy, he falls into the order of justice." London, BL, MS. Burney 131, fol. 47v, translated in D. W. Robertson, *Preface to Chaucer* (Princeton, N.J.: Princeton Univ. Press, 1962), 26–27.

17. Kiser, *Telling Classical Tales*, 107–9.

18. For the suggestion that Chaucer is here echoing *Purg.* 22, see Coolidge Otis Chapman, "Dante and Chaucer," *Times Literary Supplement*, Aug. 29, 1952, p. 565.

19. Medieval commentators merely identify Virgil as Reason. Contemporary commentators stress the reality of the literal level, that Virgil is first and last Virgil, but this changes not so much his significance as the way he signifies. Rather than being a "figure" for reason, analogous to a personification, now he exemplifies the class of ancients of which he is the outstanding member: philosophical poets. On the traditional understanding of Virgil, see Robert Hollander (whose criticism is itself a quarrel with this traditional way of reading Dante), *Allegory in Dante's Commedia* (Princeton, N.J.: Princeton Univ. Press, 1969), 19.

20. The most recent examination of their similarities is by John Fisher, who regards them as so much of a kind that he imagines them the consequence of the same royal command (see *John Gower*, 236–50; for enumerations of their similarities, see pp. 240–41).

21. Kiser, *Telling Classical Tales*, 108–9.

22. In the Prologue, the lion is a figure for a ruler who knows how to govern with justice and mercy.

23. If the description of Cleopatra as "naked" adds to the impact of her suicide, it also recalls Dante's repeated characterization of the shades of the damned as "ignudi." The term "pit" also underscores the infernal associations of her snake-filled grave (see *Oxford English Dictionary*, def. 4). Snakes are, of course, among the most commonly depicted horrors and punishments of hell.

24. For all the romanticism here, this is analogous to the "Friar's Tale," where the fiend (in the guise of a yeoman) promises the summoner, "If that thee happe to comen in oure shire, / Al shal be thyn, right as thou wolt desire" (*CT* III, 1401–2), and no amount of revelation about the character of "oure shire" can dissuade the summoner from keeping his truth (that he may fulfill his desire).

25. Dante is confusing, or perhaps conflating, Assyrian Babylonia with the Babylon of Egypt. Chaucer applied Dante's assertion that Semiramis made love licit to Nero in the "Monk's Tale," as Singleton notes (*Inf.*, pt. 2 [Commentary], 78, n. to 52–60).

26. Lowes, "Is Chaucer's *Legend* a Travesty?" 558–64.

27. On the associations of Babylon, see D. W. Robertson, Jr., and Bernard F. Huppé, *Piers Plowman and the Scriptural Tradition* (Princeton, N.J.: Princeton Univ. Press, 1951), 14.

28. Singleton observes (*Inf.*, pt. 2 [Commentary], 91, n. to 104) that "piacer" corresponds to "bella persona" and that it often means "charm," "attraction": as he falls in love with "the beautiful Francesca," she falls

in love with "the handsome Paolo." John D. Sinclair translates "with his charm" (*Dante's Inferno* [New York: Oxford Univ. Press, 1939], 77).

29. See the analogous justification provided for Antony and Cleopatra: his conviction that nothing is "so due" to him as loving and serving her, her reciprocal love of him for his "desert" and "chyvalrye."

30. Singleton observes the simultaneous presence of two perspectives in the Paolo and Francesca episode, as in the whole of the *Inferno:* the human and the divine (*Inf.*, pt. 2 [Commentary], 92, n. to 109).

31. *Metamorphoses* 4.152–53. Perhaps Chaucer's translation only reflects his understanding of the Latin, for though the parallelism encourages one to translate "poteris nec moret revelli" as "you will not be able to be separated [from me] by death," as do all modern translations of which I am aware, the Latin can be construed to mean "you will not be able to be separated from death."

32. One notes Chaucer's omission of the ameliorating metamorphosis of the mulberry tree. Lovers being punished together are common in medieval accounts and representations of hell. For the literary tradition, apparently deriving from the *Apocalypse of Peter* and continued in the *Vision of St. Paul,* in *St. Patrick's Purgatory,* and in the *Vision of Alberic,* see E. J. Becker, *A Contribution to the Comparative Study of the Mediaeval Visions of Heaven and Hell* (Baltimore, Md.: John Murphy, 1899; rpr., 1976), 39–42. For an iconographically striking, but ideologically typical pictorial representation of lovers being punished through eternal togetherness, see the miniature depicting two lovers bound together and roasting on a spit from a fifteenth-century MS of Augustine's *City of God* in the Bibliothèque Ste. Geneviève in Paris (Robert Hughes, *Heaven and Hell in Western Art* [London: Weidenfeld and Nicolson, 1968], 210). Compare Dido, simultaneously impaling herself on a sword and throwing herself on her funeral pyre.

33. *Metamorphosis* 4.63.

34. Gower lists "folhaste" as one of the subdivisions of the sin of Wrath and tells the story of Pyramus and Thisbe to illustrate it because of their impetuous suicides. Amant confesses to a similar will because he has often wished himself dead (*Confessio* 3.1503–15). The immediate association between Chaucer's narrator and his hero and heroine is with their concupiscible, rather than their irascible, impetuosity.

35. Observing that in the *Argonautica* Hercules does not go ashore, Shan-

non suggests that his role here may have been modeled on that of Achates in the *Aeneid* (*Chaucer and the Roman Poets*, 213—14).

36. We should note that Oetes plays the same role in the Medea half of the legend, as he makes his daughter "don to Jason companye." Though Chaucer removes Guido's rebuke of Oetes for being so foolish as to place an inconstant woman beside a heroic stranger (*Historia* 2.17), the parallel between the roles of Hercules and Oetes constitutes an implicit rebuke. Cf. the role played by Colatyn in the "Legend of Lucrece."

37. Jason's noble appearance and graciousness of speech establish no debt to Dante, as these shared features derive from Ovid, esp. *Heroides* 12.

38. Frank observes, "The exposition involving Pelleas' plot against Jason is too long for the tale of which it is a part. It gives us another false man, but it contributes almost nothing to either the theme of the false lover or the theme of woman betrayed" (*Chaucer and the Legend*, 91).

39. Chaucer's immediate source for Medea's enchantments is Guido's *Historia,* in which he denounces her as a sorceress even as he denies that she could have accomplished all the feats of magic Ovid attributed to her (2.15—16). Gower tells Jason's and Medea's story (*Confessio* 5.3247—4229) to exemplify in Jason's false vows of love the sin of perjury. He does accuse Medea of beguiling her father, and he includes an account of her magical rejuvenation of Jason's father but apparently only "for the novellerie" of it. This story follows an account of the love of Achilles and Deidamia, told to illustrate the sin of false witness. Genius concludes it by asking how women can expect to find safety against lying men when they betray one another, as Thetis did Deidamia. One is reminded of Hypsipyle's conviction that she was betrayed by Medea.

40. Gower tells the story to illustrate the effects of lechery upon kingship. Rather than paying heed to the justice that belongs to the office of king, the Tarquins pursued "the fleisshes lust" with "tresoun" and "tirannie." Gower repeatedly characterizes the younger Tarquin and his behavior as tyrannical (see, e.g., *Confessio* 7.4601, 4659, 4889, 4899).

41. John of Salisbury, *Policraticus* 8.17.778a; *The Statesman's Book*, 335—36. A pictorial representation of tyranny as a diabolical horned figure is Lorenzetti's mid-fourteenth-century *Good and Bad Government* in the Palazzo Communale in Siena; on the iconography of this picture,

see Nicolai Rubinstein, "Political Ideas in Sienese Art," *Journal of the Warburg and Courtauld Institutes* 21 (1958): 179–89.

42. This dual emphasis derives from Ovid's *Fasti* 2.763–67, 771–74.

43. Compare the philosophical commonplace that evil men desire the good but are powerless to attain it (e.g., Boethius, *Consolation* 4, pr. 2). For a discussion of the medieval psychology of the tyrant, see J. D. Burnley, *Chaucer's Language and the Philosophers' Tradition* (Cambridge: D. S. Brewer, Rowman, and Littlefield, 1979), 11–28. The denunciation Gower assigns to the Romans in his version of Lucretia's story, "Awey, awey the tirannie / Of lecherie and covoitise," is seemingly directed both at the power of such passions to enslave and at the tyrannical behavior that results from them (*Confessio* 7.5118–19).

44. Gower similarly locates her motivation for suicide in her determination that "nevere afterward the world ne shal / Reproeven hire" (*Confessio* 7.5063–64), though his language hardly captures her disdain as well as Chaucer's does.

45. *Confessio* 5.5231–5493, 5551–6052.

46. Kiser, *Telling Classical Tales,* 115.

47. See *Inf.* 5.4–15; Singleton points out that Dante's conception of Minos is an adaptation of Virgil's in *Aeneid* 4.432–33 (*Inf.*, pt. 2 [Commentary], 74, n. to 4).

48. Shannon and Frank suppose that the opening reference to retribution applies to Theseus (*Chaucer and the Roman Poets,* 230; *Chaucer and the Legend,* 131); Robinson supposes that it applies to Minos (*Works,* 851, n. to line 1891).

49. Darkness ("defaute" both of "light material" and of "the sighte of God"; see the "Parson's Tale," *CT* X, 182–83) and stench are, of course, standard features of hell. Its stench is associated with both brimstone and excrement; in connection with the latter, we should note the Summoner's account of the eternal "heritage" of Friars (*CT* III, 1689–1706) and the numerous artistic representations of Satan defecating sinners.

50. Medieval representations of hell are full of analogous imagery; e.g., Francesco Triani's *Last Judgment* depicts Satan, with human form and the head of a bull, in the process of defecating a sinner. The image is conveniently reproduced in *The Tales of Canterbury,* ed. Robert A. Pratt (Boston: Houghton Mifflin, 1974), 296.

51. For the Furies, see *Inf.* 9.36–54, and the proems to Books 1 and 4 of

the *Troilus;* for the owl in the Proserpina story, see Ovid's *Metamorphoses* 5.538–50, and Chaucer's reference to "Escaphilo" in *Troilus* 5, 316–22. Reference both to the Furies and the owl are in Ovid's account of the wedding, we should note (*Metamorphoses* 6.428–34).

52. Though Lowes takes this assertion that Pandion suspected no malice as evidence that Chaucer was following Chrétien's Philomena ("Chaucer and the *Ovide Moralisé*," 310–11), the verbal similarity is with the "Legend of Lucrece." The *Philomena* (727) merely tells us that he weeps and has cause, since she will never return, "mes de tot ce ne panse il" (but of all this he does not think).

53. M. Bech long ago suggested that Chaucer's description of the storm may have derived from the *Aeneid* (see 1.85–90, 102, 142) and that line 2422 translates *Aeneid* 5.823–24 ("Quellen und Plan der 'Legende of Goode Women' und hir Verhältniss zur 'Confessio Amantis,' " *Anglia* 5 [1882]: 344–45).

54. See Bernardus Silvester, *Commentum super sex libros* 4.25.18–21, and 5.26.2–3; on this, see Wetherbee, *Platonism and Poetry*, 102–10. Also of interest is Bernardus's interpretation of Aeneas's descent into Hades as a *descensus ad inferos*, that is, as an *integumentum* for the mind's contemplation of earthly things in pursuit of wisdom (see 6.28–30).

55. Fyler, *Chaucer and Ovid*, 107; Kiser, *Telling Classical Tales*, 110.

56. Dante depicts those lacking all conviction as scorned by both justice and mercy, we should note: "misericordia e giustizia li sdegna" (Inf. 3.50). Singleton compares them to the Laodiceans (*Inf.*, pt. 2 [Commentary], 45–46, n. to 41–42).

57. Besides the *Consolation*'s interpretation of Orpheus's descent, see Bernardus Silvester's interpretation of Aeneas's descent into hell as a virtuous one, undertaken that he might come to a knowledge of the creator *"per creaturarum cognitionem"* (*Commentum super sex libros* 6.30), a passage seemingly derived in turn from William of Conches's commentary on Boethius's version of Orpheus's descent (see Jeauneau, "La notion d'*integumentum*," 40–43).

58. "Si vero accipiatur opus allegorice, subiectum est homo prout merendo et demerendo per arbitrii libertatem iustitie premiandi et puniendi obnoxius est" (Epistole 13.25, ed. Ermenegildo Pistelli, in *Le opere di Dante*, ed. M. Barbi et al., 2d ed. [Florence: The Society, 1960], 405). I quote Dorothy Sayers's translation in *The Comedy of Dante Alighieri*, vol. 1 (Baltimore: Penguin Books, 1949), 15. For a brief re-

view of the modern quarrel as to the letter's authenticity, see Hollander, *Allegory*, 40–41 n.28.

59. The unacknowledged borrowings in the *Troilus* often seem to have been selected and employed with their function and significance in the *Commedia* in mind, as when Chaucer opens the second book of the *Troilus*—which is intermediate between the "hell" of the first and the "heaven" of the third—with the lines that open Dante's *Purgatorio*. Chaucer may have accommodated his art to his reader's interests and information, but he clearly did not let their limitations determine his intention.

60. Both the principle of *contrapasso* and most of the particular punishments depicted in the *Inferno* were anticipated in the literature recounting visions of hell; besides Becker, *Mediaeval Visions of Heaven and Hell,* see Arnold Barel Van Os, *Religious Visions: The Development of the Eschatological Elements in Mediaeval English Religious Literature* (Amsterdam: H. J. Paris, 1932); and D. D. R. Owen, *The Vision of Hell: Infernal Journeys in Medieval French Literature* (New York: Barnes & Noble, 1971).

V. THE CONCLUSION OF THE LEGENDS

1. It is not clear that the nineteen ladies include Alceste: Chaucer pictures the god of Love and Alceste walking hand in hand and then observes that the god was followed by nineteen ladies, who are followed in turn by a huge "traas." The supposition that Alceste is to be counted among the nineteen derives from the fact that she is compared to eighteen ladies (and two men) in the accompanying *balade*. The further assumption that Chaucer intended nineteen legends (based on the appearance of that number in the Prologues and in three manuscripts of the Retraction) is reasonable only if the nineteen ladies of the *balade* were intended to be the nineteen heroines of the legends; however, the legends of Philomela and Medea, neither of whom is mentioned in the *balade*, invalidate this assumption.

2. Skeat, *Complete Works of Chaucer,* vol. 3, 351, n. to line 2723; Robinson, *Works,* 854, n. to line 2723. The term "application" is Robinson's.

3. See *A Parallel-Text Edition of Chaucer's Minor Poems,* ed. F. J. Furnivall, Chaucer Soc., 1st Ser. 58 (London: N. Trübner, 1879), 405.

4. William L. Sullivan, "Chaucer's Man of Law as a Literary Critic,"

MLN 68 (1953): 1–8; see also Alfred David, "The Man of Law vs. Chaucer: A Case in Poetics," *PMLA* 82 (1967): 219–21.

5. Viewing the Man of Law's prologue as a response to Gower's admonition to Chaucer to finish his "Testament of Love," Fisher (*John Gower*, 288) argues that the Man of Law's insistence that Chaucer has told all the stories there are to tell of that kind is Chaucer's way of saying he is through with the *Legend*. He is not, of course, claiming the *Legend* complete.

6. For a discussion of the Retraction reading in the light of the Manly-Rickert data (J. M. Manly and Edith Rickert, *The Text of the Canterbury Tales* [Chicago, Univ. of Chicago Press, 1940]), see Eleanor P. Hammond, "Chaucer's 'Book of the Twenty-five Ladies,'" *MLN* 48 (1933): 514–16.

7. On the MS readings, see Manly and Rickert, *The Text*, vol. 4, 477; and vol. 8, 546, n. to line 1086.

8. Robinson credits two MSS with the reading "xv;" Manly and Rickert claim that the reading in BL, MS. Lansdowne 851, is "xxv," with the "second x partly lost in [the] crease" (*The Text*, vol. 8, 546).

9. Donald R. Howard, *The Idea of the Canterbury Tales* (Berkeley, Univ. of Calif. Press, 1976), 1–2, 27–30, and passim; Northrup Frye, "The Structure of Imagery in the *Faerie Queene*," in *Fables of Identity: Studies in Poetic Mythology* (New York: Harcourt, Brace & World, 1963), 69.

10. Katherine S. Gittes, "The *Canterbury Tales* and the Arabic Frame Tradition," *PMLA* 98 (1983): 246.

11. Howard himself argues that the poem is "unfinished" because its complete idea "created a literary form . . . whose possibilities were unexhaustible" (*The Idea*, 385). Thus, though he makes no reference to Arabic frame tales, he does anticipate Gittes's stress on its open form.

12. On Harry's plan as Harry's, see Howard, *The Idea*, 28. The observation was perhaps first made by Goddard, "Chaucer's *Legend*" (1909), 88, n.1.

13. Goddard, "Chaucer's *Legend*" (1909), 87–88.

14. There is uncertainty as to the ending Chaucer ultimately intended for the "Monk's Tale." In about a third of the MSS—including those usually regarded as the most authoritative—the four tragedies of Chaucer's contemporaries, which are usually situated between Cenobia and Nero, are located at the end. Manly and Rickert adopt the

order that places Croesus last partly because it gives the necessary prominence to the Host's echo of the Croesus tragedy in the Nun's Priest's prologue, partly because its final lines seem to provide an ending for the series as a whole (see *The Text,* vol. 2, 410; vol. 4, 508, 511). For an argument in favor of placing the modern instances last—one based on the assumption that the Knight's sorrowful response to the Monk's tragedies is more appropriate when the account of the tragedy of Peter of Cyprus, with whom he presumably served, is more proximate—see Donald K. Fry, "The Ending of the Monk's Tale," *JEGP* 71 (1972): 355–68. Since the MSS that place the modern instances last are those that contain the apparently revised forms of lines 2378 and 2426, it seems likely either that they are accidentally out of order as a consequence of this rewriting or that a new order of the tales was a third revision Chaucer made at that time.

15. That the idea of tragedy enunciated in the final lines of the Croesus story does not in fact fit all the antecedent tragedies very well is widely recognized. This is not evidence that these lines were not intended as a summing up but rather that the Monk's idea of tragedy is inadequate; see Robert E. Kaske, "The Knight's Interruption of the *Monk's Tale,*" *ELH* 24 (1957): 261–64.

16. It is worth remembering that Chaucer has the narrator of the *Troilus* undertake that translation out of compassion for young lovers, "as though I were hire owne brother dere" (*T&C* 1, 51).

17. See, e.g., Vincent Hopper, *Medieval Number Symbolism* (New York: Columbia Univ. Press, 1938), 10–11, 44–45, 101–2.

VI. POETRY AS SECULAR SACRAMENT

1. Patterson, "For the Wyves Love of Bathe," 688–91.

2. In fact, her contempt for forgiveness indicates that her own honor is every bit as much on her mind.

3. Patterson, "For the Wyves Love of Bathe," 691.

4. In the *Commentary* commonly attributed to him (*Commentum super sex libros* 1.12–13), Bernardus interprets the scene in the temple analogously—though (consistent with his reading of the poem as Aeneas's *psychomachia*) with exclusive reference to Aeneas's psychology: it dramatizes (in effect) Aeneas's entrance into consciousness of this life. Aeneas fixing his eyes on the pictures in the temple represents the human spirit first acquiring sense knowledge of the "temporalia

bona," which are called pictures because temporal goods are (as Boethius says) "imagines veri boni." This all takes place in Dido's city because in this world "libido" rules (which is why the Bible calls the world Babylon or confusion). Chaucer shifts the focus to Dido, of course, and reveals that her libidinous response to Aeneas as a temporal good is dictated by culture as well as by biology.

5. One can argue that placing the "Parson's Tale" last privileges it, but one must recognize at the same time that in rejecting fables, the Parson translates himself beyond the philosophical and ethical realm proper to literature to the realm of revealed doctrine. He concludes the *Canterbury Tales* by refusing to tell a "Canterbury tale." It is not first in this kind, but another kind altogether.

6. See Muscatine, *Chaucer and the French Tradition*, 133–61; Sanford B. Meech, *Design in Chaucer's Troilus* (Syracuse, N.Y.: Syracuse Univ. Press, 1959), esp. chap. 3; Payne, *The Key of Remembrance*, 197–216; Rowe, *O Love, O Charite*, 39–56.

7. The use of the expression to characterize a recurrent element in Jean's style has been explicitly criticized by Lionel J. Friedman, who views those effects as moralizing satire ("'Jean de Meung,' Antifeminism, and 'Bourgeois Realism,'" *MP* 57 [1959]: 13–23). In its application to Jean, the terms of the expression have presumably been borrowed from now largely rejected assumptions about the substance and class origins of fabliaux (for a critique of these assumptions, see Per Nykrog, *Les Fabliaux*, 2d ed. [Geneva: Droz, 1973] xxxvii—xlii). Nevertheless, I know no better term than "realism" however anachronistic, to characterize the manner and matter (by no means exclusively satiric and moralizing in intention) that Jean opposes to Guillaume's idealism; and Chaucer, at least, seems to have associated this frame of mind with the lower bourgeois—witness the narrators in the *Canterbury Tales* to whom he assigns an analogous style and substance. (The exception, the "Merchant's Tale," systematically violates decorum.)

8. As a reading of Ovid's *Heroides*, the legends seem more in tune with Ovid's intention than do traditional medieval moralizations, to say nothing of many contemporaneous and subsequent romanticizations.

9. In the *Consolation*, see, e.g., 3, pr. 2, 3; and 3, m. 11 (where Plato's doctrine of reminiscence is appealed to), pr. 12 (where Boethius characterizes himself as having forgotten truth twice: first when he

entered the body, second when he was overcome with grief). For Plato's doctrine, see the *Phaedo* 72–76. Augustine similarly insists that all learning is remembrance, of course, though he substitutes divine illumination, Christ within, for preexistence (see *De magistro* 11–12.38–40).

10. Chenu characterizes the world's dissimilar similitude to its creator, its simultaneous capacity to manifest its maker and to reveal his inimitable superiority, as one of the "laws of symbolism" for the high Middle Ages; he derives this idea in particular from the Pseudo-Dionysius (*Nature, Man, and Society*, 131–33). See, e.g., St. Thomas's assertion that scripture prefers *vilia corpora* to *nobilia corpora* as similitudes for the divinity because we are less likely to read a figurative text literally, because they better remind us of God's transcendence, because divine things are thus better hid from the unworthy (*Summa Theologia* 1a. q.1. a.9; see *De caelestia hierarchia* 2.2, *PL* 3.137–39). To late medieval readers, much of the concept of dissimilar similitude must have seemed implicit in the *Consolation's* treatment of this world's partial goods, which are simultaneously false and an index to the true.

11. I have elected to rely primarily on the *Consolation* to illustrate the theme of the mind's ascent *per creaturas ad creatorem* because of its undeniable relevance to Chaucer's philosophical poetry. As we have seen in exploring the backgrounds to the Alceste-daisy's imitation of the sun and the narrator's imitation of the Alceste-daisy, the romance of the soul's quest to return to the stars accompanies the epic of creation in the philosophical poetry of Bernardus, Alain, and Jean (however ironically), a union of themes made possible not only by the Platonic equation of macrocosm and microcosm but also by the Christian conviction that the work of creation was both a sign and an instrumentality of the work of restoration (as in Hugh of St. Victor's *De sacramentis*). The same theme dominates the spiritual literature of the age as well, as in Bernard's *Steps of Humility* or Bonaventura's *Mind's Journey to God;* the ultimate literary expression of this preoccupation is Dante's *Commedia*.

12. On the twofold motion of the World Soul and its evidence in the motions of the celestial equator and the ecliptic, see the *Consolation* 3, m. 9, 13–17, which derives from Plato's *Timaeus* 34–37. Plato's association of the one with rationality, the other with irrationality, was assumed by Calcidius in *Commentarius* xcv. The human soul is, of

course, similar to the World Soul in this regard (see *Timaeus* 44). As we have seen, medieval commentators on 3, m. 9, usually applied Boethius's characterization of the World Soul to the human soul (see chap. 2, nn. 45, 46). That Boethius's description of the order governing all things as one that unites beginning and end—the order evident, we have seen, in the Alceste-daisy—was understood to apply to the soul's return in rational thought to its creator is clear from Michael Scot's quotation of the ending of 3, m. 2, in illustration and confirmation of John Holywood's representation of rational thought as such a movement (see Scot's commentary on Holywood's *De sphera* in Lynn Thorndyke, ed., *The Sphere of Sacrobosco and Its Commentators* [Chicago: Univ. of Chicago Press, 1949], 302–4). For citations demonstrating that associating human rationality and irrationality with these two celestial motions was a medieval commonplace, see A. B. Chambers, "'Goodfriday, 1613. Riding Westward': The Poem and its Tradition," *JEGP* 60 (1961): 31–53; John Freccero, "Dante's Pilgrim in a Gyre," *PMLA* 76 (1961): 168–81; and Wood, *Chaucer and the Country of the Stars*, 231–34. In characterizing the two motions, I paraphrase John Holywood (*The Sphere of Sacrobosco*, vol. 2, 86).

13. On the infernal descent as a metaphor both for "this life" and for the philosopher's quest to ascend to God through contemplating his traces in creation (esp. with reference to Orpheus and Hercules), see chap. 2, nn. 78, 79. The most detailed discussion of the four descents—the natural, virtuous (i.e., philosophical), vicious, and magical—is Nitzsche's *The Genius Figure*, 42–64. On the relevance of Proserpina, Criseyde, and Troilus to this quest, see Rowe, *O Love, O Charite*, 131–32, 148.

14. Compare Chaucer's similar depiction of the narrator of the *Troilus* as victim and victimizer, as when he has the narrator end Book 3 by characterizing his celebration there of Troilus's good fortune as a song and begin Book 4 by describing Fortune as so entuning her song that she deceives the foolish. The consequence is that we see the narrator as at once Fortune's fool and her instrument.

15. Patterson, "For the Wyves Love of Bathe," 686.

16. One is reminded that, for Boethius, to descend from the stellar activity of contemplating the good is to experience the psychological fragmentation that is the source of the false goods (*Consolation* 3, pr. 9).

17. The goal is that achieved by Dante when Virgil declares his will free

and upright and therefore crowns and miters him (as king and pope) over himself (*Purg.* 27.139–42): i.e., when Dante, restored to himself, regains "the blissful seat."

EXCURSUS: THE TWO PROLOGUES — LOVER OR CLERK

1. Robinson provides a bibliographical survey of the priority debate in his notes to the *Legend* (*Works,* 839). There has been no reconsideration of the question since he completed that survey. For discussion since that review of the reasons for the revision and its effects, see Baker, "Dreamer and Critic," 4–18; Gardner, "The Two Prologues," 594–611; Fisher, "The Revision of the Prologue," 75–84; and Allen, *The Ethical Poetic,* 271–75. George Kane's recent effort to discriminate between authorial and scribal revision in G assumes rather than argues F's priority ("The Text of *The Legend of Good Women* in CUL MS Gg.4.27," in *Middle English Studies Presented to Norman Davis,* ed. Douglas Gray and E. G. Stanley [Oxford: Clarendon, 1983], 39–58); he judges authorial the large block revisions with which this chapter is concerned.

2. Lowes elaborated his thesis in his two extended articles, "*Marguerite* Poems," and "Chronological Relations." His later discussion — "The Two Prologues to the *Legend of Good Women:* A New Test," in *Anniversary Papers* (Boston: Ginn, 1913), 95–104 — is unrelated in argument and seems to have had no special impact. Lowes's most explicit formulation of his own thesis occurs in a lengthy footnote to the second article (pp. 749–51 n.1) in which he responds to John C. French's objections to the argument of the first piece (see *The Problem of the Two Prologues to Chaucer's Legend of Good Women* [Baltimore: J. H. Furst, 1905], 32–38). It should be noted that the two most important texts for Lowes's argument, Deschamps's "Lay de Franchise" and Froissart's *Paradys d'amours,* cannot be regarded as certain sources (see chap. 1, n. 4). There is one respect, and that not mentioned by Lowes, in which F is more like the "Lay" than G, though it hardly proves dependency or priority: the "Lay" begins with a discussion of the pleasures in the custom of honoring May and then describes the narrator's excursion on May Day to maintain the custom; the F Prologue first characterizes the narrator's habitual devotion to the daisy, his behavior every spring, and then describes the events of a particular day.

3. Lowes observes that "florouns" was a rare word in Middle English, especially in the sense of petals; he argues that its use in F, 217 and 220, where G has "floures," was due to F's proximity to Froissart's "Dit de la marguerite," which uses the term (see "Chronological Relations," 676–78). Lowes contends that in revising, Chaucer—no longer under the immediate influence of Froissart—substituted a more common English word. Though the argument as Lowes presents it seems persuasive, the situation is in fact not quite so simple. Froissart does use the term to designate the daisy's petals, but the lines in which he does so are not the source of the lines in question, where it designates the petallike protrusions on Alceste's crown of pearl. At this point in the Prologue, Chaucer was no longer looking at Froissart. It is possible that "florouns" is the revision, the substitution of a more specific term for a less precise one, even as Lowes himself argues that the "werk" of G, 79, is a revisionary improvement of "thyng" in F, 195 ("Chronological Relations," 665). "Florouns" may not have been quite so unusual as Lowes supposes. The term also occurs in line 529 of the Fairfax MS, where all the other MSS read "floures." Though Robinson thinks "florouns" the original reading (*Works*, 913), its appearance in only one MS suggests the possibility of scribal improvement, perhaps prompted by the earlier occurrences of the term in F but likely only if the scribe knew and appreciated the greater precision of "florouns." It should also be noted that Robinson does not regard the reading "floures" at G, 149 and 153, as "deliberate revision." Since the reading "floures" appears in several F MSS, an alteration presumably scribal in character, he concludes that Chaucer "used a ms. of the type which has substituted *floures*" to produce G.

4. For Lowes's discussion of the structural differences in the two Prologues, see "*Marguerite* Poems," 658–83; for the characterizations "organic" and "mechanical," see "Chronological Relations," 751 n.1. Though Gardner regards G as the revision, he too doubts Lowes's claim that the purpose of the revision was to achieve greater "clarity" and better "organization" ("The Two Prologues," 595–97).

5. The second person of direct address is in Chaucer's source for the apostrophe to the daisy, Boccaccio's *Filostrato*. Chaucer may have shifted from "she" to "ye" under its influence, but this proves nothing about priority, since these lines are found only in F. His references to the flower and leaf controversy allude to a contemporaneous debate

as to the relative merits of lovers devoted to the flower and those devoted to the leaf. The extant literature participating in the debate leaves in doubt just what was signified by devotion to the one or the other.

6. Though his view—that Chaucer's presentation of the F narrator as a lover is burlesque—is exaggerated, Gardner alone gives appropriate emphasis to this most prominent difference ("The Two Prologues," 606–9).

7. This fact was first observed by Bernhard ten Brink, "Zur Chronologie von Chaucers Schriften," *Englische Studien* 16 (1892): 16–17.

8. Culler, *The Pursuit of Signs*, 148–52.

9. Lowes, "*Marguerite* Poems," 679–80.

10. For an enumeration of the conventional content of the love-dream vision, see Sypherd, *Studies in Chaucer's Hous of Fame*, 6.

11. In G the narrator is depicted as spending the whole day walking in the fields admiring the daisies; only in F is he actually pictured as kneeling by a single daisy from before sunrise until after sunset as he follows its progress.

12. Chaucer repeatedly speculates about the validity of dreams: see *Hous of Fame*, 1–58; *Parliament of Fowls*, 92–119; *Troilus and Criseyde* 5.358–85; "Nun's Priest's Tale," *CT* VII, 2931–3153.

13. Lowes, "Chronological Relations," 786–87.

14. In the *Troilus*, Chaucer had to transform the narrator of the *Filostrato* in order to present himself as an outsider. Adopting the stance of a lover in F enabled him to use material from the *Filostrato* previously rejected: namely, the narrator's impassioned invocation of the daisy. Reading Chaucer's poetry autobiographically would require us to suppose that in the mid-1380s, when he was in his early forties, he had not yet known love but that he subsequently fell in love and told all in the F Prologue—though obviously he was only temporarily oblivious to the embarrassment if he revised F to extricate himself from it. Fisher's assertion—that while Chaucer regularly portrays himself as an outsider, he depicts himself as explicitly old only in poetry dating from the mid-1390s—is evidently somewhat circular (*John Gower*, 240–41).

15. Absent (in addition to the passionate apostrophes and the day spent hovering over the flower) is the religious language in which F couches the narrator's devotion. D. D. Griffith's contention that Chaucer revised F to remove its sacreligious parody (*Manly Anniversary Studies*

[Chicago: Chicago Univ. Press, 1923], 32–41) receives its necessary qualification in Gardner, "The Two Prologues," 597–99.

16. Kane believes G's "the lesteth" a scribal alteration of F's "the lyke." Mistaking "the finesse of Alcestis' 'even though it may not please you,'" the scribe "substituted a word implying the subsidence of desire in the Dreamer, and uncharacteristic of her general attitude to him" ("The Text of *The Legend*," 54). The change may have been scribal, but its implications suit perfectly G's different narrator and his different relationship to Alceste.

17. Arraying Cupid with flowers is of course conventional; in the *Roman de la rose* he is pictured as clothed in flowers, including a "chapelet" of roses (vv. 874–96). The sun-crown is unprecedented. The appearance of the "lilies newe," together with the absence of the reference to Anne, has led a number of critics to suppose that G allegorizes not Richard and Anne but Richard and Isabella, Richard's child bride from France. See Lange, "Zur Datierung des Gg. Prolog," 345–55, and "Neue Beiträge zu einem endgultigen Lesung der Legenden-prologfrage," 173–80. Margaret Galway advanced a similar reading, one independently arrived at, in "Chaucer, Granson, and Isabel of France," 279. This position is reasserted in Fisher, "The Revision of the Prologue," 75–84. If one assumes G the revision, reference to Chaucer's biography to explain the change from sun to garland has appeal, since the change is so difficult to comprehend on artistic grounds; nonetheless, one must question this explanation. Seeing Richard and Isabella in G presupposes Richard and Anne in F, but if Richard was as devoted to Anne and her memory as many suppose—including Fisher—he would hardly have been pleased to see a poem celebrating her, like a gift twice given, used to celebrate a marriage that was only a political alliance. Nor is it likely that Chaucer would have been so tactless. It is possible, of course, that Chaucer had not yet published F; in that case no offense would have been given.

18. For the tradition of the two Venuses, see Robert Hollander, *Boccaccio's Two Venuses* (New York: Columbia Univ. Press, 1977), 158–60 n.44; on its relevance to the *Troilus*, see Rowe, *O Love, O Charite*, 92–96. Especially relevant is Alain de Lille's depiction of two Venuses, or rather of one Venus in two states, and two gods of Love: married to Hymenaeus, Venus produces Cupid; involved in an adulterous relationship with Antigenius (or perhaps Antigamus, antimarriage), she produces Jocus (*De planctu* 10, pr. 5; *The Plaint*, 163–65). Though

Alain gives Cupid legitimacy and elevates him by providing Jocus to play the part of the god of Lust, he insists on Cupid's ambiguity, mixing praise and blame in Natura's oxymoronic description of him and terming him dishonorable unless bridled with "moderation" (*De planctu* 10, pr. 5); *The Plaint,* 154). The *Roman de la rose* provides the most influential discrimination of Cupid and Venus as *fin amour* and concupiscence respectively (see esp. vv. 10719–96).

19. This passage has occasioned considerable comment; see Robinson, *Works,* 844, for a review. Neither the general intent of the passage nor the precise identity of certain references is entirely clear. If "Valerye" refers to the *Epistola Valerii ad Rufinum ne uxorem ducat,* an antifeminist work by Walter Map that was sometimes included among Jerome's works, the inappropriateness of the god's recommended readings becomes all the more pronounced; if "Valerye" refers to the *Factorum ac dictorum memorabilium libri IX* of Valerius Maximus, which recounts the histories of a number of good women—a work often cited along with Jerome in discussions of chastity—the irony is much less pronounced. The probability is that Chaucer regarded both works as by the same Valerius. We should note that Jerome, Valerius, and Ovid are all repeatedly cited together in another of Vincent of Beauvais's *Mirrors,* the *Speculum doctrinale* 4 (*De scientia morali*), 98–100, in the chapters discussing modesty, chastity, and virginity—a fact that also reminds us that these references need not derive, as is often supposed, from the *Canterbury Tales* period when Chaucer was working firsthand with Jerome and both the texts attributed to Valerius. Similarly, though Claudyan is obviously the late Roman poet, and a reference to his *De raptu Proserpinae* serves the poet's purposes in that she is one of the models for Criseyde, why the god would cite him is not entirely clear. Finally, the fact that the references are cryptic enough to force the reader to ponder them only gaurantees the undoing of the god.

20. See chap. 1, n. 20. Also needing mention is the *Ovide moralisé,* for though there is no evidence that Chaucer was influenced by its imposed allegorizations, his narrative use of it has been demonstrated (see Lowes, "Chaucer and the *Ovide Moralisé,*" 302–25; Meech, "Chaucer and the *Ovide Moralisé,*" 182–204).

21. In contrast, in F the disparagement of the other ladies seems nothing but the conventional hyperbole of the lover celebrating his own lady. The opposition between Alceste and the others is heightened in G by

the use of the distancing demonstrative "that" rather than the inclusive "this" in the refrain.

22. Both Goddard ("Chaucer's *Legend*" [1908], 97–100) and Estrich ("Chaucer's Maturing Art in the Prologues to the *Legend of Good Women*," *JEGP* 36 [1937]: 334–35) regard G as more bluntly ironic. Conversely, Gardner judged G an effort to treat love with the same seriousness in the Prologue and legends by eliminating the comic treatment of the narrator as lover and by providing a "more elevated characterization of the god of Love" ("The Two Prologues," 605). Certainly G is less playful, its comedy less zestful, but its irony also makes its "greater elevation of the god" both a greater and a more immediate denigration of him.

23. See Walter Ong's observations about the inevitable indirection of writing in "The Writer's Audience Is Always a Fiction," *PMLA* 90 (1975): 20.

24. See Dieter Mehl, "The Audience of Chaucer's *Troilus and Criseyde*," in *Chaucer and Middle English Studies in Honor of Rossell Hope Robbins*, ed. Beryl Rowland (London: 1974), 176–77.

25. See Pearsall's observation that "its inclusion can be seen as reflecting the judgement of the manuscript's editor, publisher, or buyer that such a picture would be stylish and appropriate" ("The *Troilus* Frontispiece and Chaucer's Audience," 69).

26. See the analogous disparagement of bourgeois acquisitiveness in the consummation scene of the *Troilus* (3.1373–93), where the narrator sides with lovers.

27. See Pearsall, "The *Troilus* Frontispiece and Chaucer's Audience," 68–74, and *Old and Middle English Poetry* (London: Routledge & Kegan Paul, 1977), 194–97; Paul Strohm, "Chaucer's Audience," *Literature and History* 5 (1977): 26–41, and "Chaucer's Fifteenth-Century Audience and the Narrowing of the 'Chaucer Tradition,'" *Studies in the Age of Chaucer* 4 (1982): 3–32; V. J. Scattergood, "Literary Culture at the Court of Richard II," in *English Court Culture in the Later Middle Ages*, ed. V. J. Scattergood and J. W. Sherborne (London: Duckworth, 1983), 29–43.

28. Pearsall, *Old and Middle English Poetry*, 194.

29. The view advanced by Norton-Smith (*Geoffrey Chaucer*, 63–66) that the celebration of the Alceste-daisy as poetic inspiration reflects the role of the queen as Chaucer's poetic muse not only lacks corroboration in the historical record (see Pearsall, "The *Troilus* Frontispiece

and Chaucer's Audience," 72–73) but is in no way necessary to account for this celebration, given the ideological content of the image.

30. The initial identification of F's audience with the god's and Alceste's criticisms of the poet results both from the superiority the narrator attributes to them as lovers (cf. his appeals to them for help) and from the comic behavior of the narrator as lover, behavior that similarly invites audience condescension.

31. Reading it in conjunction with the "Wife of Bath's Tale," Lee Patterson argues that it is the point of the *Legend* in general, and the G Prologue's appeal to "the literary tradition of feminine virtue" in particular, to show this tradition "itself part of the male tyranny" the poem "relentlessly chronicles" ("For the Wyves Love of Bathe," 689). This overstates and somewhat oversimplifies the case: the Wife's tale certainly demonstrates the male penchant for using antifeminism to wield power, and the legends surely dramatize Chaucer's awareness that poets are frequently self-serving in their poetry; but the Wife herself also manipulates antifeminism to wield power, and Alceste is as active in imposing the legends on the poet as is her male counterpart. Further, the virtue Alceste embodies is clearly assumed to be real, however complicated the human motivations that prompt her, the god, and the narrator all to suppose that they are on its side. But Chaucer's dramatization of the self-serving character of all human making surely prohibits a simple endorsement of the clerical, as well as of the courtly, tradition.

Index

"This is the best study of Chaucer's *Legend of Good Women* I have seen. . . . Though it is this major poem that is Rowe's focus, he pursues the study in a fashion that is constantly illuminating and suggestive with regard to Chaucer's poetry in general, with regard to other important medieval and classical poets, and with regard to important questions in literary and intellectual history."— John V. Fleming, Princeton University.

Appearing between *Troilus and Criseyde* and *The Canterbury Tales* when Chaucer was at the height of his powers, the *Legend of Good Women* has suffered a puzzling critical neglect. Yet this major poem deals with topics that are as perennial as any in the *Tales,* and with some, like women's social status, that are especially urgent today. At the same time, it opens onto virtually every field of literary criticism, from the staunchly historical to the rigorously textual. Illuminated by the history of medieval thought and literature, *Through Nature to Eternity* offers new perspectives to readers of Chaucer's rich and complex poem.

The ten legends recount some of literature's most famous narratives of tragic love, including star-crossed destinies, variously passionate and/or perfidious seductions and betrayals, and sexual